The Future of Political Community

How should we think about the future of political community? Do we have good reason to continue to connect political community to ideas of progress and democracy? What is the likelihood of communal belonging taking post-national and even self-critical forms? Is post-territorial, border-less politics the future of political community or more to do with growing disconnection between elites and masses, whereby power becomes increasingly free from accountability? Could it even be that the boundaries of political community are necessary to ethics in world politics? How should we understand the transformation of political community as an empirical event at the global level? And what can we glean about the future of political community from the past?

Bringing major new insights to a burgeoning field of interest within international relations, the volume:

- encourages the reader to re-evaluate the concept of political community
- questions the key assumptions behind current accounts of political community's transformation
- includes contributions from internationally-renowned scholars

This volume will be of major interest to students and scholars of International Relations, International Political Theory, and Social and Political Science.

Gideon Baker is Senior Lecturer in Politics at Griffith University, Queensland, Australia.

Jens Bartelson is Professor of Political Science at the Department of Political Science, Lund University.

Routledge/ECPR Studies in European Political Science
Edited by Thomas Poguntke
Ruhr University Bochum, Germany on behalf of the European
Consortium for Political Research

The Routledge/ECPR Studies in European Political Science series is published in association with the European Consortium for Political Research – the leading organisation concerned with the growth and development of political science in Europe. The series presents high-quality edited volumes on topics at the leading edge of current interest in political science and related fields, with contributions from European scholars and others who have presented work at ECPR workshops or research groups.

1   **Regionalist Parties in Western Europe**
    Edited by Lieven de Winter and Huri Türsan

2   **Comparing Party System Change**
    Edited by Jan-Erik Lane & Paul Pennings

3   **Political Theory and European Union**
    Edited by Albert Weale and Michael Nentwich

4   **Politics of Sexuality**
    Edited by Terrell Carver and Véronique Mottier

5   **Autonomous Policy Making by International Organizations**
    Edited by Bob Reinalda and Bertjan Verbeek

6   **Social Capital and European Democracy**
    Edited by Jan van Deth, Marco Maraffi, Ken Newton and Paul Whiteley

7   **Party Elites in Divided Societies**
    Edited by Kurt Richard Luther and Kris Deschouwer

8   **Citizenship and Welfare State Reform in Europe**
    Edited by Jet Bussemaker

9   **Democratic Governance and New Technology**
    Technologically mediated innovations in political practice in Western Europe
    Edited by Ivan Horrocks, Jens Hoff and Pieter Tops

10 **Democracy without Borders**
    Transnationalisation and conditionality in new democracies
    Edited by Jean Grugel

11 **Cultural Theory as Political Science**
    Edited by Michael Thompson, Gunnar Grendstad and Per Selle

12 **The Transformation of Governance in the European Union**
    Edited by Beate Kohler-Koch and Rainer Eising

13 **Parliamentary Party Groups in European Democracies**
    Political parties behind closed doors
    Edited by Knut Heidar and Ruud Koole

14 **Survival of the European Welfare State**
    Edited by Stein Kuhnle

15 **Private Organisations in Global Politics**
    Edited by Karsten Ronit and Volker Schneider

16 **Federalism and Political Performance**
    Edited by Ute Wachendorfer-Schmidt

17 **Democratic Innovation**
    Deliberation, representation and association
    Edited by Michael Saward

18 **Public Opinion and the International Use of Force**
    Edited by Philip Everts and Pierangelo Isernia

19 **Religion and Mass Electoral Behaviour in Europe**
    Edited by David Broughton and Hans-Martien ten Napel

20 **Estimating the Policy Position of Political Actors**
    Edited by Michael Laver

21 **Democracy and Political Change in the 'Third World'**
    Edited by Jeff Haynes

22 **Politicians, Bureaucrats and Administrative Reform**
    Edited by B Guy Peters and Jon Pierre

23 **Social Capital and Participation in Everyday Life**
Edited by Paul Dekker and Eric M Uslaner

24 **Development and Democracy**
What do we know and how?
Edited by Ole Elgström and Goran Hyden

25 **Do Political Campaigns Matter?**
Campaign effects in elections and referendums
Edited by David M. Farrell and Rüdiger Schmitt-Beck

26 **Political Journalism**
New challenges, new practices
Edited by Raymond Kuhn and Erik Neveu

27 **Economic Voting**
Edited by Han Dorussen and Michaell Taylor

28 **Organized Crime and the Challenge to Democracy**
Edited by Felia Allum and Renate Siebert

29 **Understanding the European Union's External Relations**
Edited by Michèle Knodt and Sebastiaan Princen

30 **Social Democratic Party Policies in Contemporary Europe**
Edited by Giuliano Bonoli and Martin Powell

31 **Decision Making Within International Organisations**
Edited by Bob Reinalda and Bertjan Verbeek

32 **Comparative Biomedical Policy**
Governing assisted reproductive technologies
Edited by Ivar Bleiklie, Malcolm L. Goggin and Christine Rothmayr

33 **Electronic Democracy**
Mobilisation, organisation and participation via new ICTs
Edited by Rachel K. Gibson, Andrea Römmele and Stephen J. Ward

34 **Liberal Democracy and Environmentalism**
The end of environmentalism?
Edited by Marcel Wissenburg and Yoram Levy

35 **Political Theory and the European Constitution**
Edited by Lynn Dobson and Andreas Follesdal

36 Politics and the European Commission
Actors, interdependence, legitimacy
Edited by Andy Smith

37 Metropolitan Governance
Capacity, democracy and the dynamics of place
Edited by Hubert Heinelt and Daniel Kübler

38 Democracy and the Role of Associations
Political, organizational and social contexts
Edited by Sigrid Roßteutscher

39 The Territorial Politics of Welfare
Edited by Nicola McEwen and Luis Moreno

40 Health Governance in Europe
Issues, challenges and theories
Edited by Monika Steffen

41 Republicanism in Theory and Practice
Edited by Iseult Honohan and Jeremy Jennings

42 Mass Media and Political Communication in New Democracies
Edited by Katrin Voltmer

43 Delegation in Contemporary Democracies
Edited by Dietmar Braun and Fabrizio Gilardi

44 Governance and Democracy
Comparing national, European and international experiences
Edited by Yannis Papadopoulos and Arthur Benz

45 The European Union's Roles in International Politics
Concepts and analysis
Edited by Ole Elgström and Michael Smith

46 Policy-making Processes and the European Constitution
A comparative study of member states and accession countries
Edited by Thomas König and Simon Hug

47 Democratic Politics and Party Competition
Edited by Judith Bara and Albert Weale

48 Participatory Democracy and Political Participation
Can participatory engineering bring citizens back in?
Edited by Thomas Zittel and Dieter Fuchs

49 **Civil Societies and Social Movements**
Potentials and problems
Edited by Derrick Purdue

50 **Resources, Governance and Civil Conflict**
Edited by Magnus Öberg and Kaare Strøm

51 **Transnational Private Governance and its Limits**
Edited by Jean-Christophe Graz and Andreas Nölke

52 **International Organizations and Implementation**
Enforcers, managers, authorities?
Edited by Jutta Joachim, Bob Reinalda and Bertjan Verbeek

53 **New Parties in Government**
Edited by Kris Deschouwer

54 **In Pursuit of Sustainable Development**
New governance practices at the sub-national level in Europe
Edited by Susan Baker and Katarina Eckerberg

55 **Governments, NGOs and Anti-Corruption**
The new integrity warriors
Edited by Luís de Sousa, Barry Hindess and Peter Larmour

56 **Intra-Party Politics and Coalition Governments**
Edited by Daniela Giannetti and Kenneth Benoit

57 **Political Parties and Partisanship**
Social identity and individual attitudes
Edited by John Bartle and Paolo Belucci

58 **The Future of Political Community**
Edited by Gideon Baker and Jens Bartelson

Also available from Routledge in association with the ECPR:

Sex Equality Policy in Western Europe, *Edited by Frances Gardiner*;
Democracy and Green Poltical Thought, *Edited by Brian Doherty & Marius de Geus*; **The New Politics of Unemployment**, *Edited by Hugh Compston*;
Citizenship, Democracy and Justice in the New Europe, *Edited by Percy B. Lehning & Albert Weale*; **Private Groups and Public Life**, *Edited by Jan W van Deth*; **The Political Context of Collective Action**, *Edited by Ricca Edmondson*;
Theories of Secession, *Edited by Percy Lehning*; **Regionalism Across the North/South Divide**, *Edited by Jean Grugel & Wil Hout*

The Future of Political Community

**Edited by Gideon Baker
and Jens Bartelson**

Routledge
Taylor & Francis Group

LONDON AND NEW YORK

First published 2009
by Routledge
2 Park Square Milton Park Abingdon Oxon OX14 4RN

Simultaneously published in the USA and Canada
by Routledge
52 Vanderbilt Avenue, New York, NY 10017

*Routledge is an imprint of the Taylor & Francis Group,
an informa business.*

First issued in paperback 2013

Typeset in Times New Roman by Swales & Willis Ltd, Exeter, Devon

British Library Cataloguing in Publication Data
A catalogue record for this book is available
from the British Library

Library of Congress Cataloging in Publication Data
A catalog record for this book has been requested

ISBN13: 978–0–415–84787–2 (pbk)
ISBN13: 978–0–203–88264–1 (ebk)
ISBN13: 978–0–415–46820–6 (hbk)

Contents

Contributors   xi
Series Editor's preface   xiii
Acknowledgements   xv

Introduction: The future of political community   1
    GIDEON BAKER AND JENS BARTELSON

PART 1
Assumptions of political community: progress,
democracy and boundaries in question   13

1   **Dream or nightmare? Thinking the future of world politics**   15
    KIMBERLY HUTCHINGS

2   **Globalising the democratic community**   36
    JENS BARTELSON

3   **The politics of hospitality: sovereignty and ethics in political**
    community   51
    GIDEON BAKER

PART 2
Political community and the postmodern   71

4   **What future for the European political community?**
    Nietzsche, nationalism and the idea of the 'good Europeans'   73
    STEFAN ELBE

5   **Constituting community: Heidegger, mimesis and critical belonging**   90
    LOUIZA ODYSSEOS

6   **The limits of post-territorial political community: from the cosmopolitan politics of global civil society to the biopolitics of the multitude**   112
    DAVID CHANDLER

PART 3
Learning from the past and understanding future transformations   127

7   **Rethinking political community from neglected places**   129
    GIUSEPPE BALLACCI

8   **Homer, Virgil and identity in international relations**   144
    RICHARD NED LEBOW

9   **Political community formation beyond the nation-state**   175
    BENJAMIN HERBORTH

    Epilogue: Community rethought   204
    GIDEON BAKER AND JENS BARTELSON

    Index   208

Contributors

Gideon Baker is Senior Lecturer in Politics at Griffith University, Queensland, Australia. He is the author of *Civil Society and Democratic Theory: Alternative Voices* (2002) and co-editor of *Global Civil Society: Contested Futures* (2005).

Giuseppe Ballacci is in the Department of Political Science and International Relations at the Universidad Autónoma de Madrid. He is the author of 'Giambattista Vico y Eric Voegelin: fundamentos y lenguaje simbólico', in B. Hammar (ed.) *Democracia y retórica* (forthcoming).

Jens Bartelson is Professor of Political Science at Lund University. He is the author of *A Genealogy of Sovereignty* (1995); *The Critique of the State* (2001) and *Visions of World Community* (2009).

David Chandler is Professor of International Relations at the University of Westminster. He is the author of *International Statebuilding* (2008); *Empire in Denial: The Politics of State-Building* (2006); *Constructing Global Civil Society: Morality and Power in International Relations* (2004); *From Kosovo to Kabul: Human Rights and International Intervention* (2002); and *Bosnia: Faking Democracy after Dayton* (2000).

Stefan Elbe is Reader in International Relations at the University of Sussex. He is the author of *Global Health and Security* (2009); *Strategic Implications of HIV/AIDS* (2003); and *Europe: A Nietzschean Perspective* (2003).

Benjamin Herborth is Lecturer in International Relations at Johann Wolfgang Goethe-University, Frankfurt am Main. He is the co-author of 'De-Europeanization by Default? Germany's EU Policy in Defense and Asylum', *Foreign Policy Analysis* (2005) and co-editor of *Die Anarchie der kommunikativen Freiheit: Jürgen Habermas und die Theorie der internationalen Politik* (2007).

Kimberly Hutchings is Professor of International Relations at the London School of Economics. She is the author of *Time and World Politics: Thinking the Present* (2008); *Hegel and Feminist Philosophy* (2003); *International Political*

Theory: Re-thinking Ethics in a Global Era (1999); and *Kant, Critique and Politics* (1996).

Richard Ned Lebow is James O. Freedman Presidential Professor of Government, Dartmouth College. His recent books include *A Cultural Theory of International Relations* (2008); *Forbidden Fruit: Counterfactuals and International Relations* (2008); *The Tragic Vision of Politics: Ethics, Interests and Orders* (2003); and *Conflict, Cooperation and Ethics* (2006).

Louiza Odysseos is Senior Lecturer in International Relations at the University of Sussex. She is the author of *The Subject of Coexistence: Otherness in International Relations* (2007) and co-editor of *The International Political Thought of Carl Schmitt: Terror, Liberal War and the Crisis of Global Order* (2007) and *Gendering the International* (2002).

Series Editor's preface

This book is very timely. It is published in a period of (almost) unprecedented global economic upheaval that has clearly demonstrated that there is one global economic community. Yet, at the same time, the global financial crisis reminds us that politics is much less globalized than many political analysts have claimed for many years. While the institutions of global economic governance including the World Bank and the IMF were, mainly within their institutional limits, capable of reacting to the challenges of the credit crunch, a global (or at least European) political community which would have furnished political decision-makers with the legitimacy to counter the economic crisis by concerted supranational action was largely absent.

Instead, national politics dominated. In the end, national policy-making prevailed despite some high-level meetings of global and European leaders. Virtually all measures to save the global financial system were national, initiated by national governments who legitimized their enormous financial guarantees to banks within their jurisdiction by reference to the need to first and foremost protect the functioning of their national economies and the savings of their national constituencies. Admittedly, the recipients were mainly banks with a global scope of business. Yet, at the end of the day, it was national governments which used national revenue to partially nationalize banks. Similarly, the huge spending programmes launched to alleviate the economic downturn were almost exclusively national and attempts to set up a EU spending plans failed not least because national governments wanted to spend their national tax revenue within their own country.

These examples remind us that it is not only national political structures which have remained more relevant and powerful than we have become used to thinking over the past decades marked by the increasing globalization of the economy. It also reminds us that in times of crisis the national political community is a powerful point of reference – and a source of legitimation – for political action. As Jens Bartelson writes in his chapter: 'If democratic governance presupposes a community in order to be legitimate, global governance cannot be democratically legitimate since there is no corresponding community at the global level that could bestow it with legitimacy', and this explain why there was little basis for joint supranational action.

To be sure, this statement is a point of departure for the current volume and does by no means represent something like a definitive conclusion. Rather, it highlights the essence of the debate: How can we conceive of political community as a basis for legitimate democratic governance in a globalizing world? The contributions to the volume address this question from a multitude of different perspectives, discussing the role of boundaries, the (potential) relevance of common institutions and competing or complementary sources of identity like language, culture or history. In their epilogue, the editors remind us of the ambivalence of community because it always carries the dangers of exclusion or, worse, tyranny. Yet, a global community as the ultimate source of political legitimacy may be more of theoretical speculation rather than a realistic option. Hence, they conclude that they see their volume as a 'small corrective to the reification of the global, and to narrowly pejorative readings of territory, belonging and boundaries'. It is a safe guess that the current economic upheaval and the dominance of national reactions to it will add additional weight to such considerations. We will certainly not see the end of globalization – economical and political. As a matter of fact, the global scope of the problems might induce a renewed effort to create stronger institutions of global governance. At the same time, however, nation states have reasserted their role as central location of economic policy-making because they are still capable of generating sufficient legitimacy and hence support needed for raising the massive revue for combating the economic crisis.

Thomas Poguntke, Series Editor
Florence, January 2009

Acknowledgements

The chapters in this collection arose out of an ECPR workshop by the same name at the ECPR Joint Sessions of Workshops in Nicosia, Cyprus in April 2006. We would like to thank the participants in this workshop for their contributions to an exhilarating series of discussions, the insights of which have enriched each of the contributions here.

Gideon Baker would like to thank his wife, Julia Rudolph, for her solidarity and support in this project, as in so much else. Thanks also to Lotte and Atticus for tearing his attention away at frequent intervals.

Introduction

The future of political community

Gideon Baker and Jens Bartelson

The concept of community

According to what has become a standard story in the social sciences, the increasing mobility of people and information has made nations much less homogeneous than they once were, with political authority evaporating to levels above that of the state. Since such global flows allegedly undermine the foundations of the modern nation state, traditional conceptions of community have lost much of their analytical and normative import. In response to this challenge, many scholars have tried to articulate new conceptions of political community better suited to make sense of the contemporary world. Behind this quest for community lies the widespread conviction that *some* conception of community – whether democratic or not – is necessary in order to justify emergent forms of political authority beyond or below the state level.

While most contributors to this volume share this basic conviction, their responses represent different ways of defining and defending conceptions of community beyond that of the nation. Doing this, they all have had to confront the same basic philosophical challenge. How to redefine the concept of community without thereby reproducing a nationalistic ontology? Responding to this challenge, the contributors have been forced to deal with the semantic baggage which the concept of community has accumulated through its trajectory within modern social theory. Hence they also reflect a considerable dissatisfaction with many existing attempts to rethink the concept of community in the light of the above challenges, on the grounds that these have been largely unsuccessful in this regard.

This tendency to reproduce nationalistic assumptions is manifest in many contemporary attempts to theorize the concept of community. Most of these attempts have taken place in two distinct but increasingly overlapping theoretical debates, those of *cosmopolitanism* and *multiculturalism* respectively. In the first debate, several attempts have been made to redefine the concept of political community in order to justify the authority of global governance institutions with reference to a corresponding democratic community of all mankind. But even if these theories often assume that the nation today is obsolete as a source of community, they nevertheless proceed by identifying what they take to be the basic requirements of *any* community – such as being sufficiently *homogeneous* – and then project this requirement onto the global level. The result is that the 'new' form of political community thus envisaged is little but the good old nation writ large by means of domestic analogies, albeit now in a more permeable shape than before (Held 1995; 1998; 2003; Archibugi, Held, and Köhler 1998; Archibugi 2003; Linklater 1998; Bauböck 2002). So when cosmopolitans try to redefine the concept of community to meet the challenges posed by globalization, they do so by presupposing that a community must be based on some degree of sameness among its members. The cosmopolitan argument is therefore open to the objection that global cultural diversity coupled with the pluralistic structure of the international system not only make the creation of a world community difficult, but that the very attempt to do so in the name of one particular set of values is likely to provoke rather than to resolve global conflicts.

In the second debate, several attempts have been made to redefine political community from within, in order to justify individualization as a response to increased cultural pluralism within domestic societies. But to the extent that these theories have retained thin conceptions of community by advocating tolerance as a way of handling clashes between incommensurable values, they have done so while assuming that communities have to be *bounded* in order to remain sources of social cohesion and belonging. Again, the 'new' form of political community thus envisaged is blueprinted on the nation, yet admittedly in a more pluralistic guise than before (Bader 1997; Hollinger 2001; Hall 2002; Smith 2003). So when multiculturalists try to redefine political community to meet the challenges posed by globalization, they do so by presupposing that a community must somehow be bounded in order to qualify as a community in the first place. The multicultural argument is therefore open to the objection that the need for social cohesion coupled with the monistic foundations of the sovereign state put effective limits on how much pluralism can be tolerated before the community in question disintegrates into its component groups.

The problems and solutions discussed within these two debates are mirror images of each other. But taken together, they indicate where the real problems lie for anyone who would try to redefine political community today. Arguably, the sources of this problem are the mutually reinforcing assumptions of *sociocultural homogeneity* and *territorial boundedness*. Most efforts to redefine political community today try to question or remove one of these assumptions, but never both simultaneously. The reason for this is simple, since removing both of these requirements simultaneously would make it hard to speak of community in any recognizably modern sense of this term. Speaking of human community as something boundless and heterogeneous is of course possible and sometimes necessary, but such usages of the concept will invariably be cases of conceptual stretching, in which the concept of community is used to describe forms of human association that could be described equally well in other logically less demanding terms. The attributes of being bounded and homogeneous therefore seem to be integral to the identity and intelligibility of the concept of community, and these attributes in turn make it difficult to describe unbounded and heterogeneous forms of human association as communities other than in a loose and metaphorical sense, such as the 'scholarly community' or the 'business community'.

The very concept of community thus brings an amount of nostalgia for a distinct type of human association of which the modern nation is the token. From this viewpoint, the entire project of rethinking political community reflects a sense of imminent loss, and a concomitant effort to restore what some authors fear is gone forever (Bauman 2001; Delanty 2003). Curiously, this situation is not very different from the predicament in which our modern conceptions of community first emerged. As has been pointed out many times, the resurgence of the concept of community within social theory during the late nineteenth century was accompanied by a growing sense of disenchantment with the modern world. In this context, the concept of community and its semantic equivalents were used to describe social relations between individuals and groups in traditional societies, in sharp distinction to contractual and legalistic forms of human association thought to be characteristic of modernity. While this is not the place to dwell on the details of its trajectory within early social theory, it is important to note that it was in these writings that the concept of community was finally given many of its current particularistic connotations. Before the concept of community was recycled and redefined within nineteenth century social and political theory, the attributes of being bounded and homogeneous were not integral to its intelligibility. Even further back, the concept of community was frequently understood to be coextensive with mankind as a whole, however defined (Schofield 1991). Therefore, many of the present connotations of the concept of community, along with the restrictions they impose on political imagination, can be seen as the outcome of a highly successful *nationalization* that gradually made its range of meaningful reference coincide with the boundaries of the modern nation state – a process which culminated in the writings of Durkheim (1964), Tönnies (1957) and Elias (1991).

If this is the case, our present effort to theorize the future political community can be understood as an attempt to restore the default settings of political reflection. Most of our core social and political concepts have taken on many of their present connotations as a result of their involvement in the shaping of the nation state during the twentieth century. Today, when it is widely believed that this institutional framework is being challenged by global forces, those concepts have become unsuitable for the new and daunting task of understanding and explaining the emergence of new forms of community and authority. But if the concept of community carries so much baggage over from the very same past we are trying to escape, why do we not simply get rid of the concept of community and start to think afresh by means of *new* concepts, better suited to make sense of the *new* world that is opening up in front of us?

The contributors to this volume share the broadly hermeneutic conviction that it is not possible to proceed from such a clean semantic slate, since our thinking always necessarily will have to take place by means of concepts whose connotations have been accumulating through prior usage. But rather than either blindly reproducing inherited meanings, or naively believing that we can simply transcend the present by reinventing our political vocabulary wholesale, the contributors to this volume try to come to terms with the wide range of connotations that the concept of community has acquired in different contexts, in order to distinguish those meanings which are merely contingent upon past arrangements from those which might be useful in order to understand the present and the future. In this volume, this is done by systematically unpacking lost meanings and forgotten inferential connections with the aim of addressing salient problems in contemporary political theory and academic international relations. Hence, the objectives of this volume are both philosophical and historical in character, seeking to bring both forms of knowledge to bear on the challenges posed in the present to the possibility of political community in the future.

This basic philosophical commitment is also reflected in the attitude to present debates about the nature of political community. During the past decades, perhaps too much intellectual energy has been devoted to the question of whether communities are real or constructed. According to the former view, human communities exist by virtue of being repositories of collective memories that springs from a common past or perhaps even a common ancestry. According to the latter, communities are more or less deliberately constructed by political elites in order to facilitate ruling, drawing on all available myths, symbols, and rituals in the process. The ensuing debate between those positions has been animated by a series of unresolved tensions resulting from a selective and sometimes distorted uptake of insights from the linguistic turn within the social sciences. Yet as soon as we advance beyond those tensions, we are likely to discover that there is no profound contradiction between being real and being constructed. Indeed, being constructed is the defining property of all social reality. Hence it does not matter whether communities really are real or constructed: What matters in the present context is how this distinction between the real and the imagined *itself* has been drawn, and how it has been used in order to legitimize political communities in the past as well as in the present (Bonnell and Hunt 1999).

Another and closely related debate concerns the relationship between the community and the individual. The tension between communitarian and individualistic accounts of social order has not only been a central concern to modern social theory, but has also been a sticking point within political philosophy during the last decades. While many political philosophers have tried to strike a balance between the virtues of community and those of individualism at the domestic level, remaining ontological differences between these viewpoints have continued to fuel debate between communitarians and cosmopolitans at the global level (Benhabib 2004; Tan 2004). The old tension between the individual and the community has thereby been translated into a tension between particularistic and universalistic accounts of global ethics and politics. If the difficulty of making coherent sense of the concept of a global community indicates the extent to which the nationalization of the concept of community has been successful, the difficulty involved in justifying the existence of particular communities indicates the extent to which universalistic sensibilities remain integral to ethical reasoning. Most contributors to this volume are therefore less interested in the reconciliation of these perspectives, but more interested in how they emerged in opposition in political theory and practice, as well as what kind of arrangements this opposition serve to legitimize.

Therefore, the overarching ambition of this volume is *not* a matter of exploring what might be happening to political community as a consequence of globalization. Such accounts are already in abundance. Rather, while parts of this diagnosis provide this volume with its necessary starting points, our joint ambition is to explore the possibilities and limits of the concept of community in response to this predicament. What happens when the range of applicability of the concept of community is extended to cover forms of human association that do not conform to the ideal type of the nation state? What are the possible sources of human community once we have discarded the requirement that communities must be homogeneous and bounded? What happens when we discard inherited preconceptions of what constitutes the basic requirements of a life lived in common among human beings? What draws people together in the absence of such contingent constructs such as nations and states?

These are the questions that are of interest to the contributors to the present volume. The book is divided into three sections. Below we will say a few words about how the different themes discussed in these sections interconnect, and how they individually as well as taken together contribute provisional answers to the above questions.

Part 1. Assumptions of political community: progress, democracy and boundaries in question

The first section considers the challenges facing attempts at rethinking political community. It seeks to establish the true scale of these challenges in the face of a wider literature that has significantly underestimated just how difficult it is to break with the past of political community when imagining new futures. Taking as our point of departure the most extensive attempt to date at such new thinking – the now significant literature on cosmopolitan political community – we see that despite seeking to transcend state-centrism, many of the categories of statism are implicitly reproduced in cosmopolitan discourse. Let us briefly consider an example of this – the paradoxical denunciation of state sovereignty in the very language of sovereignty itself, as we see clearly in the call for international or humanitarian interventions. Here we find sovereignty problematized in a way that invites sovereign responses from those states that are now defined as setting the benchmark for 'responsible' sovereignty. While many have noted the ways in which this discourse undermines international notions of a state's right to sovereignty in favor of cosmopolitan human right, it surely also describes cosmopolitan obligations in ways which enable some states to be more sovereign than others, reproducing the hierarchies of international society in the process (see, for example, the International Commission on Intervention and State Sovereignty's report on *The Responsibility to Protect*, which is unconvincing in its denial that identifying a responsibility to protect is the same thing as providing a new right of intervention).

Another aspect of this problem is that new visions of political community seem to rely as heavily as their predecessors on a series of binary oppositions – their conceptual vocabulary shares a tendency to reproduce rigid either/or thinking. Take, for example, the binary opposition between the universal and particular character-istic of the debate between cosmopolitans and defenders of state sovereignty – a binary opposition which, despite the fury of the debate between each of these two poles, fundamentally limits the ability of its interlocutors to think differently. Thus while advocates of state sovereignty charge cosmopolitans with insufficient atten-tion to global difference, there is arguably as much universalism involved in view-ing the state as a universal structure of particularity as there is in cosmopolitan universalism. For their own part, the cosmopolitans' attempts to provide a univer-sal account of particularity in world politics via the concept of global civil society paradoxically reflects the ongoing influence of an international politics defined by state sovereignty on our attempts at new thinking about political community. There is a similarly dialectical attempt to finally resolve the tension between universal and particular in world politics; this attempted synthesis is made in both cases in the name of universality rather than particularity; and this putatively universal resolu-tion is easily shown in each case to be deeply particular (the universal claims of global civil society activists are as dependent on particular forms of transnational action as the universal claims of states were dependent on particular groups of citi-zens) (Walker 1993: 63). Again, perhaps none of this should surprise since our very notions of global identity and difference are produced by, rather than being inde-pendent of, an international politics made up of nation-states (Bartelson 1995: 262–263).

These examples of the statist implications of aspects of contemporary discourse on political community is just one of many. Significantly, however, the contribu-tors to this section do not believe such critiques go far enough in understanding the reasons why such attempts to 'go beyond' the state so often, and so paradoxically, reproduce it. In short, there are deeper ontological reasons – reasons which the con-tributions to this section are anxious to explore – why a modernist framing of the horizon of political possibilities continues to exert its hold. One aspect of this prob-lem that is unearthed here (see Chapter 1) is that critics of political modernity often rely just as heavily as the targets of their critique on the assumption of unified world-political time and its corollary – uni-directional history. However differently the *direction* that this history takes is characterized – and the pessimistic tone of some of the critics of political modernity certainly sounds different to modernist assumptions of unifying progress in history – the shared assumption, which is only reversed rather than overcome, is that human history has a *telos*, and an apocalyp-tic one at that. Both visions of the future of political community, the optimistic and the pessimistic, therefore remain encumbered with a universalizing view of the time of political community as 'known but not yet'. Crucially, these universalizing claims only seem plausible as against accounts which emphasize the inherent con-tingency of world political time if the theorist is implicitly understood to be a prophet or time-traveler.

Another example of this problem identified here (see Chapter 2) is that the con-cept of democracy (central to considerations of legitimacy and political commu-nity) has been stealthily but thoroughly nationalized in modernity, with the result that accounts of democracy at the global level are hampered by the assumption that, to be legitimate, democracy has to represent a particular people. But how is 'the people' to be democratically constituted? The short answer is that it cannot be, and so modern political thought had to introduce an ontology of nation in order to justify the democratization of territories defined initially by that antithesis of the demos – the prince. In other words, by conceptualizing the nation as the original source of political authority, modern political thought could naturalize the boundaries of the state and thereby lay a smoke screen over the paradox that democratic legitimacy was being claimed for a 'people' itself not legitimately constituted from the standpoint of democracy. The startling upshot of this insight is that democracy cannot, on its own terms, be legitimately bounded. Only approval by a global demos could grant legitimacy to territorially delimited democracy.

Having reconsidered the received wisdom of political community in relation to progress and democracy, this section finishes by revisiting the issue of the *boundaries* of political community (see Chapter 3). Again, what stands out is that, despite their profound political differences, commentators on this issue tend to share a common and restrictive starting-point, in this case that forming an inside of political community creates relative moral indifference to outsiders. On this even Carl Schmitt and the neo-Kantians can agree, even if this leads the former to affirm such indifference as the essence of the political while the later seek to overcome it by proposing cosmopolitan political community in which there is no more outside. But what neither of these positions allows for is the ethical significance of boundaries, specifically that the inside/outside of political community may be necessary to an ethics of *hospitality*. Absent some division between political inside and outside – one that preserves the 'at home' of political community and thereby also the distinction between self/citizen and Other/foreigner – hospitality is nothing, having no home to open up and no strangers to welcome. Thus while the boundedness of political community may be democratically illegitimate, from the standpoint of hospitality it is irreducible. However, irreducible does not mean unproblematic. Beyond the narrow confines of the cosmopolitan-communitarian debate hospitality requires that boundaries be neither removed (cosmopolitanism) nor reified (communitarianism). Working out what this means for the practice of political community is challenging to say the least.

Part 2. Political community and the postmodern

Looking at the limitations of our conceptual language of political community – a language which limits our attempts to think differently about, which is also to say difference in, political community – is only one way in which it is important to face up to the challenge of rethinking political community. There is also the question of how, if at all, the *practice* of political community might escape from modernist, statist assumptions of identity, of an identity between sovereignty, state, people and territory in particular. This is a critical question since post-structuralist critiques have already deeply problematized, in the sense of denaturalizing, all identity claims. Think, for instance, of the crisis post-structuralism engenders for representative claims; for traditional notions of interest; for the assumed self-identity of the nation state – in short for the political subject of modernity, whether based on class or nation, itself.

Yet post-structuralism has sought not only to critique a modern politics – there is also now a richly suggestive body of thought as to what the political might mean in the postmodern condition, and it is to this thought, to date neglected, that this section turns in its reflections on political community. The key questions here, though they pose yet more questions rather than suggesting easy answers, are put well by Jacques Derrida. When Derrida talks about a European identity which must avoid being identical with itself – of not *not* having an identity, but of having an identity which is not able to identify itself – what can this mean for political community as previously understood (Derrida 1992: 9)? Or when Derrida identifies the other as being the first condition of an identity that is not destructive of self and others, what does this imply for a politics defined by inside-outside, by the friend-enemy distinction still so familiar to us today (Derrida 1992: 15)? In sum, what does a politics of alterity look like, or is this a very contradiction in terms?

The contributions to this section face up the considerable challenge posed by this question by asking whether we can indeed go beyond essences (be they national, class-based, religious, etc.) in our thinking about the future of political community. Can we (asks Chapter 4, by way of a reflection on Nietzsche's idea of the 'good Europeans') have political community based not on some essentialist idea of identity but instead on an openness or radical freedom in which the good citizen refuses any identifier other than radical contingency itself? And if this implies a form of belonging or community that is simply too thin or too demanding (or both), then can the problem be re-posed (see Chapter 5) as one of 'critical belonging' to one's political community? Can we acknowledge our inevitable situatedness in community while yet avoiding a conservative reluctance to be questioning of that community? More challenging still, can we glean this thought of 'critical belonging' from the work of Martin Heidegger who himself infamously failed to *critically* belong in Nazi Germany?

Also necessary to this process of reflection on the possibility of postmodern political community is the question, already implied above, of whether we are still talking about a *politics* here. According to one argument, there is a large question-mark over the very possibility of political community today, given the apparent 'missing middle' or lack of mediation between the individual and the global characteristic of our present condition. Absent convincing avenues for the articulation of collective political subjectivity (class and nation in particular) the postmodern individual is at once highly individuated and, by extension, also immediately global. It is arguably easier for the postmodern subject to identify, in a highly individualistic, often confused and contradictory way, with a variety of self-chosen causes at the global level (an 'end to world poverty' along with 'saving the planet' from ecological catastrophe, perhaps?) than it is for her to make the accommodations necessary to collective action at a more local level. The postmodern individual is charged, in short, with exhibiting a subjectivity characterized by a peculiarly narcissistic form of depoliticisation. Is he, then, suitable material for a postmodern politics at all?

This is the debate at the heart of this section and, indeed, at the heart of any analysis of contemporary political possibilities. Can we have postmodern political community which succeeds in going 'beyond' essences, or is our very 'freedom' to engage in politics thus, to choose our identities and campaigns, reflective of a *lack* of social ties and social engagement? Arguing this case (see Chapter 6) involves re-reading the 1990s against the grain of those celebratory accounts which point to the emergence of new forms of post-national political community. Instead, we can see this decade as witnessing an *implosion* of political community as political engagement was increasingly evaded by liberal cosmopolitans claiming the elite rights of advocacy on behalf of the excluded and the marginal. But from this perspective, the radical critique of liberal cosmopolitanism that has emerged in the last decade from neo-Foucauldian theorists has similarly failed to identify a political subject. The result has been that liberal cosmopolitan advocacy on behalf of the Other has merely been replaced by respect for and awareness of the Other. Neither of these idealized routes to political engagement, it can be argued, offer any possibility of real political engagment and therefore lack a meaningful account of political community. The provacative implication of this analysis is that self-styled radicals need to eschew the global space of identity politics and instead experiment with building up social bonds with their peers in ways that limit their freedoms and develop their sense of responsibility and accountability to others. Under modern conditions these social connections will presumably have to be artificially constructed and their value justified through a demonstrable ability to engage with, understand, critique, and ultimately overcome the political practices and subjectivities of our time.

Part 3. Learning from the past and understanding future transformations

This section turns to the important question of what we can learn about the future of political community from the past. What comes to light when we consider the classical and humanist traditions of reflection on politics is that, unlike the moderns, and thus quite differently from the spirit of this book too, critique is not the exclusive vantage point taken. According to the tradition of rhetoric (see Chapter 7), it is not enough merely to attend to the coherence of an argument; ingenuity must be used and fantasy deployed in order to provide new perspectives on it. The importance of this insight to our collection is that it provides one possible resource for escaping the modernist ruts that our reflections on political community repeatedly fall into despite attempts at new thinking, the problem highlighted in section one. One important aspect of this problem that the neglected tradition of rhetoric might help us to avoid is that of the highly restrictive dependence of all critical approaches on the position that they seek to critique. Contra critique, with its exclusive search for Truth, rhetoric, with its love of eloquence, is more attuned to the problem of how to maintain political community. Indeed, for Cicero, in holding out the possibility of maintaining cities in peace and justice rhetoric brings its practitioners as close to divinity as is humanly possible.

A second stuck-in-a-rut modern thought of political community that the ancients may help us to get out of concerns the place of 'others' in the formation of a state's identity. The received wisdom is that such 'othering' is a *sine qua non* of political community formation, but drawing on the *Iliad* and the *Aeneid* throws doubt on this assumption (see Chapter 8). In both these ancient texts, 'others' feature centrally (as Trojans in the *Iliad* and as an assortment of non-Romans in the *Aeneid*), but largely not as essentialized and demonized outsiders and often as courageous fellow warriors who share the same basic values and practices and compete for the same honour. In this, Homer and Virgil find agreement with some of the findings of modern psychology, where identities can form effectively in the absence of others and where in-group solidarity is compatible with positive feelings towards outgroups. Echoing the nature of the conflict between the Greeks and Trojans as evoked in the *Iliad*, even in a situation of mutual hatred respect may be present and stereotyping largely absent. In sum, political community formation, as much for the future of political community as for the ancients, may be consistent with respect for, and inclusion of, 'others'. Perhaps political community is not the fiend many critically-minded people today take it for after all.

Finally, having built a sense of just how difficult it is to transform our understanding of political community or to think differently about its practices, our focus in the final part of this section turns appropriately to the question of just how political community *is* transformed. For, regardless of how well we can describe it, the transformation of political community happens, and it is in understanding this change that out best hope of thinking and speaking differently of political community lies. Where our conceptual language lags so far behind these changes themselves, this more applied approach is a crucial complement to the theory of the previous two sections.

When considering how the transformation of political community occurs in practice, we need to know what the primary drivers of this change are today. For, contra most accounts of political life, where the sovereign state is removed from history and portrayed as a timeless universal with no beginning or end, the challenge accepted here is to understand under what particular conditions the emergence of new forms of political community are likely and how these conditions are tied into new forms of authority and sociability.

Taking this process of change at the global level, we need to ask whether current descriptions of an epochal shift from a national to a post-national politics actually tell us anything about processes of political community formation at the global level. For example, the claim by much of the cosmopolitan literature that a global public sphere is emerging as the basis for global democratic law and rights appears as more a statement of normative intent than an analysis of political possibility. We are left wondering whether the very notion of democratic law and rights on a cosmopolitical scale presuppose that which is absent in world politics – the political subject of such rights, that is a global citizenry that might lay claim to the idea of popular sovereignty at a global level. Rather than presupposing the emergence of post-national or cosmopolitan forms of political community simply because this is deemed normatively desirable, then, we should instead ask what new forms of global political *authority* are emerging and how *these* are shaping new forms of political community rather than vice versa. And indeed (see Chapter 9), analyzing the emergence of political authority at the global level, and the constraints to this new form of authority imposed by a world society that is brought into existence by and in response to it, points us to the constitutive tension between society and community that is always at stake in processes of political community formation.

Political community formation at the global level, as elsewhere, does not require that first there be legitimacy for such a project, but rather that the authority effects of global governance come to be authorized in some way. For this to happen depends on whether the outcomes of global governance are, first, perceived as of public relevance and, second, whether the participants in global governance recognize each other as legitimate subjects of a common political enterprise. The messy complexity of the struggles that these two conditions give rise to, far from indicating a legitimation crisis at the transnational level, are always a central part of political community formation, representing as they do the opposition necessary to any political process. It is precisely ongoing contestation of what is included and what excluded (the 'inclusion of exclusion') from a political community that leads to its integration in the first place. Indeed, this open historical process of contestation lay at the heart of the emergence of the nation-state itself. To what extent postnational process of political community formation lead to forms of political community deemed to be legitimate is, of course, an open question. What is certain, however, is that the contestation which drives political community formation is ongoing.

Bibliography

Archibugi, D. (ed.) (2003) *Debating Cosmopolitics*, London: Verso.

Archibugi, D., Held, D. and Köhler, M. (eds) (1998) *Re-Imagining Political Community*, Oxford: Polity Press.

Bader, V. (1997) 'The Cultural Conditions of Transnational Citizenship. On the Interpenetration of Political and Ethnic Cultures', *Political Theory*, 25(6): 771–813.

Bartelson, J. (1995) 'The Trial of Judgment: A Note on Kant and the Paradoxes of Internationalism', *International Studies Quarterly*, 39: 259–285.

Bauböck, R. (2002) 'Political Community Beyond the Sovereign State, Supranational Federalism, and Transnational Minorities', in S. Vertovec and R. Cohen (eds) *Conceiving Cosmopolitanism. Theory, Context, Practice*, Oxford: Oxford University Press.

Bauman, Z. (2001) *Community*, Cambridge: Polity Press.

Benhabib, S. (2004) *The Rights of Others. Aliens, Residents and Citizens*, Cambridge: Cambridge University Press.

Bonnell, V.E. and Hunt, L. (1999) *Beyond the Cultural Turn*, Berkeley: University of California Press.

Delanty, G. (2003) *Community*, London: Routledge.

Derrida, J. (1992) *The Other Heading: Reflections on Today's Europe*, trans. P.A. Brault and M.B. Nass, Bloomington: Indiana University Press.

Durkheim, E. (1964) *The Division of Labor in Society*, New York: Free Press.

Elias, N. (1991) *The Society of Individuals*, Oxford: Polity Press.

Hall, S. (2002) 'Political Belonging in a World of Multiple Identities', in S. Vertovec and R. Cohen (eds) *Conceiving Cosmopolitanism. Theory, Context, Practice*, Oxford: Oxford University Press.

Held, D. (1995) *Democracy and the Global Order. From the Modern State to Cosmopolitan Governance*, Cambridge: Polity Press.

—— (1998) 'Democracy and Globalization', in D. Archibugi, D. Held and M. Köhler (eds) *Re-Imagining Political Community*, Oxford: Polity Press.

—— (2003) 'Cosmopolitanism: Globalization Tamed?' in *Review of International Studies*, 29(4): 465–480.

Hollinger, D.A. (2001) 'Not Universalists, Not Pluralists: The New Cosmopolitans Find Their Own Way', *Constellations*, 8(2): 236–248.

International Commission on Intervention and State Sovereignty (2001), *The Responsibility to Protect*, report available at: www.iciss.ca/pdf/Commission-Report.pdf, (Accessed 23 May, 2008).

Linklater, A. (1998) *The Transformation of Political Community. Ethical Foundations of the Post-Westphalian Era*, Cambridge: Polity Press.

Schofield, M. (1991) *The Stoic Idea of the City*, Cambridge: Cambridge University Press.

Smith, R. (2003) *Stories of Peoplehood*, Cambridge: Cambridge University Press.

Tan, K.-C. (2004) *Justice Without Borders: Cosmopolitanism, Nationalism, and Patriotism*, Cambridge: Cambridge University Press.

Tönnies, F. (1957) *Community and Society*, East Lansing: Michigan State University Press.

Walker, R.B.J. (1993) *Inside/Outside: International Relations as Political Theory*, Cambridge: Cambridge University Press.

Part I

Assumptions of political community

Progress, democracy and
boundaries in question

1 Dream or nightmare?

Thinking the future of world politics[1]

Kimberly Hutchings

The focus of this volume is on different ways in which we can theorize the future of political community at the beginning of the twenty-first century. In this chapter, rather than developing a substantive account of what the future might hold my concern is with analysing what it means to theorize the future of politics in the first place. In particular my concern is to examine the assumptions about time that underpin influential accounts of both the present and future of world politics. Since 1989 a variety of theories of the temporal trajectory of world politics have flourished. These include accounts of the world-political present as embedded in narratives of progress in which a cosmopolitan future is immanent, and much more apocalyptic accounts which describe or foretell a situation in which politics is exhausted and the existence of the world itself is in question. I will argue that such analyses rely on theorizing time in ways that are fundamentally at odds with the actual temporal plurality (heterotemporality) of world politics and that are therefore unhelpful for addressing the question of the future of political community in a hierarchically organized, plural and interconnected world. The argument proceeds in four sections. First, I examine how the time of politics is constructed in the Western tradition of political thought as produced through the interaction of two different forms of temporality: *chronos* and *kairos*. In the second and third sections I examine the arguments of two influential theorists of the future of political community, Habermas and Agamben, who exemplify respectively the cosmopolitan and apocalyptic tendencies referred to above. In the final section, I argue that the alternative approach to political temporality found in Connolly's work provides a more productive starting point for theorizing political futures.

Political time: *chronos* and *kairos*

The *chronos/kairos* distinction is often traced back to ancient Greek thought. In this context, a contrast was drawn between time as quantitatively measurable duration, associated with the inevitable birth-death life cycle of individuals (*chronos*), and time as a transformational time of action, in which the certainty of death and decay is challenged (*kairos*) (Smith 1969; 1986; Lindroos 1998: 11–12). The contrast between *chronos* and *kairos* in Greek thought captures a range of meanings. It distinguishes both analytically and evaluatively between normal and exceptional time. Analytically, it presents exceptional time as challenging or interrupting normal time, and it links 'normal' to the idea of time as a quantitatively infinite, divisible medium within which finite lives are lived out, and 'exceptional' to a qualitative event that creates, arrests or changes time, rather than endures it. Normatively, it links the *kariotic* challenge to *chronos* with an idea of 'timeliness', in which the overcoming of human subordination to natural *chronotic*[2] temporality is celebrated (Smith 1969).[3]

Most mundane ways of breaking down social time depend on thinking of time as a medium, which can be represented and subdivided in a range of ways.[4] The prevailing version of *chronos* in modern societies rests on Newtonian assumptions about time, in which time as linear, infinite succession conditions the possibility of counting time by means of the clock (Nowotny 1994: 13–14). On this account, time is universally the same, it proceeds at a constant pace, and it is infinitely divisible and linear. It is also a neutral medium and measure, events and experiences happen within it, novel and familiar, but time itself does not change qualitatively. The notion of time as a neutral, constant, measurable and measuring medium opens up a variety of possibilities for thinking about the relation of present to past and present to future in the natural and social sciences. For instance, it becomes possible to divide the past into specific periods, to make direct comparison between events at the *same* time or at *different* times, to make judgments about the sameness or novelty of now as opposed to then, and to speculate about the near or distant future. Newton's theory of time does not presume an 'arrow of time', but eighteenth- and nineteenth-century developments in physics (thermodynamics) and biology (evolution) suggested that time was not only infinite and linear but also uni-directional and irreversible.[5] On this view, *chronos* becomes bound up with a particular account of causation, in which, because time is irreversible, cause must precede effect, and in which the sequence of events potentially becomes the key to their explanation, whether in the natural or the social world.[6] It therefore becomes possible, with hindsight, to identify patterns of cause and effect, which in turn may enable prediction of what is to come.

However, if clock and causal chronologies open up a variety of possibilities for how to think about the relation between past and present in the social world, it does not exhaust those possibilities. In modern European thought, alongside *chronotic* conceptions of time, we also find a variety of ways of thinking about time that simultaneously rely on and are in *kairotic* tension with those conceptions. These ways of thinking about time establish patterns for political time that work across and through *chronotic* time, in a way reminiscent of the Greek interruption of *chronos* by *kairos*. They draw on qualitatively specific temporal categories, such as beginnings, ends, novelty, repetition, stasis and change. And they superimpose alternative linear and cyclical temporalities on the infinite, indifferent time of the clock.

In a meditation on the relation between 'politics' as a practice in the present and 'history' as the inheritance of the past, Pocock refers to two of the ways in which the *chronos/ kairos* distinction has been theorized in western political thought:

To the Florentines she was the maenad Fortune, an irrational and irresistible stream of happenings. To the Romantics she was (and is) the Goddess History, of their relationship with whom they expect a final consummation, only too likely to prove a *Liebestod*.

(Pocock 1973: 271)

The figures of Fortune and the Goddess History are drawn from a Machiavellian understanding of political time on the one hand, and, on the other, from teleological eighteenth and nineteenth century theories of history. In the case of Machiavelli, the temporality of politics is understood as an ongoing struggle between fortune and *virtú* for control.[7] Both fortune and *virtú* have the capacity to direct natural *chronotic* time, though in rather different ways. Whilst fortune is *kairotic*, an external, arbitrary power behind what 'happens', *virtú* is the (always temporary) capacity to tap into that *kairotic* power, and re-shape what 'happens'. Politics, as opposed to nature, is the sphere of a re-shaped nature, emerging out of the potential of *kairos*, whether as fortune or *virtú*, to interrupt *chronos*.

For Machiavelli, the struggle between fortune and *virtú* is not capable of being won by one side or the other. The most virtuous leader is liable to come unstuck through bad luck, the most profound bad luck may still be countered and even exploited by the 'virtuous' leader. For this reason, the combination of *chronos* and *kairos* in Machiavelli's thinking about the temporality of politics results in a cyclical understanding of politics as the rise and fall of power. In contrast, according to the Romantic theories of history to which Pocock is referring, political time is structured in relation to a specific end, which can be understood in positive or negative terms. Instead of the Machiavellian struggle and its cyclical implications for the understanding of politics, here we find an eschatological temporal trajectory, which may provide grounds for either hope or despair.

In terms of theories of contemporary world politics, it isn't difficult to identify assumptions about political time that echo Machiavellian or Romantic themes. In this chapter I will focus on examples of the latter. However, whether one operates with an account of political time in terms of repetition, progress or apocalyptic end there are certain implications that are common when it comes to considering the future of political community. The first is that the account of time operates as a unifying principle, enabling the possibility of making judgments about world politics as a whole, in spite of its plurality and complexity. The second is that such assumptions about time situate the theorist as holding the key to the *kairotic* possibility of controlling and shaping the everyday time of *chronos*. Machiavelli sought to show how the man of *virtù* could tap into the power of *kairos* to create a new political time that was reducible to neither nature nor chance. Thinkers such as Rousseau, Kant, Hegel and Marx laid claim to grasping the *kairotic* principles that shape the direction of history, thereby enabling timely intervention into the ongoing *chronos* of empirical events.

Cosmopolitan futures: Habermas and the 'Kantian project'

Habermas's critical theory has been formulated over the past half-century and encompasses a wide variety of arguments in philosophy and social theory, as well as shifts in ideological orientation, from its beginnings in the neo-Marxist tradition of the Frankfurt School. However, one of the threads that has persisted in his work throughout this time, from the *Structural Transformation of the Public Sphere* (1989) to the legal and political theory presented in works such as *Between Facts and Norms* (1996) and the essays recently gathered together in translation, *The Divided West* (2006), is the historical significance of modernity. Even in his earlier work, in which Habermas focused on the legitimacy crisis in modern social demo-cratic states, he nevertheless found the solution to modernity's problems within modernity itself (Habermas 1979). In his mature work, this solution is located in the presuppositions of communicative action, which underpin both Habermas's 'dis-course ethics' (1990; 1992)[8] and the evolution of societies from traditional to mod-ern forms (1979). They are also at the heart of the self-reflexive capacity of 'lifeworld' in modern societies to act as critical constraint on 'system' (1984; 1987).[9] And they ground the necessity of the link between popular sovereignty and human rights foundational to the constitution of the modern democratic state, and to the extension of constitutionalism beyond the bounds of the state (1996; 1997; 1998; 2006). Habermas's social, political and ethical theories build on the work of Kant, Hegel and Marx, but also on that of theorists as diverse as Austin and Luhmann, and he denies that his diagnosis of modernity and of the possibility of progress within it relies on a philosophy of history. Nevertheless Kant has become the most significant reference point in Habermas's defence of the progressive potential of modernity in the post Cold War world, and the latter's argumentative strategies are increasingly reminiscent of Kant's arguments in his political writings on peace and universal history (Kant 1991). This is evident in Habermas's argu-ment for the continuing robustness of what he terms the 'Kantian project' of 'con-stitutionalizing' international law, in the face of a variety of other interpretations of the direction of world politics after the Cold War and 9/11.[10]

In his essay 'The Kantian Project and the Divided West' (2006: 115–193), Habermas defends the ongoing 'juridification' of international politics through a combination of philosophical and socio-historical argument, in which the ques-tions of what international politics is and what it ought to be are inextricably entan-gled with one another. The essay begins with a historical claim:

> Following two world wars, the constitutionalization of international law has evolved along the lines prefigured by Kant toward cosmopolitan law and has assumed institutional form in international constitutions, organizations and procedures.

> (2006: 115)

Habermas explains this historical trend as the product of collective learning processes (2006:147), of a double kind. These learning processes reflect the lesson of the horrors of war but also the lesson learned *within* the modern constitutional state that law, properly understood, rationalizes power in a normatively positive way (138–139;148–150). It is the latter lesson that is most crucial, since it demonstrates the connection *in principle* between law and peace. This conceptual connection, which Habermas elucidates at length in *Between Facts and Norms*, derives from the formal properties of law itself, first properly unpacked in the social contract theories of Rousseau and Kant (2006: 131). On Habermas's reading of Rousseau's and Kant's arguments, law puts an end to the wars of the state of nature not because it equates to the sword in the hands of leviathan, as for Hobbes, but because the universal form of law presupposes conditions of equality and impartiality that can only be fully satisfied if positive law is grounded in a constitution in which democratic will-formation and fundamental rights are embedded. Civil peace within the state, therefore, is only ultimately to be found within the constitutional state and, for similar reasons, peace between states could only be ensured for Kant if they (states) entered a law-governed condition under a cosmopolitan constitution (2006: 121–22). According to Habermas, this explains Kant's arguments for reading history from a cosmopolitan point of view (2006: 122).

Habermas reads the idea that there is a conceptual connection between peace and law back into the logical and historical implications of international law, which, he argues, have become increasingly, though still inadequately, constitutionalized during the twentieth century. He departs from Kant, however, in refusing the two options Kant presents for the *telos* of inter-state relations, that of constitution as a world republic on the one hand (2006: 123), and that of the 'league or confederation of nations' on the other (2006: 124). Instead, Habermas goes on to build on Kant's analysis in a different way, arguing that the constitutionalization of international law is complementary rather than analogous to the constitutionalization of law within the state (2006: 134). Habermas suggests that the constitutionalization of international law is not necessarily tied to the idea of a world republic, since the key actors involved are collectives (states) rather than individuals (citizens) and the purpose is not to constitutionalize (rationalize, constrain) an already existing political power but to enable the fulfilment of diverse functions, many of which do not require a supranational level of authority (2006: 134). According to Habermas, the kind of constitution already implicit in supranational and transnational organizations implies a multi-level system of authority. He sees the constitutions (founding treaties and charters) of existing organizations such as the United Nations, the World Trade Organization and, above all, the European Union, as foreshadowing the shape that such a multi-level constitutionalized global order is likely to take (2006: 134; 140). At the supranational level, Habermas suggests that legal authority would (and should) be largely confined to the preservation of peace and the protection of human rights:

> Supranational constitutions rest at any rate on basic rights, legal principles, and criminal codes which are the product of prior learning processes and have been tried and tested within democratic nation-states. Thus, their normative substance evolved from constitutions of the republican type. This holds not only

for the UN Charter and the Universal Declaration of Human Rights, but even for the treaties underlying GATT and the WTO.

To this extent, the constitutionalization of international law retains a derivative status because it depends on 'advances' of legitimation from democratic constitutional states.

(2006: 140–1)

The conceptual connection between law and peace is carried historically by 'democratic constitutional states', and the 'prior learning processes' embodied in them, and transferred by those states to the realm of international law. However, Habermas is not only suggesting that the limited requirements to 'not – engage in wars of aggression and not – commit crimes against humanity' (2006: 143) are presupposed empirically in existing, partial constitutionalizations of international law. In addition, he argues that these requirements are universally valid beyond the 'thick' claims of differing identities and cultural traditions.[11]

Habermas's adaptation of the 'Kantian project' attempts to draw out the logic implicit in the idea of law, but, as with Kant, goes beyond the realm of the 'idea' by tracing that logic within empirical history (*chronos*), specifically the empirical history of Western modernity. As with Kant also, however, Habermas is insistent that the necessary links between law and peace may not be empirically realized within the workings of *chronos* (2006: 144) and that this therefore necessitates philosophical history:

the idea of a cosmopolitan condition, however normatively well founded, remains an empty, even deceptive, promise without a realistic assessment of the totality of accommodating trends in which it is embedded.

(2006: 144)

Kant, Habermas argues, used his philosophy of history to help render the cosmopolitan condition empirically probable and plausible (2006: 145). According to Habermas, Kant's identification of cosmopolitan historical trends in his philosophy of history suffered from blind-spots inherent in his time and place, but nevertheless remains significant in principle insofar as it rests on 'the cognitive procedure of universalization and mutual perspective-taking which Kant associates with practical reason and which underlies the cosmopolitan transformation of international law' (2006: 146). Habermas therefore undertakes to read the history of international law and international politics in a way that does better justice to Kant's insights into the real meaning of progress in history. He does this by identifying those historical developments that 'meet the Kantian project halfway' (2006: 143) and by setting his reading of history against alternative possibilities, which put international politics beyond law or reduce international law to an instrument of power politics or cultural identity (2006: 148–9). In doing this, Habermas acknowledges the depth of conflict over different interpretations of international law and of the history of international law, but argues that this conflict itself militates against a reduction of international law to power, since the relation asserted between law and power is 'affected by the normative self-understanding of state actors', a self-understanding shaped by the constitutional history of the state actor in question (2006: 150).

Habermas goes on to offer a reading of the history of international politics and successive institutionalisations of international law that point to ways in which it accords with, and ways in which it runs counter to, any cosmopolitan promise. In his account, the UN Charter plays a particularly significant role in relation to three of its features. First, in the connections it makes between securing peace and human rights. Second, in the link made between prohibitions on the use of violence and the threat of prosecution and sanctions. Third, in the inclusivity of the UN's membership and the universal validity claimed for the law it enacts (2006: 160–166). For Habermas all three of these features make explicit the link in principle between law, democracy and rights and thereby represent moves towards a cosmopolitan constitution. However, evidence in both Cold War and post-Cold War periods for the consolidation of this cosmopolitanism is, as Habermas acknowledges, ambiguous (2006: 161; 168–69). As well as cosmopolitan innovations in international law, such as the spread of international human rights law in the Cold War period or the humanitarian interventions of the 1990s, there are also many examples of the redundancy and manipulation of the UN and its founding principles. In addition, these developments in the 'high politics' of international relations are situated in a wider context, 'the emergence of a world society, chiefly as a result of the globalization of markets and communication networks' (2006: 175). Globalization, Habermas argues, is a set of systemic processes that has led to the multiplication of international organizations and the intensification of global governance, taking the world into a new 'postnational constellation' that, it turns out, 'meets the constititutionalization of international law halfway' (2006: 177).

Although he does not claim that globalization is straightforwardly progressive (in his terms) in its effects, nevertheless Habermas does claim that the pressures of globalization tend to strengthen the common interest of states in the rule of law and also socialize state actors to act in ways that acknowledge mutual dependence and increasingly undermine the distinction between domestic and foreign policy (2006: 177). The latter reinforces the principled link between all law and its (rationally required) legitimate grounding in democratic will-formation and fundamental human rights. This is exemplified, for Habermas, by the case of the EU in which 'if the chains of democratic legitimation are not to break, civic solidarity must extend across former national borders within the enlarged communities' (2006: 177). In this respect, globalization reinforces the previously relatively weak link between international law and 'world citizens' (2006: 135) and greatly enhances the chances of the cosmopolitan logic of international law unfolding historically.[12]

For Habermas, the world-historical significance of Western modernity lies in its institutionalization of practices of communicative, as well as instrumental, rationalization at the phylogenetic (socio-political) level. Just as for Kant, only societies that embed the principle of right in a republican constitution can bring politics into accord with the demands of practical reason, so for Habermas, only those societies that embed the possibility of discursive validation of claims to truth and justice can take forward the *telos* immanent in communicative action. Like Kant, Habermas, having identified the ideal *telos* of history, recognizes that development towards that *telos* is not inevitable, and that one must distinguish between empirical and philosophical history. Like Kant also, however, he sees the task of the philosopher as being to forge a link between philosophical and empirical accounts by reading history 'from a cosmopolitan point of view'. In doing this, however, the nature of the link between empirical and philosophical remains ambiguous. On the one hand, the philosopher's reading of history represents a transcendental moral judgment of what 'ought to be' a categorical imperative for those dedicated to progress. On the other hand, the reading of history is presented as immanent to historical development, a truth that can be read off by an impartial observer of the 'logic' of modernity. On the one hand, progress is carried self-consciously by principles of self-reflexivity built into complex societies, on the other hand it is carried willy-nilly by processes such as globalization that intensify that complexity and carry it beyond state borders. Habermas's argument replicates Kant's in its reliance on a particular relation between *chronos* and *kairos*, in which the latter is carried through, but also shapes the former, and in which there is a constant dialectic between determinism (fate) and self-determination (autonomy). The role of the philosopher is both to interpret the meaning and direction of political time and to intervene to push historical development in the 'right' direction. His insights are a product of his time and place (western modernity) but they are also universally valid and applicable.

Apocalyptic time: Agamben's messianic moment

Agamben comments in *Homo Sacer* (1998) (and again in *Means Without End: Notes on Politics*, 2000) that in order to grapple fully with the meaning of the present in world politics, one needs the capacity to think the end of history and the end of the state simultaneously and to mobilize the one against the other (1998: 60; 2000: 111). Following the footsteps of Benjamin,[13] and to a lesser extent, Arendt, Derrida and Foucault, Agamben's work deconstructs the claims of modernist philosophy of history and the sovereign authority of the modern state, and looks for an alternative conception of politics, beyond historicism and law. Conceptions of time and temporality are crucial to Agamben's deconstructive and constructive arguments. In an early text, *Infancy and History: essay on the destruction of experience* (2007), Agamben engages critically with two prevalent ways of approaching the understanding of human culture: historicist (diachronic) and structuralist (synchronic) (2007: 85). Agamben argues that diachronic and synchronic temporalities can be found in all cultures. However, neither of them in isolation captures the meaning of human temporality (historicity), instead this is to be found in the interplay between them:

> in historically cumulative societies the linearity of time is always arrested by the calendrical alternation and repetition of holiday time; in historically stationary societies circularity is always interrupted by profane time.
>
> (2007: 86)

In effect, Agamben is arguing that human temporality is located in the ways in which *chronos* (clock-time, profane time) and *kairos* (calendar time, sacred time) interrupt each other. And he argues that the condition of possibility of this interruption lies in the relation between human beings and language. The origin of human relation to language is marked by difference and discontinuity. Each 'speaker' is only able to enter language (and therefore enter culture and history) by differentiating him/herself in infancy from language within language as the 'I' that speaks (2007: 59). This originary splitting is what makes history, as opposed to biological evolution, possible. And it also underwrites foundational distinctions between nature and culture, private and public, time (*chronos*) and history (*kairos*) (2007: 93).[14] This means that history is, in principle, not about linear continuity (2007: 60). Nevertheless, Agamben goes on to argue, because different experiences and conceptions of time condition different conceptions of history, modern political thought has tended to fall into the trap of equating human, historical time with the linear time of *chronos* (2007: 99).

Following Benjamin, Agamben suggests that the way in which to approach an alternative experience of being-in-time, which would be more adequate to the 'original dimension of man' is to concentrate on moments in which the line of time is experienced as broken or halted. One dimension of experience in which this happens is in pleasure, and Agamben makes a direct analogy between the experience of pleasure and the nature of revolutionary action, in which time is qualitatively altered:

> For history is not, as the dominant ideology would have it, man's servitude to continuous linear time, but man's liberation from it: the time of history and the *cairós* in which man, by his initiative, grasps favourable opportunity and chooses his own freedom in the moment.
>
> (2007: 115)

Agamben's account of human temporality in *Infancy and History* depends on a differentiation between human and animal. Animals do not enter language, but humans do, and thereby condition the distinctions between animal/human, nature/culture, private/public, time/history that make politics possible (2007: 59; 1998: 8). The crucial difference between politics today and classical politics is that these distinctions have been undermined by the modern state. In the classical polis *zoē* (simple, natural life, shared by animals and humans) is excluded from the realm of politics proper, and is confined to the private realm of the household. This kind of life is clearly distinguished from *bios*, 'the form or way of living proper to an individual or a group' (1998: 1), which takes place in the public sphere. The classical polis depends on marking the distinctions between these two different realms of existence. In contrast, in the modern state, the realm of *zoē* becomes increasingly politicized and its distinction from *bios* disappears from view. Instead, politics becomes bio-politics, devoted to the production and preservation of natural life. The result of this is twofold, on the one hand, as Foucault has shown, there is a proliferation of disciplinary technologies through which individuals are produced as 'docile bodies'. On the other hand, there is a massive increase in the power of the state to control all aspects of human existence. In *Homo Sacer* and various later volumes, Agamben aims to elucidate these conditions and their implications and to examine the possibilities for an alternative politics (1998: 10–11).

In accounting for the nature of sovereign power, Agamben utilizes two figures: the sovereign authority whose right to decide on the exception underpins law (1998: 26) and *homo sacer* (1998: 81–83). *Homo sacer* is the figure who, in Roman law, marks the boundary between political life and natural life as a being that may not be sacrificed but may be killed. What is important about both of these figures is the way in which both represent zones of indistinction between what lies inside and outside of the polis. The sovereign power of exception is both law and not law; *homo sacer* is both included and excluded from both nature and politics, his life is 'bare life', not even the simple, natural life of *zoē*:

> At the two extreme limits of the order, the sovereign and *homo sacer* present two symmetrical figures that have the same structure and are correlative: the sovereign is the one with respect to whom all men are potentially *homines sacri*, and *homo sacer* is the one with respect to whom all men act as sovereigns.
>
> (1998: 84)

This symmetrical relation between sovereignty and the bare life of *homo sacer* is, Agamben argues, fundamental to all sovereign power, whatever the specific form taken by polis or state. In the modern state, however, the moment of inclusive exclusion, that in the classical polis confirmed and protected the distinction between political life and natural life through the production of bare life, has become more than a moment of exception. This is because the dependence of the exercise of sovereign power on its inclusive exclusion of life has shifted from the margin to the centre of politics. This follows the growing importance of the needs and interests of whole populations to the perpetuation of state power since the seventeenth century, accompanied by the discourse of 'rights of man' that sought to challenge but actually reinforced new biopolitical forms of sovereign power (1998: 121).[15] Within the modern state, all citizens can be said 'in a specific but extremely real sense, to appear virtually as *homines sacri*' (1998: 111). In other words, the moment of exception, in which politics is constituted through sovereign exclusion of life, has become the predominant mode in which politics is conducted. It is for this reason that Agamben sees the camp as the 'biopolitical paradigm of the modern'. Although Agamben's focus is very much on the western philosophical tradition and the western 'Westphalian' state, he extends this analysis to the situation of humanity in general in the context of globalization. In contrast to Habermas, he identifies the rise of humanitarian intervention in the 1990s as an example of totalizing power. The problem is how to get away from the totalization and reinvent a different form of politics. For Agamben, the answer has to come from starting with the zones of indistinction characteristic of contemporary world politics. Engaging with the relation between sovereign power and sacred life with a view to transcending it, involves bringing together the thought of the end of the state with the thought of the end of history, and making a connection between human temporality and the space of exception.

Agamben's answer to the problem of a new politics is developed in the text in which he returns to the idea of a conception of human temporality (historicity) different from that embedded in chronology and philosophies of history, *The Time That Remains: a commentary on the letter to the Romans* (2005b). This text consists in an analysis of the opening passages of Paul's 'Letter to the Romans' in the Christian *New Testament*. This is a text written in order to convey the meaning of 'messianic time', the time of an exigent present, a kind of dislocation between chronological time and its apocalyptic end (2005b: 62). For Agamben, it is a text with extraordinary relevance for our time ('timeliness') because it articulates a time that is neither eschatological nor chronological, and which is also simultaneously within and without the spaces of state and law. Paul is writing about a time in which the end of both history and state power are immanent. It is this same kind of time, Agamben argues, that is at issue in Benjamin's notion of 'messianic time' in the *Theses on the Philosophy of History*.[16] For Agamben, it is through re-connecting with the experience of messianic time in both Paul and Benjamin that the opening into '*nonstatal and nonjuridical*' politics may become possible:

> the messianic vocation is a movement of immanence or, if one prefers, a zone of absolute indiscernability between immanence and transcendence, between this world and the future world. This will be important in understanding the structure of messianic time.
>
> (2005b: 25)

Agamben tries to capture the meaning of messianic time in terms of the modality of 'exigency'. In unpacking this concept, he echoes Benjamin's critique of victors' history in *Theses on the Philosophy of History* and calls for a similar mode of relating present to past. For Benjamin, the task of the historical materialist is to identify those moments in the past that call the present into question and fuse with the present in a making of history in which time comes to a standstill (Benjamin 1999: 245–6). For Agamben, this means an acknowledgement in the present of responsibility to the exigency of the 'forgotten', all of the moments that will never be remembered because they are not part of victors' history. This responsibility is not about writing alternative subaltern histories, but about recognising the dependence of the present on the forgotten past, and therefore the existence of an ongoing claim of the past upon the present (1991: 40–1). The weak messianic power inherent in the present, to which the apostle testifies, must be firmly distinguished from the figures of both prophecy and apocalypse as well as from standard secular readings of chronological time. Prophecy relies on the idea that the future is knowable. Apocalypse is the end of secular time in the time of eternity. But messianic time neither knows its future nor escapes from secular time (*chronos*), rather it is a time in which the whole of secular time contracts (is redeemed) in a present in which eternity is immanent: 'the time that remains between time and its end' (1999: 62–63).

It is a time that disrupts but also relates chronological (*chronos*) and eschatological time (*kairos*), and therefore an experience of temporal non-coincidence (1999: 62–4).

Agamben interprets current world politics as the generalization of a state of exception, the loss of the differentiation of life from politics (2005a). He sees the problems of the present as stemming from the failure to sustain, or if necessary inaugurate the distinctions that make politics possible. The developments that he takes as exemplifying the parlous state of the current world order include the workings of the global political economy, the development of biotechnology and humanitarianism (2004: 77). In both intra and inter-state relations, Agamben sees a potential for tyranny, which essentially stems from the global reach of the 'spectacular' democracies of the West (1993; 2000: 86–7; 16). Within this context, the distinction between law and violence is lost and the former collapses into the latter. Nevertheless, Agamben suggests the possibility of challenges to this pessimistic scenario. In *Means Without End: notes on politics*, he refers to the ways in which spectacular democracies also produce 'singularities', those subversive movements and events that are unrepresentable by the state and articulate a messianic interruption of state representation (2000: 114–16). However, in general Agamben's discussion of such challenges relies on a highly formalized set of structural possibilities that are derived from the same problem of the originary distinction and confusion of the categories of human and animal, politics and life, history and time. At the root of Agamben's critique of the contemporary world is an argument about the ways in which politics is destroyed by a thinking that reduces human temporality to chronology and eschatology. Within this kind of thinking, in which the social sciences and philosophy of history work hand in hand, humanity is understood as an 'anthropological machine' with a historical destiny, and we are led into the world of bio-politics and the global confusion of sovereign and police power. In order to break away from this conception of humanity, Agamben calls for a thinking that reveals the distinction between man and animal in the 'hiatus' within man, the emptiness internal to the dislocation between language and its subject and between the experiences of operational and representational time (2004: 92). But the argument for the normative power of this hiatus is always caught up in the same paradox, either it inaugurates a new regime of normativity or it remains a 'weak' messianic capacity, which it is impossible to predict or direct, and which can accomplish nothing.

Agamben's reading of world-political time and the times of world politics, in messianic terms, present a powerful contrast to the post-Kantian optimism of Habermas. Nevertheless, although qualitatively different from Habermas in his sociological and philosophical accounts of political time, and in the normative force of his interpretation of the present, Agamben remains qualitatively the same in certain crucial respects. Like the historicists of whom he is critical, he analyses the times in terms of a tension between determinism (fate) and freedom (control/creation) and situates his analysis as 'timely'. In other words, he shares the same understanding of political time, as the task of directing or re-directing *chronotic* time in the light of the revelation of *kairos*. Indeed, partly because of the theological vocabulary in which his argument is expressed, the dualism between *chronos* and *kairos* and the association of politics with the control and banishment of *chronos* is arguably more marked in his work than it is in the argument of Habermas. In addition to the persistence of the idea of the theorist as prophet and time-traveller, Agamben also shares with cosmopolitan accounts of the times, a unified conception of world-political time and a tendency to conflate the time of western modernity with the time of world politics as such. The present of world politics is unquestioningly understood as the globalized fate of the liberal, capitalist, western state.

Thinking time differently: Connolly and heterotemporality[17]

Habermas and Agamben both give us ways of theorizing the future of world politics and the kinds of political community that might be possible within that future. However, as the earlier discussion has shown, in order to do so they rely on assumptions about political time that work to unify the time of world politics and to place the theorist in a position in which they can assert the timeliness of their insights into what *matters* in the world political present. Habermas and Agamben acknowledge the complexity of world politics, nevertheless, both thinkers confirm that the range of possibilities, and of possible remedies, inherent in world politics derive from a temporal trajectory inherent (for good or ill) in western modernity. This is not simply because of the contingent fact that western powers acquired unprecedented global power over the course of the last few centuries, but because western political time is presumed to be world-political time, the time that drives or leads historical development. This temporality enables an overarching sense to be made of foreign policy making, international law, global civil society activity, humanitarian intervention, global governance and intra and inter-state politics in general. These temporal assumptions do not prevent the theorists from acknowledging that there are a variety of phenomena and events, of other histories and experiences, that play a role in world politics (phenomena which might include authoritarian capitalist states, religion, non-western culture, clientalist politics, imperialism, colonization, the organization of reproduction, gendered relations of power). But they reduce the significance of such phenomena for the purposes of diagnosis and prediction by subsuming them under a master narrative of time, so that the idea of an alternative temporal perspective on world politics becomes literally unintelligible. The progressive and messianic narratives of Habermas and Agamben gain their persuasiveness, at least in part, from their reliance on certain meta-narratives of political time in modern western thought, that have traditionally accomplished an enormous amount of work in rendering politics as such, and world politics in particular, an intelligible subject for explanatory and normative generalization. But the question is whether these meta-narratives stand up to systematic theoretical scrutiny. William Connolly is one of a range of critical and postcolonial thinkers who has raised this question in political theory, and attempted to articulate an alternative understanding of political time that does not lapse into singular progressive or apocalyptic alternatives.

In *Neuropolitics: thinking, culture, speed* (2002) Connolly explores the temporality of thinking and how it may be connected to theorizing political temporality. The key point about the temporality of thinking is that it is not chronologically linear but an 'out of joint' emergence and coming together of a range of virtual (rather than potential) pasts in relation to an ongoing, given present which yield a previously unpredictable future (2002: 96–97). The asymmetries within the time of thinking, which perpetually destabilize and transform the temporal organization of pasts, presents and futures, have their parallel in the experience of 'out of jointness' between different public temporalities. Connolly discusses Wolin's argument that in the contemporary world, political time is not synchronous with the temporalities governing communication and culture. For Wolin, political time needs to be slow in order to allow for the possibility of democratic political action and engagement, it is therefore necessary to resist the acceleration of time embedded in non-political orders, and revive a 'politics of place' (Wolin 1997; Connolly 2002: 141). Connolly accepts the idea that there are asymmetries of temporal ordering within the contemporary world, but resists Wolin's conclusion:

> Wolin and I both reject the cyclical image of slow time adopted by many ancients. But I also find myself at odds with progressive, teleological, and linear conceptions of time set against it. Against these four images I embrace the idea of rifts or forks in time that help to constitute it as time. A rift as constitutive of time itself, in which time flows into a future neither fully determined by a discernable past nor fixed by its place in a cycle of eternal return, nor directed by an intrinsic purpose pulling it along. Free time. Or, better, time as becoming, replete with the dangers and possibilities attached to such a world.
>
> (Connolly 2002: 144)

In extrapolating on his idea of this time as becoming, Connolly explains that 'rifts in time' are to do with contingent encounters 'between complex systems with some capacity for self-organization and unexpected events not smoothly assimilable by them' (2002: 145). In *Pluralism* (2005), Connolly further unpacks the meaning of time as becoming as the interaction between immanent chronologies (2005: 103). This leads him to distinguish between politics of being and politics of becoming. A political temporality of being refers to relatively stable contexts for political judgment and action, on the basis of which one can extrapolate the meaning of progress in accordance with given, sedimented criteria. In contrast, the political temporality of becoming refers to shifting and unfamiliar contexts for political judgment and action, where criteria for the meaning of progress must be negotiated without the certainties embedded in a politics of being.[18]

From Connolly's point of view, normative theories of cosmopolitan or global politics, whether of the optimistic or pessimistic kind, have tended to remain within the temporal register of the politics of being, and have therefore been unable to do justice to either plurality or unpredictability in their diagnoses of the times. He uses the examples of the work of Nussbaum and Virilio to exemplify these different tendencies, but the argument applies similarly to Habermas and Agamben. For Connolly, such theorists, in their opposing evaluations of the promise of the world-political present, are caught up in a 'concentric' understanding of culture, in which a particular, parochial temporality generates the force that will bind increasingly distant circles of humanity together. Both cosmopolitan and anti-cosmopolitan thinkers, according to Connolly, fail to appreciate the eccentric temporal flows that cut across and disrupt the circles of a concentric vision of the world, and that do so as much within the 'inner circle' of liberalism or capitalism as in the outer circles of 'others' (Connolly 2002: 176–93; see also 2000). Connolly makes a similar criticism of Agamben's account of sovereignty and the mutual implication of the time (and end) of state and history. He argues that Agamben traps the interpretation of world-political time in an impasse in which there can be no room for a time of becoming:

> Agamben displays the hubris of intellectualism when he encloses political culture within a tight logic. Some theorists express that hubris by applying a tight model of causal explanation to social processes, others by applying a closed model of historical realization, and yet others by resolving the first two images into paradoxes so tightly defined that only a radical reconstitution of the world could rise above them.
>
> (2005: 140)

Connolly's double reading of political time offers two possible ways forward for theorizing world-political time without the 'hubris of intellectualism'. First, he shows that 'presentness' is always constituted by a plurality of 'presents' inscribed in diverse, immanent temporalities. Second, he rejects the idea that any unifying temporal orientation provides the master key to the meaning of 'presentness'. Third, he argues instead, the contingent and ongoing cross-contamination of different temporal orderings should be the starting point for understanding and judgment. So what this might mean for theorizing world politics? Without the 'hubris of intellectualism' will it be possible for 'us' to say anything about 'our' world, about where it is and where it might, or should, be going? One obvious implication of this way of theorizing political time is that theorists need to start by taking their own 'presentness' much more seriously. Rather than time being something that the theorist should be able to control through the timely recognition of the forces shaping the present, time would instead become something that the theorist, like the political actor, undergoes in all its complexity and opportunity.

To recognize one's implication in heterotemporality, and its centrality to the knowledge and judgment of one's 'own' times, is to make a start in developing one's capacity to unpick the meaning of different 'presents', and explore the possibilities as well as limitations of one's own political imagination in relation to specific problems and questions. From this starting point, understanding alternative temporalizations of the world-political present, without prior reference to a meta-narrative of world-political time, becomes much less difficult to envisage. The point to bear in mind here is that political temporalities are complicated, but they are neither secret nor untranslatable. Within predominant contemporary diagnoses of world politics the problem is not that temporal plurality goes unrecognized, so much as that its meaning is always already homogenized as part of the familiar linear or cyclical, repetitive, progressive or apocalyptic stories. In relation to globalization, thinking in heterotemporal terms not only allows for the recognition that globalization is not a singular phenomenon, it also opens up questions of explanation (why and how it happens where and when it happens) and refuses to prejudge the supposed irreversibility of globalization processes, or universalize their normative value (good or bad). In relation to humanitarianism, and in particular humanitarian intervention, a heterotemporal perspective raises the question as to why it should be taken as a sign of the distinctiveness of the world-political present in the first place. Does it mark a normative difference in the conduct of world politics or simply confirm the paternalistic patterns of a colonial or quasi-colonial past? For whom, and from whose perspective is this a novel development? Simply raising the question of novelty challenges those narratives that explain humanitarian intervention in terms of a shift in the institution of sovereignty. By drawing attention to the different presents of different sovereign states, heterotemporality pushes theories of humanitarian intervention towards contextual analysis and the possibility that there may be no unified pattern here, in terms of either how humanitarian intervention is to be explained, or of its normative implications.

An untimely approach to global justice is opposed to the kind of normative arguments that assert their own timeliness without regard for the co-existence of a multiplicity of 'clocks' by which world-political punctuality may be measured. Without *kairos* to shape and control the temporal ordering of multiple, intersecting chronotic systems, heterotemporal normative judgment has to recognize its own historicity and that it partakes of the partiality and revisability of the presents to which it is immanent. But this does not preclude normative critique and prescription. If humanitarian intervention is identified with the potential globalization of justice, then heterotemporality would suggest that what is needed is to begin by acknowledging and examining political temporalities of violation, in order to understand the meanings of injustice in the present. This would enable judgment of the likely effects of the institutionalization of particular normative priorities in the principles and practices of international humanitarianism. But it would also open up the question of what kinds of violation matter and why, and offer a different route to the establishment of international hierarchies of outrage than that reflected in the moral priorities of existing international human rights regimes. The world's 'clocks' may or may not already chime in harmony on these issues, but from the viewpoint of heterotemporality this is something to be discovered rather than assumed:

> To insist on the value of untimely political critique is not, then, to refuse the problem of time or timing in politics but rather to contest settled accounts of what time it is, what the times are, and what political tempo and temporality we should hew to in political life.

> (Brown, 2005: 4)

In summary, a heterotemporal account of world-political time does not identify it with a unifying logic or with the idea that politics emerges out of the controlling and re-shaping of *chronos*. It displaces the theorist from the position of prophet, not because it is impossible to theorize the multiple, parallel and interacting presents that make up world politics, but because of the sheer volatility and unpredictability of temporal becoming. In these respects, it avoids not only the unsustainable position of those theorists who are able to render engagement between different presents only by a temporal subsumption in which one present is more genuinely 'the present' than others. But it also avoids the temptation of engagement with other times having to be articulated only in terms of a formal commitment to a difference that conditions time but cannot be grasped in 'this worldly' terms.

When it comes to normative theories of international or global politics, abandoning unifying *kairotic* accounts of world-political time is doubly disorienting for the theorist interested in the question of the future of political community. It is disorienting because it undermines the theorist's capacity to represent and speak for the future in terms of the present, whether that future takes the form of cosmopolitan democracy or of the generalized state of exception. It is also disorienting because it challenges the theorist's role of time traveller and prophet, the spectator that knows where world-political time is headed but also has the responsibility to direct or re-direct the arrow of time. But for theorists such as Connolly or Brown (quoted earlier), this double disorientation does not need to be disabling for either understanding or judgment. Rather, through limiting the 'hubris of intellectualism', normative theory is able to cultivate self-criticism, appreciate the possibilities for change inherent in contingency, and multiply the possibilities for critical engagement, negative and positive.

Notes

1 I am grateful to Manchester University Press for permission to reproduce material from my forthcoming book, *Time and World Politics: thinking the present* (Hutchings 2008).
2 I use the term *chronotic* here rather than 'chronological' because I am using it to encompass the ways time is thought to work naturally as well as the ways in which natural time is represented as working chronologically through human social life.
3 The link between *kairos* and the capacity for timeliness runs through western traditions of thinking both about politics and about political theory. The point about being timely is that it involves either a prospective or retrospective grasp of what it means to be in time (punctual), which in turn means having some kind of external perspective on what the time is. Timeliness is important for politics because it is inherent in models of political agency, and accounts of the difference between natural and political events and phenomena. Timeliness is important for political theory, in particular since the speculative philosophies of history of Kant, Hegel and Marx, because the point and purpose of such theories is supposed to be their capacity to diagnose and prescribe for the times, whether with the virtues of hindsight or foresight. See Isaac 1995, and responses to his argument by Brown, W. 1997; Patton 1997; Wolin 1997, also discussed in Chambers 2003: 73–90. See also Chambers 2003.
4 *Chronotic* time is always *spatialized*, in the sense that it is represented in spatial, quantitative terms (see Smith 1986; Agamben 2005b: 63–5).
5 See Adam 1990: 53–75.

6 The question of an 'arrow of time' is a point of significant differentiation between modern physicists on the one hand and biological and social scientists and historians on the other. The prevailing view amongst physicists is that time is 'tenseless', and there is no qualitative difference between what was, is and will be, with some arguing that time travel is possible in principle (Lockwood 2005). Biologists, social scientists and historians, in contrast, treat time as essentially 'tensed' and irreversible (Adam 1990: 81–2). The question of the relation between time and causation remains a subject of contention between philosophers (Tooley 1999).

7 The translation of 'virtue' for Machiavelli's *virtú* would be misleading, since it does not refer to virtue in terms of traditional ideas about goodness. For Machiavelli, *virtú* is better understood as 'virtuosity' or 'ability'. It refers to the capacity of political leaders to foresee and control events, in contrast and opposition to the blind workings of fortune (see Machiavelli 1988: 103–6).

8 The key principle of discourse ethics is that in order for a moral principle to be legitimate, all those affected by a norm would have agreed to it in an inclusive dialogue conducted under conditions of fair argumentation (See Habermas 1990; 1992; Benhabib and Dallmayr 1992).

9 In his *Theory of Communicative Action* (1984; 1987), Habermas distinguishes two modes of action in modern societies: strategic action is driven by instrumental rationality, and involves functional responses to the requirements of complex economic and political problems, for instance the design of monetary or bureaucratic systems; communicative action, by contrast, is grounded in communicative rationality, in which certain normative pre-requisites are embedded, and is at work in the development of public spheres, human rights and democratic politics. The latter 'lifeworld' aspects of modern society, in Habermas's view need to regulate and constrain the former 'systemic' aspects.

10 These alternative interpretations include realist, liberal (neo-conservative), neo-liberal, post Marxist and Schmittian (based on the work of Carl Schmitt) 'hemispheric' arguments (Habermas 2006: 179–93). For a more in-depth discussion of Habermas's relation to Kant, see Hutchings 1996: 58–80.

11 Here Habermas is using his distinction between 'morality' and 'ethics'. According to Habermas, 'ethics' refers to those normative values that reflect specific conceptions of the good and are embedded in cultures and ways of life. Ethical principles are not inherently universal, but make sense in relation to particular contexts, languages and histories. 'Morality', in contrast, refers to those principles of justice that transcend cultural difference and are genuinely universal in their appeal. This universality echoes Kant's account of practical reason and the moral law, but is grounded instead in a theory of language and the necessary presuppositions of communication (Habermas 1990; 1992). On Habermas's account, we can test out the universality of claims of justice through an actual or virtual discursive procedure, in which all affected by the claim in question are involved. The conceptual connection between law and peace at the global level is secured ultimately by their common foundation in principles of justice that are genuinely universal, because they are grounded in the presuppositions of communicative reason, and all those affected by them would endorse those principles if given the opportunity to deliberate upon them in a fair discursive procedure (2006: 143).

12 In the concluding sections of the essay, Habermas examines three alternatives to an interpretation of the times of world politics in terms of the 'Kantian project' (2006: 179–93). The first is 'hegemonic liberalism', the second, 'neo-liberal and post-Marxist arguments', and the third 'Schmittian' arguments. In each case, Habermas's defence of his Kantian alternative in contrast to these others rests on its claim to offer a more plausible understanding of the nature of law, and the analytical and normative implications of that understanding.

13 Benjamin's aphoristic reflections translated as 'Theses on the Philosophy of History' (1999) and his essay 'Critique of Violence' (1978) are particularly influential for Agamben's thinking about time, politics and the present.

14 In this section of the text, Agamben, discussing the distinction between time and history as it originates in Greek thought, uses the term *aion* to refer to the temporal principle of qualitative change, as opposed to *chronos* – the spatially representable infinite succession of instants (2007: 93), although elsewhere he introduces the term *kairos* to capture the same meaning (2007: 115). The distinction maps on to that between *chronos* and *kairos* as used in this chapter, since it is a distinction between natural time on the one hand and the time that shapes and interrupts natural time on the other.

15 Agamben is following Foucault here, but also echoing arguments already discussed made by Hardt and Negri and Virilio about the biopolitical trajectory of the sovereign power of the modern state (Foucault 1976; 1977; 1980). He shares with Hardt and Negri and Virilio the view that contemporary humanitarianism is part of 'empire' rather than a challenge to it.

16 Indeed, Agamben identifies Paul as the theological dwarf under the table in Benjamin's opening aphorism, and suggests that Benjamin had Paul's argument in mind when he wrote the text (Agamben 2005b 138; Benjamin 1999: 245).

17 I take the term 'heterotemporality' from Chakrabarty's work (Chakrabarty 2000).

18 Connolly suggests that we can talk about 'politics of being' in situations in which there is a high level of political homogeneity, and presumably a high level of consensus in political memory and the collective reading of time's arrow. Whether or not such political communities exist, in the case of world politics it is clear that 'politics of being' could not possibly describe its temporality, although, as Connolly argues, political theorists persistently attempt to read it in this register.

Bibliography

Adam, B. (1990) *Time and Social Theory*, Cambridge: Polity.

Agamben, G. (1991) *Language and Death: The Place of Negativity*. Trans K. E. Pinkus and Mi. Hardt Theory and History of Literature, Vol. 78. Minneapolis: University of Minnesota Press.

Agamben, G. (1993) *The Coming Community*, trans M. Hardt, Minneapolis & London: Minnesota University Press.

—— (1998) *Homo Sacer: sovereign power and bare life*, Stanford CA.: Stanford University Press.

Agamben, G. (1999) *The Man Without Content*. Trans G. Albert, Stanford: Stanford University Press.

—— (2000) *Means Without End: Notes on Politics*, trans. V. Binetti & C. Casarino, Minneapolis & London: University of Minnesota Press.

—— (2004) *The Open: man and animal*, trans. K. Attell, Stanford CA: Stanford University Press.

—— (2005a) *State of Exception*, trans. K. Attell, Chicago: Chicago University Press.

—— (2005b) *The Time That Remains: a commentary on the Letter to the Romans,* trans. P. Dailey, Stanford CA.: Stanford University Press.

—— (2007) *Infancy and History: essay on the destruction of experience*, trans. L. Heron, London: Verso.

Benhabib, S. and Dallmayr, F. (eds) (1992) *The Communicative Ethics Controversy*, Cambridge: Polity.

Benjamin, W. (1978) 'Critique of Violence', in P. Demetz (ed.) *Reflections: Walter Benjamin, essays, aphorisms, autobiographical writings*, New York: Schocken Books.

—— (1999) 'Theses on the Philosophy of History', in H. Arendt (ed.) *Illuminations*, London: Pimlico.

Brown, W. (1997) 'The Time of the Political', *Theory and Event*, 1(1): http://muse.jhu.edu/journals/theory_and_event/v001/1.1brown.html.

—— (2005) *Edgework: critical essays on knowledge and politics*, Princeton and Oxford: Princeton University Press.

Chakrabarty, D. (2000) *Provincializing Europe*, Princeton: Princeton University Press.

Chambers, S.A. (2003) *Untimely Politics*, New York: New York University Press.

Connolly, W.E. (2000) 'Speed, Concentric Cultures and Cosmopolitanism', *Political Theory*, 28(5): 596–618.

—— (2002) *Neuropolitics: thinking, culture, speed*, Minneapolis and London: University of Minnesota Press.

—— (2005) *Pluralism*, Durham and London: Duke University Press.

Habermas, J. (1979) *Communication and the Evolution of Society*, Boston: Beacon Press.

—— (1984) *The Theory of Communicative Action Volume 1*, Boston: Beacon Press.

—— (1987) *The Theory of Communicative Action Volume 2*, Boston: Beacon Press.

—— (1989) *The Structural Transformation of the Public Sphere*, Cambridge MA: MIT Press.

—— (1990) *Moral Consciousness and Communicative Action*, Cambridge: Polity Press.

—— (1992) 'Discourse Ethics: notes on a program of philosophical justification' in S. Benhabib and F. Dallmayr (eds) *The Communicative Ethics Controversy*, Cambridge: Polity Press.

—— (1996) *Between Facts and Norms*, Cambridge: Polity Press.

—— (1997) 'Kant's Idea of Perpetual Peace with the Benefit of 200 Years Hindsight' in Bohman and Lutz-Bachmann (eds) *Perpetual Peace: essays on Kant's cosmopolitan ideal*, Cambridge MA: MIT Press.

—— (1998) 'Remarks on Legitimation Through Human Rights', *Philosophy and Social Criticism*, 24(2,3): 157–71.

—— (2006) *The Divided West*, trans. & ed. C. Cronin, Cambridge: Polity Press.

Hutchings, K. (1996) *Kant, Critique and Politics*, London: Routledge.

—— (2008) *Time and World Politics: thinking the present*, Manchester: Manchester University Press.

Isaac, J. (1995) 'The Strange Silence of Political Theory', *Political Theory* 23(4): 636–52; 681–8.

Kant, I. (1991) *Political Writings*, trans. N.B. Nisbet, H. Reiss (ed.), Cambridge: Cambridge University Press.

Lindroos, K. (1998) *New Time/Image Space: temporalization of politics in Walter Benjamin's Philosophy of History and Art*, Jyväskylä: SoPhi, University of Jyväskylä.

Lockwood, M. (2005) *The Labyrinth of Time: introducing the universe*, Oxford: Oxford University Press.

Machiavelli, N. (1988) *The Prince*, Q. Skinner and R. Price (eds), Cambridge: Cambridge University Press.

Nowotny, H. (1994) *Time: the modern and postmodern experience*, trans. N. Plaice, Cambridge: Polity.

Patton, P. (1997) 'The World Seen from Within: Deleuze and the Philosophy of Events', *Theory and Event*, 1(1): http://muse.jhu.edu/journals/theory_and_event/v001/1.1patton.html.

Pocock, J.G.A. (1973) *Politics, Language and Time: essay on political thought and history*, New York: Atheneum.

Smith, J. E. (1969) 'Time, Times and the "Right Time": Chronos and Kairos', *The Monist,* 53(1): 1–13.

Smith, J. E. (1986) 'Time and Qualitative Time', *Review of Metaphysics,* 40(1): 3–16.

Tooley, M. (ed.) (1999) *Time and Causation,* New York and London: Garland Publishing Inc.

Wolin, S. (1997) 'What Time is It?', *Theory and Event,* 1(1): http://muse.jhu.edu/journals/theory_and_event/v001/1.1wolin.html.

2 Globalizing the democratic community

Jens Bartelson

Today leading political theorists believe that globalization constitutes a threat to modern democracy by undermining its foundations: state sovereignty and national identity (Tully 2002; Rosanvallon 2006: 189–234). Since most of these theorists would like to save democratic institutions and practices without sliding back into nationalist nostalgia, they have explored a variety of ways to widen the scope of democratic governance beyond the boundaries of the state. Yet these efforts have been constantly compromised by what looks like an insurmountable problem. If democratic governance presupposes a community in order to be legitimate, global governance cannot be democratically legitimate since there is no corresponding community at the global level that could bestow it with legitimacy. But this problem is neither new nor specific to the global level. In order for *any* political authority to be legitimate in democratic terms, it must be based on the actual or hypothetical consent of a people or community. But since the identity of that people or community is difficult to account for in terms themselves democratic, most theories of democratic legitimacy issue in paradoxes that cannot be satisfactorily resolved by modern political theory (Doucet 2005). As Van Roermund (2003: 41) has eloquently put this problem, 'self-representation never seems to capture the self that is representing itself'.

Since the people cannot decide on its own composition, many political theorists have assumed that democratic community and its boundaries are outcome of historical accidents and therefore cannot be judged according to *any* standard of legitimacy (Nässtrom 2007). While being essential to democratic legitimacy, the political community and its boundaries are themselves outside the purview of normative reasoning. This insight has led to despair among those who argue in favor of global democracy, sometimes to the point of conceding that talk of democratic legitimacy at the global level is pointless in the absence of a world government that first could reconstitute mankind into one single political community. Since such world government presently seems to be out of reach, global democracy therefore looks equally utopian. Others have responded more optimistically to this lack of democratic legitimacy by trying to find viable substitutes for a global *demos*, such as a global civil society or an increased responsiveness and accountability among global governance institutions (Keane, 2003; Kuper 2004; Buchanan and Keohane 2006). But these latter solutions presuppose that the global realm display some features that could permit common norms to emerge and become institutionalized independently of what goes on at the domestic level. So while there is no *demos* to be found at the global level, it is reasonable to expect a global society based on democratic values to emerge from the interplay of global political institutions and those affected by their decisions.

But why is it so hard to make coherent sense of the concept of a global *demos*? Answering this question is the task of the present chapter. Instead of trying to solve the problem of democratic legitimacy, I will try to explain how this problem came into being, and, by implication, why it might be less of a problem for *global* democracy. As I shall argue, the difficulties we experience when we try to widen the scope of democratic governance beyond the boundaries of individual states have nothing to do with the characteristics of global society, but result from the underlying assumption that a political community has to be *bounded* and based on *consent* in order for democratic legitimacy to be possible. From this point of view, the perennial paradoxes of democratic legitimacy look like little but residuals of earlier attempts to *nationalize* the concept of political community by making this concept semantically equivalent to that of the nation, and taking the hypothetical consent of its members to be the source of *its* legitimacy. This is to say that claims to particularity cannot be justified in universalistic terms, only in terms themselves particularistic. Accordingly, once we let go of the idea that political communities have to be bounded and based on consent in order to qualify as democratic ones, the paradox of democratic legitimacy will look like a category mistake rather than an inescapable obstacle to democratic governance.

Pursuing this argument, I will proceed in three steps. First, I will take a critical look at some contemporary attempts to widen the scope of democratic governance beyond the boundaries of individual states. Second, I will briefly describe how democratic legitimacy became a problem of modern political theory, and why the conventional solutions to this problem issue in paradoxes that have resisted resolution. Third, I will suggest a way of redefining political community that makes it possible to dissolve the paradoxes of democratic legitimacy by suggesting that the only *prima facie* legitimate *demos* must be coextensive with mankind as a whole.

I

The idea that globalization constitutes a threat to modern democracy can be formulated in at least two ways. First, if we take globalization to bring a virtually unrestricted flow of capital and the reign of market forces at a transnational level, it becomes tempting to focus on the corrosive effects of this on state autonomy. As Held (1999: 96–97) states, '[m]odern democratic theory and practice was constructed upon Westphalian foundations. National communities, and theories of national communities, were based on the presupposition that political communities could, in principle, control their destinies'. When domestic politicians seek to regain control over national economies, they do so by ceding at least some autonomy to supranational institutions lest they lose out completely to the corporate world. Yet such ceding of autonomy comes at a price, since they then effectively move formal authority as well as control over outcomes outside the scope of domestic democratic institutions. What once was within the purview of due democratic deliberation is now more a matter of multilateral agreements between government officials at different levels (Scholte 2000: 132–158; Goldmann 2001: 74–106; Sassen 1996: 51–58). Deprived of any real power, domestic democratic institutions become increasingly hollow. From this follows two strategic options for the democratically minded: either to increase the independence *both* from global forces and supranational institutions, or, to opt for democratization of those supranational institutions in order to tame these forces and restore some consensual legitimacy to their decisions. Otherwise nobody is in charge and no one is accountable, and we will have no way left to influence our destiny as citizens (Archibugi 2002; Held 1998; 2003).

Second, if we take globalization to bring a virtually unrestricted flow of information and people at the transnational level, it becomes tempting to focus on the corrosive effects on the identity of national political communities. Transnational flows might compromise the cultural homogeneity of a people, and since it takes a people to constitute the *demos* necessary for democratic institutions to be legitimate, those transnational flows might subvert the foundations of democracy by pushing cultural plurality to an intolerable limit. In order for a people to govern itself, its members need to know who they are: a people and not just a multitude of strangers (Scholte 2000: 159–83; Goldmann 2001: 107–25; Bauman 1998: 55–76). The democratically minded again have two options at their disposal: they can either move in a nationalist direction by trying to preserve the uniqueness of their own community against the onslaught of global mobility, or, they can move in a cosmopolitan direction by trying to extend the scope of democracy beyond the boundaries of particular political communities while trying to become as tolerant as possible within each of them (Bader 1997; Seglow 1998; Chea 1998; Honig 1998; Hollinger 2001; Hall 2002; Benhabib, 2002, 2004).

Let us disregard the nationalistic option for a moment, and focus on current attempts to globalize democratic governance. Theories of cosmopolitan democracy usually buy into some version of the above diagnosis, and then proceed by rethinking political community in light of these challenges (Linklater 1998; Bellamy and Castiglione 1998; Bauböck 2002). They frequently begin their argument by pointing out that democracy – in the shape we know it – has been closely associated with the nation state. They then argue that if the nation state indeed is about to lose its status as the predominant locus of political authority and community, then the only way to save democracy is by redefining political community in such a way that it can include people *irrespective* of their citizenship in particular communities. Instead of several mutually exclusive *demoi*, we need to create one inclusive *demos* to cater to the demands of popular sovereignty in an increasingly globalized world (Held 1995; 1998; 2005). But as Buchanan and Keohane (2006: 416) have argued, 'the most obvious difficulty with this view is that the social and political conditions for democracy are not met at the global level'. This is so because there is 'no worldwide political community constituted by a broad consensus recognizing a common domain as the proper subject of global collective decision-making'. But nevertheless, in the absence of *any* kind of community at the global level, the very aspiration to democratic legitimacy would be rather pointless.

But how, then, can a global *demos* be constructed and justified? Two main ways of constructing a global *demos* compete in the literature. First, we find the idea that a global *demos* ought to include *all* human beings. Each human being should have an equal voice since each serious political concern is likely to be of global scope (Archibugi and Held 1995; Linklater 1998: 193–212; Archibugi 2004). Second, we find the idea that those who are *affected* by a particular decision should be included in the *demos*, so what constitutes the scope of the *demos* in question will vary with the nature of the decision. Each issue should therefore be settled by those affected by the outcome in each particular case, not by mankind as a whole (Archibugi 1998). But as Näsström (2003) and Wendt (1999) have shown, justifying these solutions is very difficult, since the transition from our present situation in which political communities are bounded to an unbounded global community of all mankind has to take the present situation into consideration: in order for this new community to enjoy democratic legitimacy, it has to be considered legitimate by its prospective citizens. That is, it must be democratically constituted, rather than forced upon them by some global political authority. But this merely begs the question of who these citizens are, a decision that itself cannot be settled by any democratic process, since that process then would presuppose exactly what it is supposed to yield.

The second solution is equally problematic, since we then have to face the question of how to determine who is affected and who is not by a particular decision, and that this might of course lead to divergent interpretations in each individual case. But if democratic legitimacy is wanted, who is affected and who is not should be settled in ways themselves democratic, that is, by those affected. Ergo: who is affected should be decided by those affected. Thus, both ways of justifying a global democratic community in terms themselves democratic presuppose the prior existence of that community, trapping these attempts to construct a global *demos* in a vicious circularity.

In response to these difficulties, some authors have tried to find routes to global democracy that rely on other sources of democratic legitimacy, such as deliberation and contestation. One of these goes through transnational institutions. The relocation of political authority to the transnational level might yield decentralized forms of authority that eventually will chime well with a world of territorially unbounded communities. Hopefully the collective allegiance to the procedures of deliberative democracy would then generate overlapping and constantly fluctuating *demoi*, each being relative to the issue area at hand (Dryzek 1999). From this perspective, we would not need any *demos* to keep democracy alive at the global level, only a proper differentiation into different spheres of social and political action, and the maintenance of democratic conduct within each of them from the bottom up (Cochran 2002). Another solution would be to accept the existence of a multiplicity of different *demoi*, and opt for the gradual democratization of the *relations* between them by strengthening the transnational public sphere and its institutions (Bohman 2004, 2005). Yet in both cases, it is difficult to see how and why the allegiance to democratic values and procedures could be safeguarded through the transnational dispersion of political authority, since the warrant of democratic deliberation seems to be some normative authority *prior* to the structure of authority legitimized by means of the same set of procedures. So rather than finding ourselves lost when it comes to justifying a global *demos*, we are lost when it comes to justifying the authority necessary to uphold standards of democratic deliberation within as well as across different *demoi* in democratic terms.

The second route goes through negotiating the paradox of democratic legitimacy. Even grated that not all communities are the outcome of popular consent, the democratic paradox nevertheless becomes inescapable whenever we want to justify these communities and their boundaries in democratic terms. To Benhabib (2007: 70), the way to negotiate the resulting paradoxes is by means of iterations of democratic practice which could allow a given *demos* to redefine itself in the face of ongoing 'political contestation in which the meaning of rights and other fundamental principles are reposited, resignified, and reappropriated by new and excluded groups'. To Honig, the paradoxes of democratic legitimacy are integral to the possibility of democratic governance and productive of its widening scope beyond the boundaries of individual communities. To her, 'democracy is always about living with strangers under a law that is therefore alien [and] about being mobilized into action periodically with and on behalf of people who are surely opaque to us and often unknown to us' (2001: 39). Thus, the paradox of democratic legitimacy is 'the condition in which we find ourselves when we think and act politically' (2007: 15). But if people and political communities owe their existence to the contingencies of history, why should we bother justifying them at all? Worse still, why should democratic practices then be confined to bounded communities thus constituted? Answering these questions will force us to take a closer look at the problem of democratic legitimacy and the paradoxes its solutions give rise to.

II

How and why did we end up with the problem of democratic legitimacy? Before answering this question, I think it is important to note that this problem presupposes that democratic communities have to be bounded and based on consent. In a world without boundaries, the boundary problem would not be a problem. In a community without consent, legitimacy would have to be derived from other sources. Thus, if we want to understand why democratic legitimacy is a problem, we should start by asking how the concepts of boundaries and consent once were married in political theory. As I would like to suggest, this particular union was the outcome of a broader trend to *nationalize* sociopolitical concepts that went hand in hand with efforts to justify the modern sovereign state. This nationalization implied that the range of reference of sociopolitical concepts was made to coincide with the boundaries of the sovereign state, and that their meaningful usage was equally restricted by the imagined necessity of such boundaries: all I can offer is a brief sketch of how this happened in political thought.

To the ancients, democratic legitimacy had been less of a problem. They could largely take the existence of the *polis* for granted, and if ever in doubt, they could point to the founding authority of a Solon or a Lycurgus, or appeal to the conventions embodied in ancient customs and institutions (Castoriadis 1983; Veyne 1983; Meier 1990). When democratic forms of government later fell into disrepute, this was largely because of the intrinsic difficulty in determining the scope of the relevant *demos* without thereby inviting its corruption in a world in which boundless and universal forms of community constituted the given starting point for most attempts to justify political authority. When democratic ideals started to resurface during the Enlightenment, however, these ancient roads to legitimacy had been blocked by the secular and revolutionary aspirations of that age, and the pitfalls of democratic government well forgotten (Bourke 2008). Without the city-state as the given point of reference and with a universalistic framework still in operation, it was also hard to come up with reasons why democratic governance should be restricted to particular communities, rather than applied to mankind as a whole, irrespective of its division into distinct communities. Hence, for writers like Diderot, Raynal, Paine and Condorcet, the global spread of popular sovereignty was seen as a way of overcoming what they saw as a tragic division of mankind into distinct communities of unequal standing, and the immoral impact this had on their intercourse. As Diderot argued, the general will is universal and

> forms the rule binding the conduct of an individual towards another in the same society, together with the conduct of an individual towards the whole society to which he belongs, and of that society itself towards other societies ... submission to the general will is the bond which holds all societies together.
>
> (1992: 21)

But as Robert Wokler (1975) has shown in admirable detail, the paradox of democratic legitimacy arises the moment Rousseau tries to restrict the scope of this general will to a particular community by demanding that the community in question ought to be based on the consent of its members. Taking such consent as his starting point, Rousseau discovered that the boundaries of a democratic community cannot be justified in terms themselves democratic, since the people cannot constitute itself *ex nihilo*. If sovereignty has to derive from the people, and if the people by definition cannot be defined by itself – that is, democratically – then how is it possible for a people to be both ruler and ruled all at once? As he stated the resulting paradox:

> For a young people to be able to relish sound principles of political theory and follow the fundamental rules of statecraft, the effect would have to become the cause; the social spirit, which should be created by those institutions, would have to preside over their very foundation; and men would have to be before the law what they should become by means of law. The legislator therefore, being unable to appeal to either force or reason, must have recourse to an authority of a different order, capable of constraining without violence and persuading without convincing.
>
> (1990: 216)

While the city republic continued to evoke nostalgic pangs in his imagination (Kelly 1987), Rousseau had to make his case for democracy from scratch. In order for democracy to be possible, there has to be a people united by means of common laws, yet these laws would have to derive their legitimacy from the same people. But how could the people ever be constituted in the absence of a founding authority, and how could the proper boundaries of the political community be drawn without thereby presupposing the existence of that people? Since the above problem could not be solved by logical means, it quickly became a matter of finding a pragmatic solution that catered to the political agenda of the Revolution while concealing its paradoxical character. What Emmanuel de Sieyès did in this respect may seem self-evident to us who have been accustomed to take parts of his solution for granted: he introduces the concept of the *nation* in order to define the proper boundaries of the political community, thereby also justifying the exercise of popular sovereignty within it. As he asked rhetorically,

> [h]ow can one believe that a constituted body may itself decide on its own constitution […] Power belongs only to the whole … From this it follows that the constitution of a country would cease to exist at the slightest difficulty arising between its component parts, if it were not that the nation existed independently of any rule or any constitutional form.
>
> (Sieyès 1963: 129)

To Sieyès, the nation is logically prior both to sovereign authority and to the corresponding *demos*. As he explains, '[t]he nation is prior to everything. It is the source of everything. Its will is always legal; indeed, it is the law itself' (Sieyès 1963: 124). By conceptualizing the nation as the original source of political authority, Sieyès could brush the paradox of democratic legitimacy under the carpet. As Näsström (2003) has summarized this move, it was a matter of placing the nation rather than the individual in an imaginary state of nature, and spelling out the consequences for the inner workings of the political community. And as Wokler remarked on the end result,

> in addition to superimposing undivided rule upon its subjects, the genuinely modern state further requires that those who fall under its authority be united themselves – that they form one people, one nation, morally bound together by a common identity … the modern state generally requires that the represented be a moral person as well, national unity going hand in hand with the political unity of the state.
>
> (1998: 30)

In the French context, it was then left to the next generation to bring the nation into existence through an array of clever propagandistic measures (Bell 2003: 140–97; Hazareesingh 2004).

But in the guise in which it first emerged during the Revolution, the concept of the nation did not presuppose cultural homogeneity or a common identity. To

Sieyès, as to many liberals after him, what makes it possible for the people to appear as a unity is not the *sameness* of the citizens, but rather the fact that the nation is something more than the sum of its parts, irrespective of the individual characteristics of the citizens (Jaume 2003). Not only did this way of defining the political community circumvent the problem of democratic legitimacy as it had been posed by Rousseau, but it had obvious practical advantages compared to competing definitions, since it made it possible to articulate a view of popular sovereignty based on *representation* rather than on the *participation* of all citizens (Hont 2005: 447–528). Later, in those times and places where the legitimacy of a political community was in doubt, the link between state and nation could be reinforced by appealing to a common culture or the common historical memory of a people (Ringmar 1998; Benhke 1997). Consequently, in many cases, *ethnos* and *demos* have become inseparable expressions of the same quest for popular sovereignty and democratic legitimacy (Yack 1998; 2001).

At this point, it is common to point out that this transition was greatly facilitated by the fact that writers like Bodin and Hobbes had already justified the principle of indivisible sovereignty and that the territorial framework of its exercise had already been established a long time before. All that Rousseau and Sieyès had to do was to replace the King with the people as the ultimate source and locus of that indivisible sovereign authority within an already territorially demarcated community. But how was this transition from kings to people carried out within political thought? I think important clues can be found in the ways the concept of a general will was defined and used before Rousseau made it the touchstone of popular sovereignty. For when he distinguishes between a general will and the will of all, he does so by identifying the former with the formal sovereignty of the people as a whole, and the latter with an aggregate expression of individual wills. The general will is never wrong, since 'the people is never corrupted, but it is often deceived' (1990: 203), while particular wills often are misguided. Now these different wills can only be brought to coincide if individual wills are considered in their individuality, that is, in strict isolation from any other association than the state itself, since such 'partial societies' are potent sources of corruption. As Rousseau rephrases Machiavelli's warning against factionalism, 'if groups, sectional associations are formed at the expense of the larger association, the will of each of these groups will become general in relation to its own members and private in relation to the state' (1990: 204). Thus, a viable political community requires that the people consist of nothing but individuals, each standing in an equal relationship to the indivisible authority of their totality. Only then can the differences between individual wills be cancelled out and ultimately reconciled with the general will through representation or deliberation. Thus the very concept of a general will presupposes that the people is categorically distinct from the individuals that compose it, and hence also that the people thus constituted can act wholly independently of their individual wills, however combined. Now this assumption is hard to reconcile with the idea that the people itself is constituted by a prior contract between its individual members to enter as free and equal members into the political community *before* they can consent to *any* sovereign authority, even granted that this authority emanates from their wills at the very same moment they enter into the political community. The tension between the general will and the will of all therefore remains unresolved within the contractual framework as long as the latter is supposed to be a precondition of the former.

But what if the general will actually is a precondition of the will of all? As Foucault has reminded us, before the triumph of modern democracy, there was an art of government that took its object of governance to be a *population*, and which regarded the happiness of its members as a means to the survival and smooth functioning of the state (Foucault 1988). If we step outside the contractual framework for a moment and unpack some of its underlying assumptions, I think that some clues to how this transition was carried out can be found in the theory of political will which Rousseau borrows from his absolutist predecessor Marquis d'Argenson. In fact, d'Argenson furnishes the missing link between the concept of population as an object of governance and the idea of a people able to govern itself. By breaking down the people into individual wills, d'Argenson is able to argue that there is no basic difference between the will of the sovereign and the will of the people, only a numerical distinction between different wills that only can be handled through the use of political arithmetic by the sovereign. Through this investigation, writes the Marquis solemnly, 'I hope to show that popular administration can be exercised under the authority of the Sovereign, without diminishing the public power which it instead increases, and that this is the source of happiness of the people' (1787: 2). In order to bring about this outcome, the sovereign must learn how to control the manifestations of particular wills at different levels of society, this royal control sometimes includes giving people latitude to deliberate and act independently whenever it is suitable from the perspective of the sovereign. As a consequence, the sovereign will strengthen his power, benefit the community, as well as get an edge in international affairs (1787: 22–5). So perhaps we are forced to admit that modern democracy is a manifestation of a prior will to govern, a will that first constitutes the people as an *object* of government and then turns it into a *subject* of government in order to legitimize itself.

Now this foray into the prehistory of modern democratic theory does nothing to solve the problem of democratic legitimacy, but it does help us to understand a few things better. First, it makes us aware that the problems faced by democratic communities today cannot be blamed on globalization, but rather are to be found at the very origin of modern democratic theory. The paradox of democratic legitimacy has been around since democracy was nationalized, and the paradigmatic way of handling this problem since then has been to use the concept of the nation – however defined – in order to square the circle and brush the question of what makes nations legitimate under the carpet. The revolutionary concept of the nation was created precisely in order to furnish democratic governance with legitimacy, to the same extent as popular rule itself was necessary in order to justify the existence of indivisible sovereign authority within bounded political communities. Second, the above account helps us to understand why emancipation from this state of affairs today is perceived as so urgent by so many. If the revolutionary solution consisted in substituting the nation for the individual in an imaginary state of nature, this move had the inevitable side effect of actually realizing that nasty state of affairs *among* political communities. In order to enjoy the benefits of democracy domestically, we have had to accept that sovereign authority ultimately is justified with reference to the state of exception prevailing in the international realm precisely as a consequence of democratic legitimacy. Therefore, it seems as if the revolutionary solution to the problem of democratic legitimacy has backfired, since the cash value of the above arrangement is that mankind now oppresses itself – in a perversely democratic way – by consenting to remain confined into particular communities whose bounded character is also the very condition of possible warfare between them. Hence, democratic governance at the domestic level is an obstacle to be overcome if we want to emancipate ourselves from the costly illusion of being human by virtue of being members of a 'people', as well as from the corollary and even costlier reality of being stuck in an international state of war.

III

But how can we escape this predicament? Ironically, our situation with regard to the problem of democratic legitimacy is not unlike that of Rousseau, insofar as his solution is as irrelevant to us as those of the ancients were to him. We no longer live in a world in which bounded communities remain the predominant loci of political authority and the ultimate sources of human belonging, and the way in which these once were justified today only makes sense as a source of nationalist nostalgia. The way in which boundaries are drawn and peoples defined cannot be justified with reference to theories of democracy, since they presuppose exactly that which stands in need of justification. This insight has led to a widespread cynicism with regard to the possibility of justifying democratic governance at *any* level, since it is tempting to argue that *all* communities ultimately owe their existence to more or less violent relocations of political power rather than to the consent of their members. If this is the case, political authority is nothing more than power having been around long enough to become taken for granted by those subjected to it, and peoples and boundaries are but outcomes of successful efforts to homogenize an arbitrary multitude of human beings into citizens. By implication, our theories of democratic legitimacy are but ideologies designed to conceal the violence of such founding acts and their consequences (Derrida 1992).

Many people believe that this is what is happening today at the global level as well. If this pattern were to repeat itself at the global level, this would entail that questions of legitimacy can only be meaningfully posed if and when a global structure of authority has been firmly established (Nagel 2005: 146–47). This implies that the creation of a global *demos* would require a prior concentration of power at the global level in order to be possible. Since there is no global culture or common historical memory which could provide the symbolic foundations of a global political identity or citizenship, the creation of a single *demos* of a planetary scope would require allegiances to particular political communities to be gradually undone through a global process of homogenization. Only when this process has been completed could global political institutions start to enjoy legitimacy by commanding consent among their members.

But such domestic analogies merely make us forget what made them possible, namely conceptual nationalization. Through these processes, the meaningful usage of the concept of democracy was restricted to bounded political communities, and democratic legitimacy within such communities was supposed to derive from the consent of their members. But would it be possible to make coherent sense of democracy in the absence of both boundaries and consent? I think an affirmative answer to this question becomes possible when we realize what makes both boundaries and consent possible. Such claims to particularity are only *possible* against the backdrop of characteristics that are universally shared by human beings, yet these characteristics themselves do not confer any automatic legitimacy upon such claims. That claims to particularity have to be justified in universalistic terms also make them reversible, since these claims could equally well be contested on the same universalistic grounds. The same set of reasons used to legitimize a particular people or community in terms of consent could equally well be used to dispute its legitimacy on grounds of its boundless contestability.

In fact, before the process of nationalization gained momentum, the predominant way of understanding political community in Western political thought was by regarding mankind as one immanent and universal community, by virtue of the *sociability* of its members. The idea that consent ought to constitute the only legitimate foundation of authority was closely connected to the ambition to nationalize the concept of political community, insofar as such consent was also essential to the identity of the political community. But the idea of consent derived from the very same sources as human sociability: the universal human capacity to form social bonds by means of the use of language and reason. But as long as human sociability provided the foundation of most attempts to legitimize political authority, it was hard to come up with reasons why political communities should be bounded or based on consent, given the fact that the capacity to form social bonds by means of language and reason are innate characteristics of all members of the species. All the way from the Stoics to Kant, such assumptions of a universal community of all mankind provided the starting point of much Western political and legal thought, as well as for subsequent critiques of despotism, imperial expansion and colonial exploitation (Schofield 1991; Headley 2002; Muthu 2003). While many of those universalistic conceptions of human community are difficult to defend in scientific and secular terms, they provided the conceptual foundations for subsequent attempts to legitimize particular peoples and communities in terms of consent, as well as for most attempts to *contest* the legitimacy of the same peoples and communities in universalistic terms.

Such universalistic conceptions of political community might contain some of the things we need in order to make coherent sense of democracy in the absence of a unifying global authority or a common global culture, without reducing humanity to a mere multitude of unencumbered selves. This being so since universalistic conceptions of community understand mankind to be a unity categorically distinct from the mere sum total of its individual members, constituted not by their sameness but rather by their radical diversity. However different each people or community might be from each other, they nevertheless share the attribute of being different in common, which is the condition of their basic unity. From this point of view, communities of lesser scope are but instantiations of a shared capacity among human beings to form social bonds by means of the use of language and reason, rather than manifestations of *particular* principles or reason or expressions of *particular* linguistic communities. This entails that the basic modern requirement of democratic legitimacy – the existence of bounded communities based on the consent of their members – must be seen as the outcome of a prior differentiation of mankind that is essentially contestable since it is *not* based on the universal consent of all mankind but on historical contingencies alone. Thus, what has to be justified in democratic terms is not the existence of this or that particular people and the boundaries they have drawn around themselves, but the very division of mankind that has made such claims to particularity possible in the first place.

So instead of asking under what conditions globalization might bring about a transition to global democracy, and how the desired end result of such a transition might be justified, I think we should reverse the thrust of the entire argument. Such a reversal might help us understand why the existence of particular communities and their boundaries have been so hard to justify in *democratic* terms, once we realize that the members of different *demoi* share some characteristics in common that are essential for the formation of *any* political community of whatever scope and size. If we are willing to admit that mankind as a whole ought to be considered the ultimate source of legitimacy by virtue of these shared capacities for social life, the burden of proof would no longer rest with those who argue in favor of considering mankind as a single *demos*. Rather it would rest with those who argue that *any* people or community could enjoy legitimacy *independently* of its hypothetical contestation by mankind as a whole, not only since each member of the former necessarily also is a member of the latter, but since these capacities themselves are universal.

Thus it also becomes plain why democratic governance must be global in scope in order for democratic legitimacy to be possible, and why the paradox of democratic legitimacy is a category mistake rather than a genuine logical paradox. For democratic governance to be legitimate in terms themselves democratic, all claims to particularity must be open to contestation at the global level before democratic communities of lesser scope and size can be considered democratically legitimate. Those issues that must be settled either by or with reference to mankind as a whole if the outcome is to be legitimate in democratic terms thus concern whether this or that particular people or community are legitimate sources of political authority and hence also entitled to sovereignty. All such claims would ultimately have to be settled with reference to the contestability of the community in question. For a community and its boundaries to be contestable in practice means that barriers – legal as well as cultural – to entry and exit are low or non-existent. Thus, the easier it is for members to exit and non-members to enter and remain within a given community, the more democratically legitimate it is, as well as conversely. This implies that the existence of a global *demos* at least has to be assumed before claims to legitimacy by any people or community can be conclusively settled in terms themselves democratic. And this leads to the conclusion that all particular claims to democratic legitimacy must be considered invalid in principle until they have been opened to such contestation. Until then the legitimacy of each particular people or community will remain wholly contingent on the historical accidents that brought them into being, and they will therefore remain wholly provisional sources of democratic legitimacy. Now most of those who have wrestled with the paradox of democratic legitimacy have resisted this obvious conclusion. The logical difficulties we encounter when we try to justify particular claims to democratic legitimacy indicate that these claims simply are invalid on their own terms, and are based on lingering nationalist intuitions rather than on logical analysis. This is not to say that all particular peoples or communities necessarily lack democratic legitimacy, only to say that such claims will have to be evaluated against a framework that takes mankind as a whole into consideration, since a global *demos* is the only *demos* that could enjoy *prima facie* democratic legitimacy. Nor is this to say that all boundaries between communities necessarily are illegitimate, only to say that the question of their legitimacy can only be settled democratically with reference to the wider community of all mankind. Hence, to put it simply, democracy has first to become global before it can be a democratically legitimate form of governance at any other level.

Bibliography

Archibugi, D. (2004) 'Cosmopolitan Democracy and Its Critics: a review', *European Journal of International Relations*, 10: 437–73.

—— (2002) 'Demos and Cosmopolis', *New Left Review*, 13: 24–38.

—— (1998) 'Principles of Cosmopolitan Democracy', in D. Archibugi, D. Held and M. Köhler (eds) *Re-Imagining Political Community*, Oxford: Polity Press.

Archibugi, D. and Held, D. (1995) *Cosmopolitan Democracy: an agenda for a new world order*, Cambridge: Polity Press.

Argenson, M. de (1787) *Considérations sur le Gouvernement Ancien et Présent de la France, Comparé avec Celui des Autres États*, Liege: C. Plompteux.

Bader, V. (1997) 'The Cultural Conditions of Transnational Citizenship: on the interpenetration of political and ethnic cultures', *Political Theory*, 25: 771–813.

Bauman, Z. (1998) *Globalization: the human consequences*, Cambridge: Polity Press.

Bauböck, R. (2002) 'Political Community Beyond the Sovereign State: supranational federalism and transnational minorities', in S. Vertovec and R. Cohen (eds) *Conceiving Cosmopolitanism: theory, context, practice*, Oxford: Oxford University Press.

Bell, D.A. (2003) *The Cult of the Nation in France: inventing nationalism, 1680–1800*, Cambridge MA: Harvard University Press.

Bellamy, R. and Castiglione, D. (1998) 'Between Cosmopolis and Community: three models of rights and democracy within the European Union', in D. Archibugi, D. Held and M. Köhler (eds) *Re-Imagining Political Community*, Oxford: Polity Press.

Benhabib, S. (2007) *Another Cosmopolitanism*, Oxford: Oxford University Press.

—— (2004) *The Rights of Others: aliens, residents, and citizens*, Cambridge: Cambridge University Press.

—— (2002) *The Claims of Culture: equality and diversity in the global era*, Princeton: Princeton University Press.

Benhke, A. (1997) 'Citizenship, Nationhood and the Production of Political Space', *Citizenship Studies*, 1: 243–65.

Bohman, J. (2005) 'From Demos to Demoi: democracy across borders', *Ratio Juris*, 18: 293–314.

—— (2004) 'Republican Cosmopolitanism', *Journal of Political Philosophy*, 12: 336–52.

Bourke, R. (2008) 'Enlightenment, Revolution and Democracy', *Constellations*, 15: 10–32.

Buchanan, A. and Keohane, R.O. (2006) 'The Legitimacy of Global Governance Institutions', *Ethics and International Affairs*, 20: 405–37.

Castoriadis, C. (1983) 'The Greek *Polis* and the Creation of Democracy', *Graduate Faculty Philosophy Journal*, New School for Social Research, 9: 79–115.

Chea, P. (1998) 'Given Culture: rethinking cosmopolitical freedom in transnationalism', in C. Pheng and B. Robbins (eds) *Cosmopolitics: thinking and feeling beyond the nation*, Minneapolis: The University of Minnesota Press.

Cochran, M. (2002) 'A Democratic Critique of Cosmopolitan Democracy: pragmatism from the bottom-up', *European Journal of International Relations*, 8: 517–48.

Derrida, J. (1992) 'Force of Law: the mystical foundation of authority' in D. Cornell, M. Rosenfeld, and D. Gray (eds) *Deconstruction and the Possibility of Justice*, London and New York: Routledge.

Diderot, D. (1992) *Political Writings*, Cambridge: Cambridge University Press.

Doucet, M. (2005) 'The Democratic Paradox and Cosmopolitan Democracy', *Millennium: Journal of International Studies*, 34: 137–155.

Dryzek, J. (1999) 'Transnational Democracy', *Journal of Political Philosophy*, 7: 30–51.

Foucault, M. (1988) 'The Political Technology of Individuals', in L.H. Martin, H. Gutman, and P.H. Hutton (eds) *Technologies of the Self*, London: Tavistock.

Goldmann, K. (2001) *Transforming the European Nation-State*, London: Sage.

Hall, S. (2002) 'Political Belonging in a World of Multiple Identities', in S. Vertovec and R. Cohen (eds) *Conceiving Cosmopolitanism: theory, context, practice*, Oxford: Oxford University Press.

Hazareesingh, S. (2004) *Saint-Napoleon: celebrations of sovereignty in nineteenth-century France'*, Cambridge, MA: Harvard University Press.

Headley, J.M. (2002) 'The Universalizing Principle and Process: on the West's intrinsic commitment to a global context', *Journal of World History*, 13: 291–321.

Held, D. (2005) 'Principles of Cosmopolitan Order', in G. Brock and H. Brighouse (eds) *The Political Philosophy of Cosmopolitanism*, Cambridge: Cambridge University Press.

—— (2003) 'Cosmopolitanism: globalization tamed?', *Review of International Studies*, 29: 465–480.

—— (1999) 'The Transformation of Political Community: rethinking democracy in the context of globalization', in I. Shapiro and C. Hacker-Cordón, *Democracy's Edges*, Cambridge: Cambridge University Press.

—— (1998) 'Democracy and Globalization', in D. Archibugi, D. Held and M. Köhler (eds) *Re-Imagining Political Community*, Oxford: Polity Press.

—— (1995) *Democracy and the Global Order: from the modern state to cosmopolitan governance*, Cambridge: Polity Press.

Hollinger, D.A. (2001) 'Not Universalists, Not Pluralists: the new cosmopolitans find their own way', *Constellations*, 8: 236–48.

Honig, B. (2007) 'Between Decision and Deliberation: political paradox in democratic theory', *American Political Science Review*, 101: 1–17.

—— (2001) *Democracy and the Foreigner*, Princeton: Princeton University Press.

—— (1998): 'Ruth, the Model Émigré: mourning and the symbolic politics of immigration', in C. Pheng and B. Robbins (eds) *Cosmopolitics: thinking and feeling beyond the nation*, Minneapolis: The University of Minnesota Press.

Hont, I. (2005) *Jealousy of Trade: international competition and the nation-state in historical perspective*, Cambridge, MA: Harvard University Press.

Jaume, L. (2003) 'Citizens and State during the French Revolution', in B. Stråth and Q. Skinner (eds) *States and Citizens*, Cambridge: Cambridge University Press.

Keane, J. (2003) *Global Civil Society?*, Cambridge: Cambridge University Press.

Kelly, C. (1987) 'To Persuade without Convincing: the language of Rousseau's legislator', *American Journal of Political Science*, 31: 321–335.

Kuper, A. (2004) *Democracy beyond Borders? justice and representation in global institutions*, Oxford: Oxford University Press.

Linklater, A. (1998) *The Transformation of Political Community: ethical foundations of the post-Westphalian era*, Cambridge: Polity Press.

Meier, C. (1990) *The Greek Discovery of Politics*, Cambridge MA: Harvard University Press.

Muthu, S. (2003) *Enlightenment against Empire*, Cambridge MA: Harvard University Press.

Nagel, T. (2005) 'The Problem of Global Justice' *Philosophy and Public Affairs*, 33: 113–47.

Näsström, S. (2007) 'The Legitimacy of the People', *Political Theory*, 35: 624–58.

—— (2003) 'What Globalization Overshadows', *Political Theory*, 31: 808–34.

Ringmar, E. (1998) 'Nationalism: the idiocy of intimacy', *British Journal of Sociology*, 49: 534–49.

Rosanvallon, P. (2006) *Democracy Past and Future*, New York: Columbia University Press.

Rousseau, J.-J. (1990) *The Social Contract: the Social Contract and Discourses*, London: Everyman's.

Sassen, S. (1996) *Losing Control? Sovereignty in an age of globalization*, New York: Columbia University Press.

Schofield, M. (1991) *The Stoic Idea of the City*, Chicago: University of Chicago Press.

Scholte, J.A. (2000) *Globalization: a critical introduction*, London: Macmillan.

Seglow, J. (1998) 'Universals and Particulars: the case of liberal cultural nationalism', *Political Studies*, 46: 963–77.

Sieyès, E. de (1963) *What is the Third Estate?*, London: Pall Mall Press.

Tully, J. (2002) 'The Unfreedom of the Moderns in Comparison to Their Ideals of Constitutional Democracy', *Modern Law Review*, 65: 204–228.

Van Roermund, B. (2003) 'Sovereignty: unpopular and popular', in N. Walker (ed.) *Sovereignty in Transition*, Oxford: Hart.

Veyne, P. (1983) 'Les Grecs ont-ils Connu la Démocratie?' *'Diogène'* 124: 3–33.

Wendt, A. (1999) 'A Comment on Held's Cosmopolitanism', in I. Shapiro and C. Hacker-Cordón, *Democracy's Edges*, Cambridge: Cambridge University Press.

Wokler, R. (1998) 'The Enlightenment and the French Revolutionary Birth Pangs of Modernity', in J. Heilbron, L. Magnusson and B. Wittrock (eds), *The Rise of the Social Sciences and the Formation of Modernity*, Dordrecht: Kluwer.

—— (1975) 'The Influence of Diderot on the Political Theory of Rousseau', *Studies on Voltaire and the Eighteenth Century*, 82: 55–111.

Yack, B. (2001) 'Popular Sovereignty and Nationalism', *Political Theory*, 29: 517–36.

—— (1998) 'The Myth of the Civic Nation', in R. Beiner (ed.) *Theorizing Nationalism*: Albany: SUNY.

3 The politics of hospitality

Sovereignty and ethics in political community

Gideon Baker

Can we conceive of the relationship between sovereignty and ethics in political community without privileging one over the other? If not, we are then led to one of two positions. Either we end up with a Schmittian ontological prioritization of sovereignty where ethics in political community is entirely overcome. Or we move towards a neo-Kantian reversal of this order of priority, in which, ideally, ethics determines sovereignty to the extent that sovereignty in political community is overcome. This, according to Emmanuel Levinas at least (to whom we shall return), constitutes an unpalatable choice between an ethics-free and a depoliticized vision of political community in which

> there would be no alternative between recourse to unscrupulous methods whose model is furnished by *Realpolitik* and ... a careless idealism, lost in utopian dreams but crumbling into dust on contact with any reality or turning into a dangerous, impudent and facile frenzy.
>
> (Levinas 1994: 194)

Is there, however, an alternative way of treating the relationship between ethics and sovereignty in political community that avoids the drive to a hierarchical arrangement of these two poles? Jacques Derrida has sought to provide just such an alternative under the heading of hospitality, and it is the aim of this chapter to analyse both the character and implications of this attempt. One implication in particular will be drawn out in the conclusion – that, from the perspective of hospitality, we are forced to reconsider the ethical implications of the boundaries of political community and to distance ourselves from the way in which the cosmopolitan-communitarian debate dominant in international political theory reduces the moral significance of boundaries to either good or ill. When it comes to hospitality, this dichotomization will not do. The boundaries of political community, it will be demonstrated, are both an enabling *and* constraining condition of an ethical relation to the Other or stranger.

Derrida insists that the 'problematic of sovereignty', understood as involving the necessity of unfounded political decision and also in relation to a claim of possession over the home, is an irreducible element of an ethics defined by hospitality. However uncomfortable a truth it might be, ethical responsibility 'engages or commits us before … *sovereignty'* (Derrida 2003a: 45, 44). However, just as much as being necessary to the practice of ethics as hospitality, sovereignty entails falling short of what is actually, for Derrida, following Levinas, an ethics of *unlimited* hospitality, in which no possession is claimed over the home that is opened up, unconditionally, to the arrival of the Other; in which no decision is made as to who is allowed in or on the terms of their entry. The sovereignty of the 'at home' is therefore both absolutely necessary and yet purely provisional in as much as the hospitality it makes possible is exceeded by the figure of an unconditional hospitality which overflows, even destroys, any sovereign container – household, city- or nation-state as that may be. In other words, less the attribution of an 'it is necessary' appears to neutralize a critical stance towards sovereignty, Derrida's intention is rather to show that, contra Bodin, Hobbes, Schmitt and other theorists of the indivisibility of sovereignty, we must, while being sovereign, yet have 'another thought' of the possibility of power, mastery and sovereignty, a thought of 'unconditionality without sovereignty' which is that *'unconditional hospitality* that exposes itself without limit to the coming of the other …' (Derrida 2003a: 34, 40).

Ethics as hospitality

> Insofar as it has to do with the *ethos*, that is, the residence, one's home, the familiar place of dwelling, inasmuch as it is a manner of being there, the manner in which we relate to ourselves and to others, to others as our own or as foreigners, *ethics is hospitality*.
>
> (Derrida 2001: 16; see also Derrida 1999a: 94)

The importance of hospitality for Derrida, and why for him hospitality *is* ethics, is that it is a – *the*? – response to the otherness of the Other for whom we are responsible. 'The face' – that is, a particular rather then generalized other – 'always lends itself to a welcome and the welcome welcomes only a face' rather than a generic, cardboard-cut-out, human being (Derrida 1999a: 20). Unconditional hospitality as a welcoming of the other as Other, 'where the other eludes the theme', points beyond all attempts at domestication of the stranger even as it envisages a welcome, a responsibility taken for that other (Derrida 1999a: 21).[1] And herein lies the paradox. Although unconditional hospitality captures the radical implications of the welcome that accepts responsibility for the other while truly acknowledging his otherness, it cannot instantiate a welcome. For it is quite literally impossible in the sense of self-defeating: an unconditional giving way to any and to all who come, leaves us with no home to offer hospitality within. But just as much, a conditional hospitality is always too conditional, always falling short of the spirit of hospitality which disavows all violence to the Other by claiming no sovereignty over the home that is opened up, by being open to the unexpected visitation rather than merely the always conditional invitation. We cannot practice ethics as hospitality – opening our door to specific, named others – without limiting it, but we cannot imagine ethics as hospitality without creating the demand for its unlimited form – a leaving open of the door to the unannounced, unexpected and unforeseeable arrival of the unknown, nameless Other. In short, the two poles, limited and unlimited hospitality, are both inseparable from and yet also irreducible to one another. They 'defy dialectics' because there is a 'double law' or double bind at play – two equally imperious imperatives pull us in different directions each time we offer hospitality (Derrida 1999a: 967). Of a final synthesis of these two laws, of a dialectical resolution, there is no prospect.

Defying dialectics changes the nature of ethics as commonly understood. Rather than being told what it is imperative that we should do, *undecidability* becomes characteristic of the question of our duties to others. Precisely because hospitality-ethics involves ceaseless competition between two determined duties (pure and limited hospitality) 'if I want to respond in the name of justice, I have to invent singularly', that is, in the absence of any norm or law (Derrida 1999b: 72). Undecidability is challenging – it can lead to confusion, stasis and a fatalism that can allow harm-doers to do their worst. But it has its rewards too. Paradoxically, it opens up space for, indeed requires, fresh decision and therefore responsibility. Indeed, to take one of Derrida's own examples, the case of a judge's decision: how else, other than by the judge taking responsibility for a unique decision based on the merits of a particular case, can we say that justice has been done?

In sum, what we find here, as the irreducible core of ethical or hospitable life, is a double figure of sovereignty. First, sovereignty is defined by the inescapable need for a decision, and responsibility for it, to be taken. The decision concerns how to render the ethics of unconditional hospitality into a practical politics or practice of hospitality in which the welcome might take concrete form. It is a real decision, in the sense of being free or unprogrammed by any law, because deciding between unlimited and limited hospitality is ultimately impossible, even if it must be done. From this paradox comes the requirement to *decide* uniquely and singularly each time how to limit, and how much to limit, unconditional hospitality. Second, sovereignty is defined by the irreducibility of the home, which, if there is to be hospitality, ultimately cannot be surrendered. Clinging, sovereignly, to a space within which we are 'at home' is necessary if hospitality is to exist in the world, even as it also presents the gravest dangers.

Ethics and sovereignty in political community: three approaches

In the terms in which political community is usually articulated, the implications of this description of the relationship between ethics and sovereignty are intriguing. The implication that ethical life is necessarily political life and that ethico-political life is necessarily sovereign (in the double sense of requiring that a decision, and thus responsibility for the decision, be taken and also that there be home-ownership, so to speak) flies in the face of much of the contemporary literature on sovereignty.

It is differentiated, first, from that perspective inspired by Carl Schmitt in particular, which pictures sovereignty as characterized by decision on the state of exception in which ethico-legal, or normative, considerations are subordinated to *realpolitik*. Here, the survival of the political community in a Hobbesian state of

nature is all. Schmittian decisionism, then, has absolutely nothing to do with ethical responsibility. Decision regarding who is a friend and who is an enemy is not
only completely other than morality in which categories of good and evil might
make sense, but is entirely its own foundation. The political, for Schmitt, rests only
on this 'ultimate distinction' between friend and enemy and this distinction is one
which the state 'decides for itself', having 'no normative meaning, but an existential meaning only, particularly in a real combat situation with a real enemy' (1996:
26) who need be neither evil nor ugly, only 'other' (1996: 27). The distinctively
political decision, then, is simply one regarding 'who the enemy is' (Schmitt 1996:
34; see also 45, 47), and he who decides this in the extreme case of war is sovereign:

> In any event, that grouping is always political which orientates itself towards
> this most extreme possibility ... If such an entity exists at all, it is always the
> decisive entity, and it is sovereign in the sense that the decision about the cru-
> cial situation, even if it is the exception, must always necessarily reside there
>
> However one may look at it, in the orientation toward the possible extreme
> case of an actual battle against a real enemy, the political entity is essential, and
> it is the decisive entity for the friend-enemy grouping; and in this (and not in
> any kind of absolutist sense) it is sovereign.
>
> (Schmitt 1996: 39)

A crucial implication of this definition of a properly political entity, Schmitt goes
on to argue, is that it 'presupposes the real existence of an enemy and therefore
coexistence with another political entity ... The political world is a pluriverse, not
a universe' such that 'Universality at any price would necessarily have to mean
total depoliticalization' (Schmitt 1996: 53, 55).

The notion that political decision might actually be *necessary* to ethical life (as a
decision necessitated by responsibility for the Other), rather than, in Schmittian
vein, fundamentally other than or hostile to ethics, is the challenge laid down by
Derrida here. One aspect of this re-reading of the ethical significance of sovereign
decision will be that the distinction between friends and enemies that sovereign
decision produces for Schmitt is replaced *not* with its antonym – a boundary-free
ethics in which there are no longer any distinctions between self/citizen and
Other/foreigner – but with a new awareness of the *ethical* significance of a sovereign distinction between inside and outside in political community. Here, it is not
'the political' that constitutes the political world as a pluriverse, but rather 'ethics
as hospitality'. And it is not the threat of depoliticization (as if human freedom
defined agonistically were self-evidently a good as Schmitt implies)[2] that is
the price to be paid for apolitical universality, but rather the threat to a universal
ethic of responsibility for the Other defined by *particular and political* acts of
hospitality.

Second, there is separation here from those neo-Kantian accounts, expressed
most clearly in the contemporary literature of liberal-cosmopolitanism, which find
sovereign claims to a bounded or bordered 'home' to be simply the problem for
ethical political community, which should ideally be cosmopolitan in scope or at

least in intent. As Andrew Linklater writes, the challenge facing cosmopolitans is to identify 'the moral resources for weaning the human species away from particularistic attachments that thwart collective efforts to control global processes in conformity with the ideals of the Enlightenment' (2007: 8; see also Linklater 1998: 211), ideals expressed most clearly in the injunction to pursue 'new forms of community that are committed to realizing the Kantian ideal of a universal kingdom of ends' (Linklater 2007: 108). The fundamental driver of such a 'post-Westphalian' or cosmopolitan political community would be an ethical 'obligation to transcend the dichotomy between citizens and aliens by establishing systems of joint rule' (Linklater 1998: 212). Here there is the unmistakeable echo of Kant's injunction, in *Toward Perpetual Peace*, that 'all politics must bend its knee before right', a right which is cosmopolitan in nature.[3]

From this liberal-cosmopolitan perspective, decisionism is also read largely pejoratively, as leaving open a space for a politics which is – dangerously, even fascistically – its own foundation. This is accused of legitimating totalitarian domination and state violence and of rejecting the critical rationality necessary to a critique of these political forms (see Habermas 1989). Political action, rather, should be understood as the application of a universal ethic orientated around individual human rights. As Linklater puts it, advocates of cosmopolitan citizenship seek to harness practices that can 'transform political communities and the global order so that they conform with universalistic moral commitments … The universal human rights culture is deemed to reveal the emerging law of world citizens' (1998: 124). Thus if Schmittians read 'real' political community as pure decisionism or sovereign particularity, neo-Kantians read it 'ideally' as pure ethics, or universality. Derrida, as we shall see, seeks rather to keep in tension the ideal and the real, the ethics and the politics, and the universal and the particular in political community. We are here 'at an equal distance from a simple deduction of politics from ethics and from a sheer pragmatics of politics' (Raffouel 1998: 282).[4]

In the light of this claim, though of course simplifying in the process, we might represent the distinctiveness of Derrida's position on political community vis-à-vis these other currently dominant positions as follows

	Schmittian	Derridean	neo-Kantian
Decisionistic*	✓	✓	✗
Cosmopolitan†	✗	✓	✓
Universal	✗	✗	✓

* politics not programmed by ethics
† recognising ethical commitments to all human beings

Given that we will focus on the gap between a Derridean and neo-Kantian conception of political community in the next section, it is important first to say something more about how Derrida and Schmitt compare. At first sight, there is less distance between Derrida and Schmitt than between Derrida and the neo-Kantians.[5] In fact, to repeat, there is considerable distance between all three. Against the tendency to conflate a Schmittian valorization of the political with post-structuralism, it will be argued that, in the case of Derrida's post-structuralism at least, there *is* a crucial distinction vis-à-vis Schmitt, a distinction which lies primarily on the ethical dimension.[6] What distinguishes a Derridean from a Schmittian position on political community is thus neither the unfounded, existential quality of the properly political decision – Derrida concurs that 'sovereignty is first of all one of the traits by which reason defines its own power'(2003a: 45) – nor the emphasis on the particular, rather than universal, quality of political association. Here there is some agreement. Instead, it is in the ethical relation to the other or stranger that we should understand the distinction. For Schmitt, the collective (that is public or political) other, though not necessarily an enemy at any given point in space or time, is always and necessarily capable of becoming an enemy (1996: 33). And, since 'War follows from enmity', the requirement for the 'existential negation' of the stranger is an ever-present political possibility. In short, there simply is no ethical relation to the non-citizen other in politics. For Derrida, as we shall see, the very opposite is true. Political sameness and Otherness (citizenship or the inside/outside of political community) attains it significance only in as much as it is necessary to an ethical relation to strangers, manifestly *not* as a valorization of any political community in and for itself. It is because our responsibility to the Other is *definitive* of the self (here, as we shall see, Derrida follows Levinas), rather than threatening to it, that the boundary between self and Other becomes significant as the threshold of an unconditional hospitality rather than an ever-present possibility of war as in Schmitt, the Hobbes of the twentieth century.

As shall become apparent, the necessarily existential quality of the political decision for Derrida then becomes one of deciding, impossibly and therefore singularly each time, how to translate an unconditional hospitality into a practical or conditional hospitality, rather than deciding on the enemy. Thus if the existential quality of the political decision for Schmitt is that, like the miracle in theology, it is unfounded in the sense of being pure or referring only to itself (Schmitt 2005: 36; see also 12, 13), the existential quality of the political decision for Derrida is that, like the miracle in a different sense, it is in the realm of the impossible and *not* because it refers only to itself. It is not irrationalism 'a pure decision not based on reason and discussion and not justifying itself' (Schmitt 2005: 66)[7] but impossibility that characterizes the decision.[8] The decision is taken not because somebody, in reference to themselves alone, is sovereign enough to decide who constitutes an existential threat but because it is only by making a real, that is a non-determined, decision that responsibility for the decision can be taken.[9] And to what or who is that responsibility directed? Not towards the preservation of the status quo, as in Schmitt, but towards the Other. For an ethics defined by responsibility for the Other, the decision is a *sine qua non* of acting ethically.[10] Politics and ethics become as indissociable from as they are irreducible to each other – knotted together, we might say. For Schmitt, they simply have no relation, being nothing less than ontologically other (1996: 26–7).

This is why, unlike Schmitt, Derrida is able to keep the critique of sovereignty alive. Sovereignty is not only 'necessary' but dangerous – an always possible 'concentration, into a single point of indivisible singularity (God, the monarch, the people, the state or the nation-state) of absolute force and the absolute exception' (Derrida 2003a: 45). In particular, for Derrida, the logic of the sovereign nation-state needs to be called into question even while avoiding an unconditional opposition to sovereignty that combats '*all* sovereignty [or] sovereignty *in general* ...' (2003a: 49). Derrida's approach to sovereignty continues to allow space for a sovereign politics or decisionism that, while it is not reducible to or programmable by an ethics, is, contra Schmitt, nonetheless amenable to ethical critique. Thus, what Derrida writes about 'reason' in the following passage might faithfully be said also of his view of sovereignty:

> Reason reasons, to be sure, it is a right, and it gives itself reason, to do so, so as to protect or keep itself, so as to keep within reason. It is in this that it is and thus wants to be itself; that is its sovereign ipseity [selfhood].
> But, to make its ipseity see reason, it must let itself be reasoned with.
>
> (2003a: 50)

Responsibility and undecidability

Turning now in some more detail to the distinction between Derrida's and neo-Kantian visions of political community, the starting point for differentiation is that, for Derrida, freedom is the opposite of Kantian and liberal autonomy, being a freedom *from* self rather than freedom of the self (Bankovsky 2005: 161). Here, as in much else, Derrida takes from Levinas, for whom freedom is freedom from egotistical 'return to the self', a turning away from what, for a creature doomed to destruction, is a perverse obsession with self-preservation towards an answer for the other, towards a defence of the 'rights of the *other* man' (Levinas 1981: 124). Foregrounding responsibility for the other in this way flows from an account of the other pre-existing, and being constitutive of, the self. In Levinas, subjectivity stems from the ego's awareness that it is not sovereign, but exists in a world which, far from being an extension of or coinciding with itself, it is fully dependent on. This then allows for a radically decentring experience of the Other and of dependence on the Other, an Other to whom I must therefore now respond (such that subjectivity is defined by openness and vulnerability rather than Kantian autonomy). Derrida radicalizes this decentring welcome, which is for Levinas originally a feminine welcome into the world, further, suggesting that I am actually constituted by the Other's hospitable welcome of me such that I am now a response to, or hostage of, the Other (Bankovsky 2005: 157–8).[11]

This Other-wise, and therefore otherwise than liberal-individualist, defence of the 'rights of man' (as 'rights of the *other* man') is also irreducibly plural. It is the right of the Other to receive a necessarily specific response to his needs arising out of my responsibility for him (Bankovsky 2005: 159). Levinasian and Derridean justice, being attentive to the singularity of the Other, and of the Other's suffering, is therefore irreducible to law or right which are necessarily expressed by the formalism of universality:

I want to insist right away on reserving the possibility of a justice, indeed of a law that not only exceeds or contradicts 'law' (*droit*) but also, perhaps, has no relation to law.

Law (*droit*) is not justice. Law is the element of calculation, and it is just that there be law, but justice is incalculable, it requires us to calculate with the incalculable ...

(Derrida 1990: 925)

The contrast here with Kant's confident claim that 'there is no conflict of politics, as doctrine of right put into practice, with morals, as theoretical doctrine of right', could not be starker (cited in La Caze 2007: 783). In Derrida, the quantifiable rights of 'man' characteristic of liberal political community give way to the 'practically infinite' right of the Other. Equity between human beings is not the abstract, formal equality of liberalism but the 'equitable honouring' of others whose otherness cannot be thematized and between whom there is 'absolute dissymmetry' (Derrida 1990: 959; see also Derrida 2003b: 43). *This* idea of ethics or justice, contra liberalism, is 'infinite because it is irreducible, irreducible because owed to the other, owed to the other, before any contract, because it has come, the other's coming as the singularity that is always other' (Derrida 1990: 965). In short, this justice, as 'the experience of absolute alterity' or otherness, is for Derrida 'unpresentable' – irreducible to a given law or right (Derrida 1990: 971).

For Levinas, human solidarity is based not on universals, whether biological, linguistic or otherwise, but rather in collective responsibility of each for everyone else, a responsibility rooted in the 'irreducible singularity', the infinity, of each and every human being (Gauthier 2007: 167):

Man understood as an individual of a genus ... has no privilege that would establish him as the aim of reality. But man must also be thought from the responsibility that [consists in] self putting himself despite himself in the place of everyone, substituted for everyone because of his very non-interchangeability; man must be thought from the condition ... of hostage, hostage of all the others who, precisely others, do not belong to the same genre as me ...

(Levinas 2006: 68)

Thus between 'the I who is what it is, singular and identifiable, only through the impossibility of being replaced' (Levinas, cited in Derrida 1999a: 6) and the other for whom I am uniquely responsible ('the uniqueness of the Ego is the fact that no one can answer in my stead') 'gapes a bottomless difference' (Levinas 2006: 33, 6). The universality of law and right, however, is possible only through abstraction – laws speak to the general rather than the particular and therefore cannot do justice to human alterity or otherness, only to a totalized humanity of 'interchangeable men'. Taken alone, law is thus tyrannical, 'it deforms the I and the other who have given rise to it, for it judges them according to universal rules, and thus in absentia' (Levinas 1981: 300).

From this perspective universals, liberalism's law or rights included, are not condemned for being universal but rather for failing to be universal enough – universal enough to do justice to particular others, that is (Derrida 2003b: 49). As Levinas puts it, 'there's no need to deny humanism as long as we recognize it there where it receives its least deceiving mode', that is at its most universal or transcendental and 'never in the zones of ... power and law, order, culture ...' (2006: 67). Residing in these zones, liberal humanism must continually be challenged and rethought. Such a negotiated approach to the question of humanism is how we might distinguish 'Derridean' political community from its liberal variant. Liberals see duties as defined by an already given humanistic ethics while for Derrida the 'ethicity' of any particular application of ethics, humanism included, is always in question:

> I would say that what is 'reasonable' is the reasoned and considered wager of a transaction between these two apparently irreconcilable exigencies of reason, between calculation and the incalculable. For example, between human rights, such as the history of a certain number of juridical performatives has determined and enriched them from one declaration to the next over the course of the last two centuries, and the exigency of an unconditional justice to which these performatives will always be inadequate, open to their perfectibility ... and exposed to a rational deconstruction that will endlessly question their limits and presuppositions, the interests and calculations that order their deployment and their concepts – beginning with the concepts of law and of duty, and especially the concept of man ...
>
> (Derrida 2003a: 42; see also 1999: 176)

From this perspective, openness concerning the 'rules' of ethical political community, even human rights laws, does not suggest the absence of rules or rights as such, but rather the irreducible 'necessity of a leap at the moment of ethical, political, or juridical decision'. In the absence of such a 'leap', a decision taken in a context of undecidability, 'we could simply unfold [ethical] knowledge into a programme or course of action' (Derrida 1999a: 117). Derrida says of this latter course of action that 'Nothing could make us more irresponsible and more totalitarian' (1999a: 117). Contra liberal cosmopolitanism, then, deducing politics from ethics remains an indeterminate activity; that is, *to be determined* (Raffouel 1998: 282). Undecidability becomes a call to responsible action – that is, for decision – rather than an excuse for inaction. Although there can be no formal deduction of politics from ethics, one must, nonetheless, 'deduce a politics and a law from ethics. There must be this deduction in order to determine what is "better" or "the least bad"' (Derrida 1999a: 198).

Before going further, let us state in summary form the argument so far. Ethics as responsibility for the Other leads to hospitality: '[H]ospitality becomes the very name of what opens itself up to the face [the Other] ... what "welcomes" it. The face always lends itself to a welcome and the welcome welcomes only a face' (Derrida 1999: 20). But just as surely as the face of the Other calls for hospitality (to the extent, indeed, that ethics *is* hospitality), hospitality produces undecidability. This is because this face of the Other

as we know from reading Levinas, must resist all thematization ... This irreducibility to a theme, this exceeding of all thematization ... is precisely what
the face has in common with hospitality. Levinas does not simply distinguish
hospitality and thematization ... he explicitly opposes them.

(Derrida 1999: 20).[12]

But despite not being able to thematize hospitality without doing violence to the
infinity of the Other, hospitality must be practiced. To practice in the absence of
thematization, as Derrida shows, is the very terrain of undecidability.
Undecidability here means to have to *decide* uniquely and responsibly each time
exactly how to offer a hospitality that, in the very offering, will reduce the stranger
to a theme, to a guest in the (sovereign) home. To this problematic, or double-bind,
we will now turn in more detail.

The 'double law' of hospitality

Derrida indicated some of the dimensions of his thinking on the double-bind of hospitality in a 1997 address to the International Parliament of Writers' (IPW). Derrida
was responding in this address to the IPW's Network of Cities of Asylum which,
following the Salman Rushdie affair, was established to provide safe havens for
persecuted writers. *The European Charter of Cities of Asylum*, launched in
Strasbourg, proposed that this city 'offer Salman Rushdie the freedom of the city
and declare itself a "City of Asylum" for persecuted intellectuals'. Strasbourg City
Council indeed adopted a 'Motion regarding Salman Rushdie and his
Commitment'. Subsequently, cities in Europe, North America and Africa have
joined the Network (becoming the International Network of Cities of Asylum or
INCA), with each one charged to provide physical, financial, and social stability for
the authors they shelter – to seek the necessary papers and deploy their security
forces as necessary (Kelly 2004).[13]

Derrida's address to the IPW called for the extension of their limited (literary)
cosmopolitan hospitality to include 'the foreigner in general, the immigrant, the
exiled, the deported, the stateless or the displaced person'. To cite only 'the best
known would risk sending the anonymous others back into the darkness from
which they find it hard to escape, a darkness which is truly the worst and the condition for all others' (Derrida 2001: 6). What Derrida sought here is to identify the
cities of refuge with the foreigner in all his foreignness, with the nameless and
homeless, something which the IPW fell short of in its call for solidarity with what
were effectively compatriots of the mind if not of the passport. In this they were
guilty of that limited hospitality offered subject to the other following our laws and
customs; in short, of hospitality as it is commonly understood, based on conditions
and (at the national or international level) laws (Derrida 2005: 7). Better by far
would be that, above and beyond according the other's rights by doing 'everything
to address the other, to accord him, even ask his name', we keep this question 'from
becoming a "condition", a police inquisition, a blacklist or a simple border control'.
For Derrida, this difference, though subtle, is fundamental; for the question in

question 'is asked on the threshold of the "home" … an entire politics depends on it, an entire ethics is decided by it' (Derrida 2005: 7). We see just how fundamental this questioning at the border, or its lack, is when we consider that the unconditional hospitality prefigured in the absence of questioning precludes even the sovereignty involved in an inviting in. *This* hospitality is always already open to whoever comes, to the uninvited, unexpected, unidentifiable, absolutely foreign visitor (Derrida 2003b: 129). Such pure hospitality, because it sets no limits whatsoever to the coming of the other, is more universal than any cosmopolitan law – it simply 'exceeds juridical, political, or economic calculation' (Derrida 2003b: 40).

But if every individual who knocks on our door is treated as an individual case without regard for the consequences, then we have a hospitality that appears entirely self-defeating since in no time at all we will no longer have a home to welcome anybody into. And indeed, Derrida tells us that absolute hospitality requires nothing less of us than that we lose our home by unconditionally opening it up not only to the foreigner, 'but to the absolute, unknown, anonymous other'; by not merely giving to the foreigner but 'that I *give place* to them' (2001: 25; see also 2000: 25). Derrida recognizes that all of this is practically impossible, that the unconditional law of hospitality requires laws, since all *finite* hospitality implies sovereignty. Short of a home we are in no position to offer any hospitality at all. Thus we cannot make of pure hospitality a set of statutes or laws; though it calls forth a welcome 'without reserve and without calculation', we must yet hold back against the unlimited arrival of the other in order to 'render the welcome effective, determined, concrete, to put it into practice'. And, from such necessary conditions, it is only a short distance to 'the rights and the duties, the borders, the passports and … the immigration laws' (Derrida 2005: 6).

More even than this, the foreigner/host relation sets the *logical* – not simply the material – limits of the practice of hospitality. Any particular, historical, mode of welcoming cannot transcend this limit: if there is to be hospitality, then there must be a foreigner; and, for the foreigner to appear foreign in the first place, there must exist hospitality of some kind. But because my 'at home' supposes a reception of the other in terms of appropriation, control, and mastery, in short 'according to different modalities of violence, there is a history of hospitality, an always possible perversion of the law of hospitality' (Derrida 2001: 17). All finite hospitality is built upon the laws or customs of the host. 'It is the familial despot, the father, the spouse, and the boss, the master of the house who lays down the laws of hospitality' (Derrida 2000: 149). Such laws construe the foreigner as welcome *provided* he can be translated into the host's language of hospitality. Under such conditions the foreigner is little more than the host's own other, the other who enables the host to establish his domesticity as proper. Hospitality is always part of the attempt to account for difference within the host's own language, thereby excluding the foreigner as foreign by reducing him to what is already known (Kelly 2004: 429).

Thus Derrida challenges the IPW, necessary though their *particular* application of the law of hospitality undoubtedly is, to remember that 'the foreigner is first of all foreign to the legal language in which the duty of hospitality is formulated, the right of asylum, its limits, norms, policing, etc. He has to ask for hospitality in a language which by definition is not his own ...' (Derrida 2000: 15; see also Derrida 2001: 15). We have already seen that, practically speaking, Derrida knows that this is inevitable. And yet, when asked whether it could be otherwise, he responds 'Yes, because it is perhaps the first violence which the foreigner undergoes: to have to claim his rights in a language he does not speak' (Derrida 2005: 7). Although Derrida answers 'yes', he does not do so with some practical reason why not, but because violence has been done, and it is responsibility for the other beyond all violence that must be hoped for even as we always, inevitably, fall short of it: 'Suspending this violence is nearly impossible, an interminable task at any rate. Another reason to work urgently to transform things' (Derrida 2005: 7).

The 'double law' of hospitality, then, far from leading to paralysis, actually spurs us on. It offers no comfort to those who would eschew all violence in their hospitality to others (declaring this to be impossible), even while it calls each attempt at hospitality insufficient for its violence to otherness. The 'double law' of hospitality 'defines the unstable site of strategy and decision' (Derrida 2005: 6; see also Derrida 2000: 147–8). Responsibility emerges from within 'an historical space which takes place *between* the Law of unconditional hospitality ... and the conditional laws of a right to hospitality' (Derrida 2001: 22; see also 45). If the unconditional law of hospitality could be written in our laws then we would know in advance what to do, there would be nothing for us to decide and therefore no responsibility. Knowledge would programme action entirely and

> the so-called responsible decision [would] become again the merely technical application of a concept. ... In order to be responsible and truly decisive, a decision should not limit itself to putting into operation a determinable or determining knowledge, the consequences of some preestablished order ... But, conversely ... who will dare call duty a duty that owes nothing ... It is necessary, therefore, that the decision and responsibility for it be taken ...
>
> (Derrida 1993: 16–17)[14]

Derrida uses the example of a judge's decision to indicate the strong connection between responsibility and justice. In order to be called responsible and just, the judge's decision must consist of a 'freely decisive interpretation', a 'reinstituting act of interpretation, as if ultimately nothing existed of the law, as if the judge himself invented the law in every case. No exercise of the law can be just unless there is a "fresh judgement"' (Derrida 1990: 961–3).[15] This requirement for fresh judgement is expressed hyperbolically, as moving us as far as possible beyond calculation, 'beyond the place we find ourselves and beyond the already identifiable zones of morality, or politics or law, beyond the distinction between national and international, public and private, and so on' (Derrida 1990: 971). Indeed, in his own reflections on politics, Derrida repeatedly makes it clear that the task is one of 'genuine innovation'; the development of 'forms of solidarity yet to be invented'; that 'this invention is our task', a task 'indissociable from 'practical initiatives' and 'political implementation' such as reforming the right of asylum; that, with regard to the 'cities of refuge', the task is to 'transform and reform the modalities of membership by which the city belongs to the state', maybe even freeing it from this membership (Derrida 2001: 4–9). What these tasks boil down to is the challenge posed by Derrida in 'Force of Law': 'how would this infinite and unconditional hospitality … operate in a practical politics?' (2001: 91). For the ethics of unconditional hospitality, which remains irreducible to politics, nonetheless always and immediately calls for a politics.

Ethics as hospitality: the irreducibility of the 'problematic of sovereignty'

Ensuring that our practices of hospitality stay as true as possible to the law of unconditional hospitality in which we have no home that we call our own requires, then, that we do *not* in fact surrender our own home but rather render it as accessible as possible, inventing in the process 'the best arrangements, the least bad conditions … that is to say some particular legislative limits, and especially a particular application of the laws' (Derrida 2005: 6). Limited hospitality, even with its exclusionary and domesticating practices, its sovereignty, is necessary in order that justice be done.

Thus the 'problematic of sovereignty', it turns out, is an irreducible component of ethics as hospitality. This is often overlooked in post-structuralist discussions of political community, where sovereignty is usually treated, in a way reminiscent of the blindness to the political in classical Marxism, as if it might one day simply 'wither away'. In an interesting critique of this myopic tendency in relation to David Campbell's influential deconstruction of 'Bosnia' as a territorially bounded political community in *National Deconstruction: Violence, Identity and Justice in Bosnia*, Dan Bulley shows that Campbell makes this mistake by setting up dichotomous territorial and non-territorial conceptions of 'Bosnia' and then privileging the latter by rejecting the territorial desire for the sovereign 'at-home'. But, as Bulley observes, this denies that which must be retained of the 'territorial' Bosnia 'the "at-home" without which hospitality is impossible'(Bulley 2006: 646). We could, along with Derrida, state this objection even more strongly in the sense that rejecting the 'at home' of hospitality, which is analogous to making a final choice for unconditional over conditional hospitality, can have terrible consequences in the sense that, offering nothing by surrendering all, it clears the way for harm-doers to do their worst: 'Left to itself, the incalculable and giving idea of justice is always very close to the bad, even to the worst, for it can always be appropriated by the most perverse calculation … And so incalculable justice requires us to calculate' (Derrida 1990: 971). This insight is an important corrective to the post-structuralist literature in IR, where Campbell is not alone in missing the irreducibility of the sovereign 'at home'. For example, Edkins and Zehfuss's call for a 'generalized international' portrays domestic politics, in a conflation of the domestic with the nation-state, as merely 'an unusual and historically specific form of association that takes place only where there are distinct states with borders and defined populations', and which looks instead to a post-domestic form of political community in which communities are 'spread around the globe, with people's subjectivities invariably hybrid, ambiguous and fluctuating' (2005: 467).

This one-sided reading of the sovereign 'at home' is present also in a recent study of the violence at the heart of Canadian hospitality. Peter Nyers has described a 'sovereign retaking' at work in the Canadian government's response, in 2002, to the activism of Montreal's *Comité d'Action des Sans-Statuts* (CASS). CASS was formed to stop the deportations of non-status Algerians living in Montréal, people whose asylum claims had been rejected but who (in a desperate irony) were not returned due to a Canadian government moratorium on all deportations to a country deemed to be too dangerous. In the face of CASS's successful campaigning on this issue, the Canadian government conceded to non-status Algerians the right to make in-land applications for permanent residence. Yet in doing so, as CASS activists argued, the Canadian government was at once able to reassert its 'sovereign capacity to decide on the exception' by excluding from this agreement those non-status Algerians living outside Quebec or with any form of criminal record – not to mention those already issued with deportation orders, already deported, or unable to pay the costly application fee of $550 per adult. As CASS activists noted, given the nature of its concession – namely that these non-status applicants were now to be taken as immigrants rather than asylum seekers – the Canadian state was also able to neutralize or capture the campaign to some extent by linking their concession to the 'worthiness' or social utility of the applicants rather than the threat of violence facing them in their country of origin (Nyers 2003: 1086–7). As Nyers sums up the lessons of the CASS campaign, while activists were successful in receiving recognition from the Canadian government, 'they were unsuccessful in defining the conditions of this recognition. The radical takings of foreigners are always at risk of being deflected and absorbed by the ... re-takings of sovereign power ...' (2003: 1090). Despite the undoubted truth of this observation, what Nyers implies here is that there could be a hospitality that went beyond sovereignty, where, as we have seen, to give way absolutely to the 'takings' of the foreigner would be to have nothing to offer at all.

Strongly related to this negative reading of the ethical significance of sovereignty is a tendency to a pejorative framing of the ethical meaning of boundaries. In an exploration of the ethics of hospitality in the case of *Fronteras Compasivas*, an NGO providing water stations for illegal immigrants thirsting in the deserts straddling the US-Mexican border, Roxanne Lynn Doty reads this practice as writing: 'unboundedness'; the possibility of completely open borders; and a demystification of 'the brutality necessary to maintain the illusion of our bounded democratic polity' (2006: 70). Doty finds in this practice of unconditional hospitality an instantiation of Simon Critchley's polis, which 'is not an enclosed structure, but a multiplication of spaces ...' (2006: 69). In sum, the ethics as hospitality described here is implicitly identified as the other of boundaries. More explicit still in drawing this binary opposition is Mustafa Dikec, who bemoans the 'exclusionary politics of home' and reads hospitality as being

> about openings, about keeping open the question of who 'the people' (the demos) is ... There is a need to reconsider the boundary, not only as separator,

but as connector as well, where hospitality comes into play pointing beyond the boundaries.

(2002: 243).

'The point then', Dikec writes, 'is to open up spaces ... [and] not merely to open spaces; more importantly, it is the keep them open. Hospitality is aimed at such a concern' (2002: 244). Hospitality *is* aimed at being impossibly open to the coming of the Other, beyond passports and border controls; but it is also premised upon a radical separation from the Other who must come from some place other than the home and whom we must be able to welcome into a space that is sufficiently bounded to be a home.

For if the perversion of the law of unconditional hospitality involves the domestication of the foreigner in our own home, then how much more perverting of hospitality-ethics is an ethics defined by the erasure of all boundaries? Hospitality, as we have seen, clearly requires two things: that I have a 'home' over which I am more or less sovereign in order to have a place to invite the other into, but also that there is a place outside the home from which the other arrives. Otherwise there is no longer any possibility of conceiving of pure hospitality, of a non-sovereign relation to the Other. If the foreigner 'was already speaking our language, with all that that implies, if we shared everything that is shared with a language, would the foreigner still be a foreigner and could we speak of asylum or hospitality in regard to him?' (Derrida 2000: 15). For Derrida, without boundaries there would indeed be no threshold, and without the threshold there would be no possibility of hospitality (2000: 65).

The problematic of sovereignty, then, is an irreducible element of ethics as hospitality – not as a distinction between friends and enemies that reifies a particular definition of 'the people', but as a necessary, though by no means fixed, division between political inside and outside that both preserves the 'at home' of political community and thereby also the distinction between self/citizen and Other/foreigner. Without these sovereign distinctions somehow and somewhere in place hospitality is nothing, having no home to open up and no strangers to welcome.

Conclusion

The most significant implication of the earlier discussion for rethinking the future of political community relates to the issue of the boundaries of political community. Despite otherwise profound political differences, commentators on this issue converge on a common and restrictive starting-point, namely that forming an inside of political community creates relative moral indifference to outsiders. On this even Carl Schmitt and the neo-Kantians can agree, even if this leads the former to affirm such indifference as the essence of the political while the later seek to overcome it by proposing cosmopolitan political community in which there is no more outside. But what neither of these positions allows for is the ethical significance of boundaries, specifically that the inside/outside of political community is necessary to an ethics of *hospitality*.

Beyond the narrow confines of the liberal cosmopolitan vs. Schmitt debate (with communitarian positions somewhere in between), hospitality requires that boundaries be neither erased (liberal cosmopolitanism), naturalized (communitarianism) nor absolutized (Schmitt). Distinct from all these positions – which variously see the boundaries of political community as either good or bad – from the standpoint of the ethics of hospitality, boundaries are necessary but always in question. This is the clear implication of the argument made in this chapter that hospitality requires a home and decision about who should be welcomed into that home – namely, a bounded space defined by a certain irreducible sovereignty. But irreducible as this sovereignty and the boundaries which they imply might be, they are always also a problem, since conditional hospitality is haunted by the figure of an unconditional hospitality which calls for the transgression of boundaries in the sense of an unlimited welcome offered to all who come.

Thus the boundary question, viewed from the standpoint of the ethics of hospitality, becomes undecidable. This does not mean unknowable, but implies rather that the ethics of hospitality does not determine or programme an answer to the question of the ethical significance of boundaries *in general*. The boundaries of political community, and the sovereignty they enclose, become both an enabling condition *and* a constraint on hospitality. Negotiating this irreducible paradox becomes the political task of any political community that would stand in an ethical relation to the Other. And it requires that, though there be boundaries, these are understood as opening onto the stranger rather than closing him out.

In the absence of such a self-critical sovereignty, one which is always putting the boundaries of political community in question, what would we find? We would find a world without public or political hospitality. This could take two forms. Either it would be a *post-hospitable* world, defined by global domestication, in which there is no longer an outside to the home (say, of cosmopolitan right) and therefore no Other left to come. Or it would be (or continue to be, since this second option looks pretty much like the world we now live in) an *inhospitable* world defined by a limited hospitality that goes largely un-challenged, one in which there is apparently no imperative to question the boundaries of the sovereign home. From the perspective of the ethics of hospitality, neither of these options looks palatable.

Notes

1   A slightly different reading of the importance of unconditional hospitality to otherness is elaborated by John Rundell (2004). For Rundell, Derrida's gesture towards unconditional hospitality is useful for giving 'content to the empty freedom of modernity as a regard for the other in their contingency' (2004: 96). Rundell sees in the idea of unconditional hospitality recognition of the other as absolute stranger rather than simply as outsider. This 'absolute stranger' perspective on the other is identified with a 'cosmopolitan attitude' in which there is indifference to the 'who' of the outsider. Rather than being read as cold or hostile, this 'indifference to the prejudgements and prejudices that are mobilized around the outsider as a stigmatized, illegal alien' allows the stranger the 'empty freedom of modernity', including 'all of its choices and cultural projects' (2004: 97).

2 See here Leo Strauss's critique of Schmitt as thus remaining trapped within the horizon of liberal morality that he seeks to refute (in Schmitt 1996: 97–122).

3 A good example of this determination of politics by ethics in Kant towards the *telos* of cosmopolitan right is found in his *Practical Philosophy*:

> the harmony of politics with morals is possible only within a federative union (which is therefore given *a priori* and is necessary by principles of right), and all political prudence has for its rightful basis the establishment of such a union in its greatest possible extent, without which end all its subtilizing is unwisdom and veiled injustice.
>
> (cited in La Caze 2007: 787)

4 Making a similar observation in relation to the Kantian end of this spectrum, Marguerite La Caze has recently observed that, though Derrida agrees with Kant that ethics has an indispensable place in politics, this does not constrain Derrida's sense of politics as much as it does Kant's: 'Rather than providing a limit to what is possible, they [ethical considerations] set up an impossible injunction that politics can only aspire to, rather than follow' (La Caze 2007: 786).

5 Although, perhaps indicating that his ethical-political thought does indeed succeed in resisting each of these two poles, Derrida is also readable as having a Kantian approach to the relationship between ethics and politics. La Caze, for example, notes that his 'linking of ethics to politics, the setting up of unconditional ideals, and his concern with cosmopolitanism, make him sound very Kantian' (2007: 791).

6 Thus while Derrida, as we shall see, continues to insist on the interrelation of ethics/law and politics, other post-structuralist accounts appear to inflate the political to a messianic realm somehow above the ethical/legal. For example, even in a post-structuralist text which takes as its starting point the critique of Schmitt, the conclusion is reached that 'The only true political action ... is that which *severs* the nexus between violence [understood, in Benjaminian vein, as non-determined or anomic human action] and law' (Agamben 2005: 88, emphasis added).

7 See also Schmitt (1996: 49) where he writes: 'There exists no rational purpose, no norm, no matter how true, no program no matter how exemplary, no social ideal no matter how beautiful, no legitimacy nor legality which could justify men in killing each other ... If such physical destruction of human life is not motivated by an existential threat to one's own way of life, then it cannot be justified'.

8 This, of course, also establishes a double distinction from Kant's position, where for Kant political 'decisions' should follow moral laws which, in terms of right, are moral only in as much as they are both realisable (politically possible) and also generalisable (universal). As La Caze puts it, 'Unlike Kant's dictum that ought implies can, Derrida's dictum is that ought implies *cannot* ... Kant's imperfect duties become perfect duties on Derrida's account. They are perfect in the sense that we cannot put limits on what it is to fulfil them, although we will inevitably fall short of their demands' (2007: 792).

9 'No knowledge [which might programme action] as such, no theoretical reason ... will ever be able to found a responsibility or a decision in any kind of sustained manner ...' (Derrida 2003a: 36).

10 See, for example, how Derrida uses the terms responsibility and decision to mean the same thing in his discussion of responsibility (2003a: 36).

11 The 'constitutive outside', an outside which is actually internal to the formation of any identity, whether singular or collective, can easily be applied to political entities like nation-states also, where we are forced to ask how a nation can possess a nationality 'prior to the advent of strangeness' (Melville 2006: 40). Melville quotes Bonnie Honig, for whom the foreigner 'disabuses' the nation of 'fantasies of identity', thereby making it 'more open to difference and otherness' (2006: 49).

12 Indeed, in *Totality and Infinity*, Levinas suggests that the 'possibility of forgetting the transcendence', or otherness, 'of the Other' is the same thing as 'banishing with impunity all hospitality ... from the home' (1981: 20; see also Levinas 1994b: 98).

13 INCA was disbanded in 2005, to be replaced by the International Cities of Refuge Network (ICORN) and Cities of Refuge North America. In its founding Charter, ICORN responds to the ongoing persecution of writers by providing 'a functioning network of cities and regions that will provide shelter for persecuted writers' (Charter available at: http://www.icorn.org/resource/userfiles/TheCharter/Eng-TheCharter.pdf). Cities of Refuge North America, meanwhile, 'helps writers, persecuted and silenced in their native countries, to find safe haven in North America ...' (http://www.citiesof refuge.com). (Accessed September 1, 2007).
14 See also *The Other Heading* (41, 45 and 72), *On Cosmopolitanism* (53–4), and 'Hospitality, Justice and Responsibility' (65–7).
15 Derrida also suggests in this text that 'a decision that didn't go through the ordeal of the undecideable would not be a free decision, it would only be the programmable application of a calculable process. It might be legal; it would not be just' (1990: 964).

Bibliography

Agamben, G. (2005) *State of Exception*, Chicago: University of Chicago Press.
Bankovsky, M. (2005) 'Derrida Brings Levinas to Kant', *Philosophy Today*, 49(2): 156–70.
Bulley, D. (2006) 'Negotiating Ethics: Campbell, ontopology and hospitality', *Review of International Studies*, 32: 645–63.
Derrida, J. (1990) 'Force of Law: "The Mystical Foundation of Authority"', *Cardozo Law Review*, 921: 929–85.
—— (1993) *Aproias*, Stanford CA: Stanford University Press.
—— (1999a) *Adieu: to Emmanuel Levinas*, trans. P. Brault and M. Nass, Stanford CA: Stanford University Press.
—— (1999b) 'Hospitality, Justice and Responsibility: a dialogue with Jacques Derrida', in R. Kearney and M. Dooley (eds) *Questioning Ethics: contemporary debates in philosophy*, London: Routledge.
—— (2000) *Of Hospitality*, Stanford CA: Stanford University Press.
—— (2001) *On Cosmopolitanism and Forgiveness*, London: Routledge.
—— (2003a) 'The World of the Enlightenment to Come (Exception, Calculation, Sovereignty)', *Research in Phenomenology*, 33: 9–52.
—— (2003b) in G. Borradori, *Philosophy in a Time of Terror: dialogues with Jürgen Habermas and Jacques Derrida*, Chicago: University of Chicago Press.
—— (2005) 'The Principle of Hospitality', *Parallax*, 11(1): 6–9.
Dikec, M. (2002) 'Pera Peras Poros: longings for spaces of hospitality', *Theory, Culture and Society*, 19(1–2): 227–47.
Doty, R. (2006) 'Fronteras Compasivas and the Ethics of Unconditional Hospitality', *Millennium*, 35(1): 53–74.
Edkins, J. and Zehfuss, M. (2005) 'Generalising the International', *Review of International Studies*, 31: 451–72.
Gauthier, D. (2007) 'Levinas and the Politics of Hospitality', *History of Political Thought*, 28(1): 158–80.
Habermas, J. (1989) *The New Conservatism: cultural criticism and the historians' debate*, Cambridge MA: MIT Press.
Kelly, S. (2004) 'Derrida's Cities of Refuge: toward a non-utopian utopia' *Contemporary Justice Review*, 7(4): 421–39.
La Caze, M. (2007) 'At the Intersection: Kant, Derrida, and the relation between ethics and politics', *Political Theory*, 35(6): 781–805.
Levinas, E. (1981) *Totality and Infinity: an essay on exteriority*, trans. M. Lingis, London: Martinys Nijhoff.

—— (1994a) *Beyond the Verse: Talmudic readings and lectures*, trans. G. Mole, London: Athlone.

—— (1994b) 'The Nations and the Presence of Israel', in *In the Time of Nations*, trans. M. Smith, Bloomington: Indiana University Press.

—— (2006) *Humanism of the Other*, trans. N. Poller, Chicago: University of Illinois Press.

Linklater, A. (2007) *Critical Theory and World Politics*, Abingdon: Routledge.

—— (1998) *The Transformation of Political Community*, Cambridge: Polity.

Melville, P. (2006) 'Staging the Nation: hospitable performances in Kant's *Anthroplogy*', *European Romantic Review* 17(1): 39–53.

Nyers, P. (2003) 'Abject Cosmopolitanism: the politics of protection in the anti-deportation movement', *Third World Quarterly* 24(6): 1069–93.

Raffouel, F. (1998) 'On Hospitality: between ethics and politics', *Research in Phenomenology*, 28: 274–82.

Rundell, J. (2004) 'Strangers, Citizens and Outsiders: otherness, multiculturalism and the cosmopolitan imaginary in mobile societies', *Thesis Eleven*, 78: 85–101.

Schmitt, C. (1996) *The Concept of the Political*, Chicago: University of Chicago Press.

—— (2005) *Political Theology*, Chicago: University of Chicago Press.

Part II

Political community and the postmodern

4   What future for the European political community?

Nietzsche, nationalism and the idea of the 'good Europeans'

Stefan Elbe

Plato once suggested that one could not imagine a city where the idea of a city was completely lost and no longer recognizable at all. Over two thousand years later, rummaging amidst the ashes of the Second World War, the architects of the emerging European community confronted this same question – albeit, of course, on a much larger scale. Would it be possible to create a genuine European political community without articulating a common idea of Europe that the various peoples of Europe could collectively embrace? Despite initially opting for a functionalist strategy revolving around economic and technical cooperation, there was no doubt in the minds of founding fathers like Robert Schuman that 'Europe cannot and must not remain an economic and technocratic undertaking. It must have a soul, awareness of its historical affinities and its present and future responsibilities and political determination in the service of a single human ideal' (Schuman 1963: 48, 78). Just as with Plato's city, the European Union would eventually have to advance an inspiring idea of Europe if it was not just to remain an expedient economic and institutional arrangement, but was also to serve as the basis for cultivating a deeper European community. Following decades of incremental and at times contradictory progress, this long awaited opportunity to define the contours of the European soul, and 'to forge a common destiny' (Preamble to the European Constitution), finally emerged on October 29, 2004 when delegates representing the member states of the European Union agreed and signed the text of the European Constitution.

The negotiations leading up to the drafting of the Constitution were predictably complex, generating considerable debate about the ideational principles upon which the Union ought to be based. An important area of disagreement was whether the Preamble of the Constitution should make an explicit reference to Europe's Christian heritage, or whether it should adopt a more secular tone. The Catholic Church and some heads of state (such as the Polish president Aleksander Kwaśniewski) argued strongly for a Christian conception of Europe, while France and others argued in favour of a decidedly secular stance. The negotiations about the Preamble to the Constitution thus formed a significant site for contesting which idea of Europe the political community ought to be based upon. In the end compromise prevailed with the Preamble now broadly 'drawing inspiration from the cultural, religious and humanist inheritance of Europe, from which have developed the universal values of the inviolable and inalienable rights of the human person, free-dom, democracy, equality and the rule of law …' (Preamble). Yet the success of this compromise would prove to be short-lived, as the French and Dutch electorates soon rejected the Constitution in their respective national referenda, effectively putting the Constitution on ice for the time being. As so often in the history of the European Union, the question 'What future for the European political commu-nity?' must be confronted anew, opening up the possibility of considering alterna-tive and more unconventional conceptualisations of the European idea.

One such account, this chapter argues, can still be found buried within the writ-ings of the nineteenth-century German philosopher Friedrich Nietzsche, where a unique but frequently overlooked idea of what it would mean to be a 'good European' within the cultural configuration of European modernity is sketched out in broad but distinctive strokes. The contours of this idea are necessarily broad because Nietzsche developed the notion of the 'good Europeans' not as a way of delineating a specific European identity that all European citizens should model themselves upon, but rather as a way of outlining a particular *ethos* that he thought Europeans might cultivate following the 'death of God'. It is the purpose of this chapter to reconstruct this ethos on the basis of a selection of Nietzsche's published writings (as well as many of his posthumously published notes), and to critically contrast this ethos with the idea of Europe embodied in the European Constitution.

This ethos of the 'good Europeans', whom Nietzsche hoped would emerge in the future, consists of three elements. First, this ethos entails a realisation that European secularisation calls into question a whole host of metaphysical ideals associated with Europe's cultural heritage, including many of those alluded to in the Preamble of the European Constitution. Second, these 'good Europeans' oppose any national response to European secularisation as being deeply inade-quate. Broadly supportive of attempts to create a closer European political commu-nity, this ethos would seek to challenge those passages in the Constitution accommodating the persistence of existing national identities. Finally, these 'good Europeans' also believe that the spirit of Europe ultimately resides not in a particu-lar political or economic institutional arrangement, but in a creative experience of freedom that is afforded to Europeans by the advent of secularisation. This ethos of Nietzsche's 'good Europeans', which is explored in greater detail below, leads to a conceptualisation of a European political community that avoids nationalist inter-pretations of community, that remains open to those who currently live outside the borders of the European Union, and that seeks to address the problem of the glob-alisation of the 'last man' by continuing to cultivate and exemplify a deep commit-ment to freedom. Most importantly of all, this ethos of the 'good Europeans' opens up a path of advancing the process of Europeanisation even when the institutional project of Europe runs into profound political difficulties.

The 'death of God' and the question of Europe

Although very much a late nineteenth-century figure, Nietzsche still remains a sig-nificant thinker for contemporary debates about the political community of Europe.

Long before the European continent was to develop such a deep addiction to war in the first half of the twentieth century, Nietzsche began to fear the collapse of a common idea of Europe within the cultural configuration of European modernity. Nietzsche anticipated that one of the greatest dangers likely to confront Europe in the course of the twentieth and twenty-first centuries would be the loss of a European voice; Europeans would increasingly lack the means with which to cultivate a common European spirit (Nolte 1991: 207). What would trigger this loss? The answer, for Nietzsche, lay in the advent of European secularisation – what he famously called the 'death of God'. Nietzsche thought that this decisive cultural shift towards more widespread secularity entailed the possibility of a vast disenchantment of European culture. The diagnosis of European culture he advanced was one of nihilism. 'Nihilism', he penned in one of his notebooks 'stands at the door'. But '[w]hat does nihilism mean?', famously providing the answer: '[t]hat the highest values devalue themselves'. It means, moreover, that in Europe the overall 'aim is lacking' and the question 'Why?' 'no longer finds an answer' (1968 §2: 9). Nietzsche thus used the word nihilism to denote that stage of Europe's historical development towards the end of the nineteenth century, during which the theistic universe of Christianity was finally starting to lose its grip on the European imagination; and as modern science progressively challenged Christianity as a pervasive cultural force in Europe, so too it became increasingly difficult to continue to conceive of Europe as essentially a Christian club. There were simply no longer enough Europeans regularly kneeling at the cross to make this a persuasive vision for uniting the continent's various peoples.

But what was Europe to be, if not a Christian continent? Here, Nietzsche detected an uncomfortable silence. While many of his contemporaries were seduced by the optimistic dream of scientific and technological progress – believing that henceforth Europe could do without the old Christian tales – Nietzsche spent much of his time worrying that science ultimately could not provide Europeans with a compelling new set of post-Christian values capable of bringing about a politically united community. Science, he warned, 'never creates values' (1967a §25: 153). Although science was undoubtedly a powerful intellectual pursuit, it could not answer the 'Why?' question, nor the question of why there should be a united European community. To the extent that modern European culture embraced, even put a primacy on, science and scientific methodology, it would also find it increasingly difficult to articulate an ideal of Europe capable of replacing its formerly Christian identity. Nietzsche took this joint 'decline of the faith in the Christian god, [and] the triumph of scientific atheism' (Nietzsche 1974 §357: 306) to be the most decisive 'European event' of modern times – decisive because the rise of modern science cast irrevocable doubt on the Christian idea of Europe without offering a new European vision of its own. Gradually the Christian ice was beginning to thaw, permitting the European continent to decompose into a set of rivalling and hostile nationalisms. In the long run, Nietzsche sensed, Europe was in peril.

Although written from the perspective of the late nineteenth century, this is an understanding of the dilemma of 'Europe' that still resonates amongst contemporary scholars. Not too long ago Anthony Smith aptly described Europe's unavoidable political dilemma between its various nation states and the European Union as 'a choice between unacceptable, historical myths and memories on the one hand, on the other a patchwork, memoryless scientific 'culture' held together solely by political will and economic interest that are so often subject to change' (Smith 1997: 338). Despite 50 years of European integration, the political project of Europe remains for too many an uninspiring and bureaucratic construct incapable of challenging the primacy of national identities. A compelling European dream no longer inhabits the European consciousness, with the result that the electorates of Europe have no qualms with rejecting a Constitution – however historic – if they do not see it as working in their immediate self-interest.

Nietzsche's idea of the 'good Europeans', by contrast, is a complex and original attempt to gradually move European culture beyond this impasse, and to keep a European dream alive in a post-Christian, secular cultural context. It is, in other words, an endeavour to reflect on this still very contemporary question of how can we have an inspiring idea of Europe that does not, on the one hand, resort to Christian or other mythologies which are no longer compelling except as matters of faith, and yet that is also not 'merely' a rationalised, technocratic and institutional enterprise on the other? Unlike many of those who today continue to argue in favour of a Christian conception of Europe, Nietzsche thought the way out of this impasse clearly could not lie with a return to Christianity – this was no longer intellectually convincing. The evolution of Christianity in Europe, along with other belief systems, was now something that was itself to be explained in scientific terms. 'Formerly', Nietzsche observed in a work from his middle period:

> one sought to prove that there is no God – nowadays one indicates how the belief that there is a God could *arise* and how this belief acquired its weight and importance: a counter-proof that there is no God thereby becomes superfluous. When in former times one had refuted the 'proofs of the existence of God' put forward, there always remained the doubt whether better proofs might not be adduced than those just refuted: in those days atheists did not know how to make a clean sweep.
>
> (1997 §95: 93)

The way forward for re-enchanting the European dream could not consist of a return to Christianity, but had to rest instead with a much more critical engagement with modern science, which had emerged as such a powerful new cultural force in Europe.

Nietzsche thought that the great achievement of modern science – and indeed the secret of its pervasive grip on European culture – lay in its appearance of being objectively true and as value-neutral in nature. Scientific knowledge is widely deemed to be universal and free of cultural or political elements. As such, its status also seems incontestable. Nietzsche's strategy for loosening the grip of modern science on the European imagination consisted of exposing this widespread perception of modern science as a profound illusion. Although on the surface science appears to be objective and value-neutral, Nietzsche thought the scientific endeavour always already embodies an implicit value – that of truth. As he argued in the *Genealogy of Morals*:

> [t]hat which *constrains* these men [the modern scientists], however, this unconditional will to truth, is *faith in the ascetic ideal itself*, even if as an unconscious imperative – don't be deceived about that – it is the faith in a *metaphysical value*, the absolute value of *truth*, sanctioned and guaranteed by this ideal alone (it stands or falls with this ideal).
>
> (1967a §24: 151)

The entire enterprise of modern natural and social science is based on the idea – always implicit but seldom consciously articulated – that we ought to pursue the truth of things.

But from where, asked Nietzsche, do scientists derive this implicit and zealous pursuit of truth? Scientists clearly do not first meditate on the value of truth versus untruth in social life, and then decide to become scientists; more often than not they are drawn to science for one reason or another, and subsequently dedicate their lives to the pursuit of truth. It is usually only when their knowledge is put to immensely inhuman use, as with the case of the development of nuclear weapons for example, that scientists begin to reflect more consciously on the value of truth and knowledge. Nietzsche argued that in fact historically this scientific belief in the value of truth is actually an unconscious remnant of Christianity. '[W]e men of knowledge of today', he insisted, 'we godless men and anti-metaphysicians, we, too, still derive *our* flame from the fire ignited by a faith millennia old, the Christian faith, which was also Plato's, that God is truth, that truth is *divine*' (1967a §24: 152). The dedicated cultivation of truth as an overriding value can already be found in Platonic philosophy, including Plato's famous allegory of the cave. In Plato's case the 'true' world that needed to be discovered and studied consisted of the non-empirical and eternal Forms – a world that was also deemed by Plato to be superior because it contained all those essential properties such as truth, identity, unity and stability that earthly existence did not possess (Toole 1998: 32). Plato thus stood at the beginning of a long European tradition that tended to denigrate the sensuous world in favour of some truer – or metaphysical – world.

Nietzsche thought that Christianity had mostly retained Plato's habit of positing a 'true' world beyond the realm of earthly existence, and substituted it with a Christian narrative; like Plato it posited a timeless and divine world separate from earthly existence where the ultimate truth about life resides (Detwiler 1990: 74). In this regard, Nietzsche mused, the Christian faith is merely a form of 'Platonism for the people' (1966 Preface: 2). The task of devout Christians, too, was to study earthly existence in order to detect traces of this divine world. This can be seen, for example, by considering the importance of the Ten Commandments, or by bearing in mind the important role that confession played in Christianity. In assuming that knowledge of truth is also knowledge of the divine, both Platonism and Christianity postulate the existence of a true world and encouraged the rigorous pursuit of truth in relation to this metaphysical world (Detwiler 1990: 74). Nietzsche referred to

this powerful impulse, which he saw as being so characteristic of nearly two millennia of European culture, as the 'will-to-truth'; and it is from this same cultural
trajectory, he argued, that modern scientists still derive their zeal and ambition to
discover the truth of existence. Modern scientists too, still believe that there is a true
world beneath the sensuous world that can be discovered through strict adherence
to the principles of science.

Not only is modern science's implicit but powerful emphasis on the importance
of truth still continuous with Christianity and Platonism, but for Nietzsche it was
also precisely the Christian emphasis on the value of truth that, over time, first gave
rise to modern science and scientific accounts of existence – accounts which would
later begin to directly challenge the Christian narrative. Put differently, Nietzsche
wished to draw attention to the immensely ironic circumstance that it was precisely
the Christian insistence on the moral imperative of truth that, in the end, demanded
that Europeans admit that the concept of God is a lie (Carr 1992: 39):

> You see what it was that really triumphed over the Christian god: Christian
> morality itself, the concept of truthfulness that was understood ever more rig-
> orously, the father's confessor's refinement of the Christian conscience, trans-
> lated and sublimated into a scientific conscience, into intellectual cleanliness
> at any price. Looking at nature as if it were proof of the goodness and gover-
> nance of a god; interpreting history in honour of some divine reason, as a con-
> tinual testimony of a moral world order and ultimate moral purposes;
> interpreting one's own experiences as pious people have long enough inter-
> preted theirs …
>
> (Nietzsche 1974 § 357: 307)[1]

The rise of modern science in Europe was therefore not simply the result of
Europeans having voluntarily turned their back on Christianity for underlying personal or sociological reasons. Rather – and this is often seen to be one of the very
strength's of Nietzsche's account – the European experience of the 'death of God'
results from the sincere and consistent application of Christian morality (Carr
1992: 39). 'We outgrew Christianity', Nietzsche maintained, 'not because we lived
too far from it, rather because we lived too close, even more because we grew out
of it. It is our strict and over-indulged piety itself that today forbids us still to be
Christians' (cited in Carr 1992: 40). The consistent pursuit of truth, cultivated initially by Platonism and subsequently popularised by Christianity, eventually gave
rise to the modern scientific conscience which pursued truth at all costs with the
result that it also felt compelled to expose Christianity as being merely a 'faith', a
'mythology', or in the case of the account of Genesis, even an outright 'lie'. This
systematic unfolding of the will-to-truth that Nietzsche retraced also explains why
he detected a kind of logic behind the advent of secularisation, and why he insisted
that this development was in a sense the necessary consequence of our valuations
so far, i.e. why in Europe the highest values began to *devalue themselves*.

But if this belief in the unconditional value of truth expressed in modern science
is itself a residue of Christianity, then the thornier and more fundamental question

arises as to how this continuing belief in the value of truth can be grounded in a secular culture following the 'death of God'. The categorical pursuit of truth is certainly intelligible within a Christian framework that posits a supreme God who shines through all aspects of human existence and thus guarantees the existence of truth, indeed, is even equated with the truth. Yet this pursuit of truth becomes much more difficult to sustain intellectually once this overarching Christian theology collapses:

> [a]t this point it is necessary to pause and take careful stock. Science itself henceforth *requires* justification (which is not to say that there is any such justification). Consider on this question both the earliest and most recent philosophers: they are all oblivious of how much the will to truth itself first requires justification; here the ascetic ideal has hitherto *dominated* all philosophy, because truth was posited as being, as God, the highest court of appeal – because truth was not *permitted* to be a problem at all. Is this 'permitted' understood? – From the moment faith in the God of the ascetic ideal is denied a *new problem arises:* that of the *value* of truth.
>
> (Nietzsche 1967a §24: 152–153)

The dilemma for modern science after the 'death of God', David Owen suggests, is that it can no longer persuasively ground itself: 'science as the will to truth cannot itself articulate a ground on which to assert the value of truth' (Owen 1994: 59).

What ought one to do in this situation? Nietzsche thought there were essentially two options. First, one could refuse to problematise the overriding faith scientists put in the value of truth, and simply continue with the scientific enterprise as many scientists have done in the past. The problem with this response, however, is that it is not very scientific if by 'scientific' one understands the open and critical evaluation and examination of all of one's assumptions. It is neither intellectually rigorous, nor consistent with the principles of science itself. Max Weber would later draw attention to this very problem in his famous lecture entitled 'Science as a Vocation' when he observed that '[s]cience ... presupposes that what is yielded by scientific work is important in the sense that it is "worth being known". In this obviously are contained all our problems. For this presupposition cannot be proved by scientific means' (cited in Owen 1994: 89). Without providing an explicit grounding for the value of the will-to-truth, the scientific endeavour itself amounts to an act of faith in the inherent value of truth.

A better strategy – and the one Nietzsche recommended to the 'good Europeans' of the future – would be to subject the value of truth to deeper intellectual scrutiny. If we really want to get to the bottom of things following the 'death of God', we must also ask where this whole European desire and quest for truth came from, and what the value of pursuing such true worlds is. Henceforth, Nietzsche insisted, '[t]he will to truth requires a critique – let us define our own task – the value of truth must for once be experimentally *called into question*' (Nietzsche 1967a §24: 153).[2] While such a response arguably remains true to the scientific spirit of critically questioning all assumptions, it also, of course, begins to undermine the entire basis of the scientific endeavour itself; for, once one begins to question the will-to-truth in the name of truth, the latter effectively begins to prey on itself. Nietzsche described this process in the following terms:

> Christianity *as a dogma* was destroyed by its own morality … [a]fter Christian truthfulness has drawn one inference after another, it must end by drawing its *most striking inference*, its inference *against* itself; this will happen, however, when it poses the question '*what is the meaning of all will to truth?*' And here I again touch on my problem, on our problem, my *unknown* friends (for as yet I *know* of no friend): what meaning would *our* whole being possess if it were not this, that in us the will to truth becomes conscious of itself as a *problem*.
>
> (1967a §27: 61)

For those willing to forge ahead this deeply, then, the advent of European secularisation ultimately calls into question not just Christianity but also modern science because the 'death of God' necessitates reflecting much more deeply on how the underlying will-to-truth at the heart of the enterprise of modern science is to be justified. There is no longer any *a priori* reason as to why modern science, which displaced Christianity as a cultural force in Europe, should be elevated as the highest European ideal in its aftermath. The status of science's claim to be the embodiment of the new European idea is itself revealed to be extremely tenuous.

Even here, however, we have not yet fully plumbed the true depths of the implications of the 'death of God'. Ultimately, the advent of European secularisation implied for Nietzsche not only that the Christian God is dead, but more importantly that '*[a]ll gods are dead*', as he had Zarathustra famously proclaim (Nietzsche 1961 Part I, 'Of the bestowing of virtue', §3: 104). Once one begins to question the will-to-truth, it is not just the God of Christianity and modern science that is called into question, but more fundamentally the entire way of rendering European existence meaningful by positing the existence of a 'true' world behind or underneath the sensuous world. As Martin Heidegger pointed out, the 'death of God' ultimately means that the 'suprasensory world is [now] without effective power. It bestows no life. Metaphysics, i.e., for Nietzsche Western philosophy understood as Platonism, is at an end' (Heidegger 1977: 61). The way in which Europeans had rendered life meaningful for more than two millennia was beginning to implode before his very eyes, which is also why Nietzsche understood himself to be living through such a crucial turning point in the history of Europe.

All of this has important implications for contemporary attempts to find a more meaningful idea of Europe that could serve as the basis for a reinvigorated European political community. This task is now revealed to be much more difficult than even many of those involved in drafting the European Constitution may have realised. For how can one possibly determine a more meaningful idea of Europe once the will-to-truth is put into question? Once one goes down this path, any attempt to posit the truth or essence of European existence around which a new European community could be built would no longer seem credible. It is also precisely the awareness of this deep impasse within secular, European culture that marks the first element of the ethos of Nietzsche's 'good Europeans' of the future. They realise that the deeper implications of secularisation entail not just the demise of Christianity, but also necessitate putting this will-to-truth experimentally into question. For these 'good Europeans' there could consequently be no return to a Christian conception of Europe, nor could Europe be built around the principles of modern science, nor even along the seemingly enlightened and progressive principles noted in the Preamble to the European Constitution – such as democracy, equality, and the rule of law. These are all attempts to determine the true meaning of Europe and what it means to be a European; as such they are also contemporary manifestations of Europe's Christian–Platonic will-to-truth that fail to adequately challenge the latter. The deeper question these 'good Europeans' confront, therefore, is if the European idea cannot be defined in such a manner, then what meaning could the European idea still have in a secular cultural context?

Nationalism as a 'metamorphosis of the cross'

How would Nietzsche's 'good Europeans' respond to this deeper rupture in European culture that necessitates calling the Christian–Platonic will-to-truth experimentally into question? Nietzsche's choice of naming his idea the 'good *Europeans'* indicates that he thought a nationalist response to European secularisation would be profoundly mistaken and inadequate. Nietzsche was convinced that at bottom modern nationalism was simply a secular replacement for the Christian God that had died. 'What is the meaning of our nationalism?' he asked, but 'the metamorphosis of the cross' (Nietzsche 1988b 7(26): 305). Nietzsche sensed that following the 'death of God' Europeans would be looking for a new purpose in their lives, and that this spiritual vacuum would provide a nourishing cultural environment within which nationalism could prosper. Nietzsche himself wished to criticise this 'old habit of supposing that the goal must be put up, given, demanded *from outside* – by some *superhuman authority*'. The response to secularisation that he nevertheless found most likely in modern Europe was that '[h]aving unlearned faith in that, one still follows the old habit and seeks *another* authority that can *speak unconditionally* and *command* goals and tasks' (Nietzsche 1968 § 20: 17). Following the 'death of God' Europeans would be seeking a 'temporary *redemption* from pessimism', and in this quest would turn, amongst other things, to 'nationalism' (Nietzsche 1988b 9(126): 410). Nietzsche thus urged his readers to understand nationalism as a modern attempt to endow European existence with a greater sense of meaning or purpose in the aftermath of secularisation (see 1968 §1: 8 and 1988b: 377).

This relationship between nationalism and secularisation was already identified quite early on in the historiography of European nationalism by pioneering scholars such as Carlton Hayes (1926: 95), Hans Kohn (1946: 8), and Arnold Toynbee (1968: 147). More recently this link has also enjoyed a resurgence amongst nationalism scholars. In his influential account, for example, Benedict Anderson broadly locates the rise of nationalism within the context of increasingly secular cultures. According to Anderson the waning appeal of religious modes of existence pointed to the need of 'a secular transformation of fatality into continuity, contingency into meaning', and in his view 'few things were [are] better suited to this end than an idea of nation' (Anderson 1991: 127). The title of Joseph Llobera's (1994) study of the rise of modern nationalism in western Europe, *The God of Modernity*, similarly evokes this relationship. Llobera argues that modern national identity appeared in western Europe at the same time that all the intermediary bonds of society were collapsing, and religion was losing its grip on the people. Religion was a ready-made model for nationalism and in many cases it was also a powerful ally, reinforcing emerging nationalism (Llobera 1994: 144). This allows him to conclude that 'nationalism has become the functional equivalent of religion; or, expressed in a more pungent way, nationalism has become a religion – a secular religion where god is the nation' (1994: 143). These studies provide much empirical and historical support for Nietzsche's earlier hypothesis that, at least in the European context, nationalism is partially indicative of a 'metamorphosis of the cross'.

Why, though, would Nietzsche's 'good Europeans' not follow this now familiar and well-trodden path? The problem with a nationalist response to European secularisation is two-fold. First, a nationalist response addresses the problem of European secularisation on too small a scale. In light of the European dimensions of the 'death of God', Nietzsche thought that a European rather than merely a national response was evidently required. The 'death of God', he noted in *The Gay Science*, was 'already beginning to cast its first shadows over Europe' (1974 §343: 279) – not just over individual nations. He thus repeatedly referred to nationalism as being 'petty' and small, and saw it as being in no way fit to address the magnitude of the phenomenon of European secularisation. These nationalist ideas are ultimately a dead-end for Europe:

> [n]ationalism, *this nervrose nationale* with which Europe is sick, this perpetuation of European particularism (*Kleinstaaterei*), of petty politics [has] deprived Europe itself of its meaning, of its reason – [has] driven it into a dead-end street. – Does anyone besides me know the way out of this dead-end street? – A task that is great enough to *unite* nations again?
>
> (Nietzsche 1967b §2: 32)

In contrast to those favouring a Europe of nation states, Nietzsche consistently thought that the problem of the 'death of God' could only be addressed on a *European* level, which is why he deliberately extolled his idea of the 'good Europeans' who would be 'laughing about the nations' (1988a 32(8): 404)[3] and 'supra-national' in outlook (1988a 26(297): 229).

The second reason these 'good Europeans' would reject a nationalist response to European secularisation is that rather than calling Europe's Christian–Platonic will-to-truth experimentally into question, as Nietzsche thought the 'good Europeans' would have to do following the 'death of God', nationalism actually seeks to reactivate it in a new, earthly guise. Nationalism is a response to European secularisation that merely seeks to replace the worship of the old God with the worship of more secular idols and ideologies. As with modern science, Europe's incessant desire to determine the deeper truth of existence – its will-to-truth – is merely redirected from the otherworldly realm to the earthly horizon. The nation is thus simply the most recent in a long line of ascetic ideals generated by Europe's Christian–Platonic heritage in order to establish the true meaning or essence of existence. If, as Nietzsche thought, the advent of European secularisation ultimately entailed putting the will-to-truth of Europe's Christian–Platonic tradition into question, then the re-activation of the will to truth under the guise of nationalist ideals was not intellectually persuasive, although such strategies might nevertheless achieve considerable popular success. 'What is called a "nation" in Europe today', Nietzsche lamented in *Beyond Good and Evil*, 'is really rather a *res facta* than *res nata* (and occasionally can hardly be told from a *res ficta et picta*) ...' (1966 §251: 188 – something made; something born; something fictitious and unreal). He had already articulated similar concerns about the constructed nature of nationalism in *Human, All too Human,* where he noted that 'this artificial nationalism is in any case as perilous as artificial Catholicism used to be, for it is in its essence a forcibly imposed state of siege and self-defence inflicted on the many by the few and requires cunning, force and falsehood to maintain a front of respectability' (1984 §475: 228).

At the root of modern nationalism, then, is the desire *not* to question the will-to-truth, but rather to escape the at times disenchanting experience of secularisation by replicating the comforting, transcendental ideals within the earthly realm. As Nietzsche noted in a passage from the *Gay Science*:

> The demand that one *wants* by all means that something should be firm (while on account of the ardor of this demand one is easier and more negligent about the demonstration of this certainty) – this, too, is still the demand for a support, a prop, in short, that *instinct of weakness* which, to be sure, does not create religious, metaphysical systems, and convictions of all kinds but – conserves them. ... Even the vehemence with which our most intelligent contemporaries lose themselves in wretched nooks and crannies, for example into nationalism [*Vaterländerei*] (I mean what the French call *chauvinisme* and the Germans 'German') ... always manifests itself above all in the *need* for a faith, a support, backbone, something to fall back on.
>
> (1974 §347: 288–289)

It is against the background of this critique of modern nationalism as a secular continuation of the will-to-truth that one must understand Nietzsche's despising of the self-intoxication of the European nations (Nietzsche 1990 Foreword: 125), as well as his ardent pleas to overcome the petty nationalism of nation-states. In one of his notes Nietzsche pleaded to '[l]et some fresh air in! This absurd state of affairs must not go on any longer in Europe! What sense is there in this bone-headed nationalism? Now that everything points to larger common interests, what is the purpose of encouraging this scurvy egoism (1988c: 92)?' In his autobiography he even called nationalism the anti-cultural sickness *par excellence* (1967b, 'The case of Wager', §2: 321).

The second element of the ethos of Nietzsche's 'good Europeans' of the future, then, is that having understood the deeper ramifications of the 'death of God', they also actively resist a nationalist response to this cultural development. The cultivation of national myths and identities not only maintains the will-to-truth under secular conditions, but also facilitates the decomposition of Europe into a set of hostile and competing nationalisms. This was no way to keep a European dream alive within the cultural configuration of European modernity. Those who propagate nationalist ideas Nietzsche accordingly deemed to be perpetuating the 'sickness of the century' and were 'an enemy of the good Europeans, an enemy of the free spirits' (Nietzsche 1988d §87: 593). In the contemporary context Nietzsche's 'good Europeans' would thus also be much more critical of national identities than those drafting the European Constitution, in the Preamble to which one finds references to following a path of 'unity in diversity' (Preamble) – which does not do much to challenge the persistence of national identities in Europe; nor does the Preamble's concession that the various people of Europe should remain 'proud of their own national identities and history' (Preamble). From this perspective, although perhaps understandable in terms of political expediency, the European Constitution still remains at times too tolerant of national ideas and identities to be the embodiment of the kind of Europeanisation that Nietzsche hoped the 'good Europeans' would cultivate. This still leaves unresolved, however, the deeper problem of how these 'good Europeans' could keep alive a common European spirit without simply replicating the logic of nationalism, and hence also of the will-to-truth, on a much larger scale. If Europe's various national ideals and identities are still manifestations of Europe's Christian–Platonic will-to-truth, then would not any attempt to replace the Christian idea of Europe with a new, more secular idea of Europe around which the European community could be structured similarly be a manifestation of this will-to-truth?

The 'good Europeans' and the experience of freedom

For the 'good Europeans' the most promising way forward would be to seek to reinvigorate the European dream not through adherence to a common European ideal, but to reorient this dream around a profound experience of freedom. This would require a fundamental revaluation of Europe's Christian–Platonic heritage whereby Nietzsche's 'good Europeans' of the future would have to begin experimenting with a way of living that could flourish without needing to fix the truth of European existence. 'One could conceive', Nietzsche noted in this vein,

> of such pleasure and power of self-determination, such a freedom of the will that the spirit would take leave of all faith and every wish for certainty, being practised in maintaining himself on insubstantial ropes and possibilities and dancing even near abysses. Such a spirit would be the *free spirit* par excellence.

(1974 §347: 290)

And indeed for Nietzsche's 'good Europeans' (or 'free spirits' as he sometimes also referred to them)[4] 'the demand for certainty is not … the inmost craving and the deepest need'. Instead he recommended to them in one of his notebooks 'the magic of the opposite way of thinking, not to be denied the stimulation of the enigmatic' (1988a 2(155): 142),[5] insisting that their starting point would have to be a '[d]eep aversion towards resting once and for all in any total interpretation of the world' (1968 §470: 262). Nietzsche's revaluation of European values, then, does not consist of articulating a new set of ideals – national, European or other – but rather of beginning to experience value in a fundamentally different way (Kaufmann 1968: 110–111). What is valuable about European culture after the 'death of God', for these 'good Europeans', is precisely that it affords them the possibility of experiencing existence in a way that is not reducible to any singular truth. As Nietzsche wrote in a letter '[m]y task is quite singular this time: I've asked myself what mankind has always hated, feared, and despised the most – and precisely out of this I've made my gold' (in Hoover 1994: 21). Nietzsche mined for his revaluation of European values where many of his contemporaries never even bothered to look.

This revaluation of values undertaken by the 'good Europeans' responds to the 'death of God' through understanding the latter as an immensely liberating cultural experience. Indeed, perhaps one of Nietzsche's most important insights about the nature of European secularisation was that, despite the fact that it was often experienced as disquieting and disorienting, it also entails a vastly creative and liberating potential. Nietzsche noted quite explicitly how his own response to the 'death of God' is 'not at all sad and gloomy, but rather like a new, difficult to describe kind of light, happiness, relief, amusement, encouragement, dawn', and that

> we philosophers and 'free spirits' feel, when we hear the news that 'the old god is dead', as if a new dawn shone on us; our heart overflows with gratitude, amazement, premonition, expectation. At long last the horizon appears free to us again.
>
> (1974 §343: 280)

Nietzsche's 'good Europeans' would thus be distinguished from contemporary Europeanists by their attempt to revalue the traditional Christian–Platonic values revolving around the will-to-truth, and their consequent unwillingness to erect new European idols in order to replace the old God that has 'died'. They would experiment instead with a way of living that rejoiced in the absence of positing a deeper essence to European existence and would understand this new form of existence as a liberation from the past constraints of Europe's Christian–Platonic culture.

In the end, it is this experience of freedom which is the 'decisive event' for the 'good Europeans', and is marked by a 'dangerous curiosity for an undiscovered world [which] flames up and flickers in all the senses' (Nietzsche 1984 §3: 6). It is also this *ethos* of Nietzsche's 'good Europeans', of pursuing a thinking that is more free than it is 'true', which can be said to constitute a vibrant alternative to the predominantly pessimistic assessments of Europe which predominate today. 'Let us not undervalue this', Nietzsche insisted: '*we ourselves*, we free spirits, are already a "revaluation of all values", an *incarnate* declaration of war and victory over all ancient conceptions of "true" and "untrue"' (1990 §13: 135). The Nietzschean perspective on the future of Europe places its wager on the possibility of a Europe consisting of 'good Europeans' who do not necessarily share a fixed idea of Europe. Nietzsche himself was even quite optimistic about this prospect in the long term, noting in *Human, All too Human*:

> [t]hat there *could* someday be such free spirits, that our Europe will have such lively, daring fellows among its sons of tomorrow and the day after tomorrow, real and palpable and not merely, as in my case, phantoms and a hermit's shadow play: I am the last person to want to doubt that. I already see them *coming,* slowly, slowly; and perhaps I am doing something to hasten their coming when I describe before the fact the fateful conditions that I *see* giving rise to them, the paths on which I *see* them coming?
>
> (1984 §2: 5–6)

Nietzsche's vision of the 'good Europeans' is his attempt to communicate to his readers the possibility of a revaluation of European values based around an experience of deep intellectual freedom that European secularisation affords. Participating in this revaluation of values marks the third and final element of the ethos of the 'good Europeans'. At long last, Nietzsche noted in this vein, 'our ships may finally venture out again, venture out to face any danger; all the daring of the lover of knowledge is permitted again; the sea, *our* sea, lies open again; perhaps there has never yet been such an "open sea"' (1974 §343: 280). Most importantly of all, this experience of freedom can also continue to be communicated even whilst the political project of Europe finds itself in crisis.

Conclusion

Having explored the broad outlines of Nietzsche's 'good Europeans', their *ethos* can finally be summarised as consisting of the following three characteristics:

i   their realization that the deeper dimension of European secularisation necessarily entails calling the Christian–Platonic will-to-truth experimentally into question;

ii   their realisation that a European rather than a national response is required to this decisive and wide-ranging cultural transformation; and

iii   their ability to experience an existence partially freed from the will-to-truth not as a paralysing and distressing one, but as an important moment of liberation from the past constraints of European culture.

The impossibility of positing a new idea of Europe, and the fact that all such ideals advanced by the European Union ultimately must remain questionable, are not a reason for despair but rather a symbol of the 'protean diversity of life' (Connolly 1996: 257–258). As Nietzsche put it:

[b]ut to stand in the midst of this *rerum concordia discors* and of this whole marvellous uncertainty and rich ambiguity of existence *without questioning*, without trembling with the craving and the rapture of such questioning, without at least hating the person who questions, perhaps even finding him faintly amusing – that is what I feel to be *contemptible*, and this is the feeling for which I look first in everybody. Some folly keeps persuading me that every human being has this feeling, simply because he is human. This is my type of injustice.

(1974 §2: 76–7)

By refusing to posit a new essence underlying European existence, such a community consisting of Nietzsche's 'good Europeans' would avoid nationalist, racist and other essentialising interpretations of Europe. In so doing, it would in principle also remain open to those who are currently outside the borders of the European Union. Finally, it is a conception of what it means to be a 'good European' that seeks to address the problem of the increasing globalisation of the 'last man' through combating the refusal to cultivate, within existence, an important reflective depth. From the Nietzschean perspective, proper Europeanisation would manifest itself not so much in the attempt to articulate a 'true' idea of Europe, but rather in the encouraging of the emergence of those 'good Europeans' who 'can actually tolerate free thoughts' (Nietzsche, cited in Hoover 1994: 18), and who can share in an experience of freedom that has long been lost in the political project of Europe.[6] 'I intend to find out', Nietzsche wrote in a letter from 1874 'to what degree our friends, who are so proud of their freedom of thought, can actually tolerate free thoughts' (in Hoover 1994: 18). To recover this experience of freedom is the challenge of Nietzsche's European thought. It is a challenge that may seem unconventional; but then again Europe would not be Europe if it were not able to find a new way out of an old dilemma (Darras 1990: 60).

Notes

1 See also *The Will to Power* where Nietzsche remarks that '[m]orality itself, in the form of honesty, compels us to deny morality' (1968 §404: 219).
2 In an unpublished note written after Nietzsche had completed Part 3 of *Zarathustra*, he had the latter claim that 'We are conducting an experience with the truth!' (1988a 25(305): 88).
3 As Nietzsche put it in a fragment, 'against the national [*das Nationale*] – the good European' (see Nietzsche 1988 25(523): 150).
4 Nietzsche often used the expression 'good Europeans' and 'free spirits' interchangeably. In the preface to *Beyond Good and Evil*, for example, Nietzsche refers to 'we *good Europeans* and free, *very* free spirits ...' (1966: 3). See also Ottmann (1987: 125) and Nolte (1991: 202). Nietzsche, moreover, continues to accord his notion of a 'good European' a central role until his collapse in 1889. (See Nolte 1991: 203).
5 What is more, he insisted, '[o]ne should not let oneself be misled: great intellects are sceptics'. Nietzsche (1990 §54: 184).
6 As John Rajchman has rightly pointed out,

Nietzsche is the philosopher who separates the problem of freedom from the problem of acquiring the truth about ourselves, who would free us from the tyrannies of such truths through an analysis of their histories. He separates our freedom from the knowledge of our nature.

(1985: 121)

Bibliography

Anderson, B. (1991) *Imagined Communities: reflections on the origin and spread of nationalism*, London: Verso.

Carr, K.L. (1992) *The Banalization of Nihilism: twentieth-century responses to meaninglessness,* Albany: State University of New York Press.

Connolly, W.E. (1996) 'Suffering, Justice, and the Politics of Becoming', *Culture, Medicine and Psychiatry*, 20(3): 79–93.

Darras, J. (1990) *Beyond the Tunnel of History,* London: Macmillan.

Detwiler, B. (1990) *Nietzsche and the Politics of Aristocratic Radicalism*, Chicago: University of Chicago Press.

Hayes, C.J.H. (1926) *Essays in Nationalism*, New York: Macmillan.

Heidegger, M. (1977) 'Nietzsche's Word God is Dead' in *The Question Concerning Technology and Other Essays*, trans. W. Lovitt, New York: Harper and Row.

Hoover, A.J. (1994) *Friedrich Nietzsche: his life and thought*, London: Praeger.

Kaufmann, W. (1968) *Nietzsche: philosopher, psychologist, antichrist*, 4th ed., Princeton: Princeton University Press.

Kohn, H. (1946) *Prophets and Peoples: studies in nineteenth-century nationalism*, New York: Macmillan.

Llobera, J. (1994) *The God of Modernity*, Oxford: Berg.

Nietzsche, F. (1961) *Thus Spoke Zarathustra*, trans. R.J. Hollingdale, London: Penguin.

——— (1966) *Beyond Good and Evil: prelude to a philosophy of the future*, trans. W. Kaufmann, New York: Random House.

——— (1967a) *On the Genealogy of Morals,* trans. W. Kaufmann and R.J. Hollingdale, New York: Vintage Books.

——— (1967b) *Ecce Homo,* trans. W. Kaufmann and R.J. Hollingdale, New York: Random House.

——— (1968) *The Will to Power*, trans. W. Kaufmann and R.J. Hollingdale, New York: Random House.

——— (1974) *The Gay Science*, trans. W. Kaufmann, New York: Vintage Books.

——— (1984) *Human, All Too Human*, trans. M. Faber and S. Lehmann, London: Penguin.

——— (1988a) *Nachgelassene Fragmente 1884–1885*, KSA 11, Berlin: Walter de Gruyter.

——— (1988b) *Nachgelassene Fragmente 1885–1887*, KSA 12, Berlin: Walter de Gruyter.

——— (1988c) *Nachgelassene Fragmente 1887–1889*, KSA 13, Berlin: Walter de Gruyter.

——— (1988d) *Menschliches, Allzumenschliches II*, 'Der Wanderer und sein Schatten', KSA 2, Berlin: Walter de Gruyter.

——— (1990) *The Anti-Christ*, trans. R.J. Hollingdale, London: Penguin.

——— (1997) *Daybreak: thoughts on the prejudices of morality*, trans. R.J. Hollingdale, Cambridge: Cambridge University Press.

Nolte, J. (1991) *Wir guten Europäer: Historisch-politische Versuche über uns selbst*, Tübingen: Narr.

Ottmann, H. (1987) *Philosophie und Politik bei Nietzsche*, Berlin: Walter de Gruyter.

Owen, D. (1994) *Maturity and Modernity: Nietzsche, Weber, Foucault, and the ambivalence of reason*, London: Routledge.

Preamble to the European Constitution, available online at: http://europa.eu.int/constitution/en/ptoc1_en.htm#a1 (Accessed March 18, 2006).

Rajchman, J. (1985) *Michel Foucault: the freedom of philosophy*, New York: Columbia University Press.

Schuman, R. (1963) *Pour L'Europe*, Paris: Les Editions Nagel.

Smith, A.D. (1997) 'National Identity and the Idea of European Unity,' in P. Gowan and P. Anderson (eds), *The Question of Europe*, London: Verso.

Toole, D. (1998) *Waiting for Godot in Sarajevo: theological reflections on nihilism, tragedy, and apocalypse*, Boulder: Westview Press.

Toynbee, A. (1968) 'Death in War', in A. Toynbee (*et al.*) *Man's Concern with Death*, London: Hodder and Stoughton.

5 Constituting community
Heidegger, mimesis and critical belonging

Louiza Odysseos

International Relations and Political Theory have long engaged with the question of community, and in particular the question about the *constitution* of political community. Seminal contributions have highlighted that thinking about community is usually pursued within a dichotomy: either there is an essence by which community is constituted (usually referred to as 'thick' conceptions of community) or community is composed of pre-formed individuals and, thus, amounts to little more than procedural co-presence (denoted as 'thin' understandings of community, cf. Walzer 1994). Awareness of this dichotomy has led to a variety of critiques, for example, questioning the conflation of the community to the state; rethinking oppression and social exclusion and their relation to civil conflict; conceptualising the 'we' outside of essentialist and, therefore, exclusionary determinations such as those of religion, ethnicity, nation, etc.; investigating the assumptions of liberal democracy about community and diversity, as well as examining the ways in which modern assumptions about the subject of politics and society entail the reduction of coexistence, and community, to the mere co-presence of pre-constituted, 'pre-social' selves.[1]

This chapter interprets the desire to think the constitution of community, and especially of *political* community, as a call to move beyond the parameters of this dichotomy – if not to transcend it, then to chart a path through it which attempts to reconcile its extremes. Prominent amongst its chief preoccupations is a concern with otherness, understood both as the particularity/otherness of the self and also the concrete other, threatened by the homologies of essence and copresence (Odysseos 2007). To navigate this dichotomy the chapter turns to Martin Heidegger, who some scholars might regard an unlikely source, and asks whether his early thought has anything to contribute to such a consideration of the constitution of political community.[2]

The impetus for turning to Heidegger comes from a set of comments made by the French philosopher Philippe Lacoue-Labarthe who remarked, when discussing Heidegger's 'politics', that there is a continuous but unanswerable question of identification, and its relation to community, in Heidegger's thought. Indeed, Lacoue-Labarthe asked (1998: 286; cf. 1990), why would the problem of mimesis and identification, the problem of 'community', not be considered the essential question of the political as such? In this chapter, I propose a consideration of precisely the question of community and mimesis, both as it operates within Heidegger's *Being and Time* (1962), and also as it continues to affect discussions on the constitution of political community today. I use the context of the debate on Heidegger's politics in order to return to Heidegger's assumed determination of community according to a nationalist essence. I suggest (cf. Odysseos 2002, 2007) that Heidegger's radically hermeneutic and heteronomous[3] analysis of existence (*Daseinanalytik*) enables us to revisit Heidegger's contentious, troubling and cryptic statements on 'community' and 'people' in the infamous paragraph 74 of *Being and Time* and reread these critically and productively. Contra the assumptions of the debate on the 'Heidegger affair', I read his discussion of Dasein's[4] relation to the historical tradition as enabling the emergence of a political selfhood that has a distinct *questioning* relationship to its historical tradition and which thus avoids positing communal constitution according to an essence (such as religion, nation, ethnos, language, etc.).

Such a rereading is primarily a *retrieval* from Heidegger's thought of a productive understanding of how community comes to be constituted through the practice of an agonistic sort of identification, which Peg Birmingham (1991) calls 'critical mimesis'. Critical mimesis or identification, I argue, points to a type of relationship towards the community's past ('the tradition') that renders the very constitution of community by its members into a type of 'critical belonging'. Critical belonging involves critique, displacement and resistance towards the historical tradition: indeed, it may be this attitude of critique, some might say, *betrayal* (cf. Cavell 1979), towards certain of the tradition's historical *possibilities* that helps constitute the communal, and the political, as such.

My purpose is not solely exegetical with respect to Heidegger's argument, however. This is a perspective of a critical and questioning mode of identification, I propose, which is extremely valuable for theorising community today. Specifically, it facilitates a conception of community constitution which lies between the two extremes of, on the one hand, mechanistic, additive and compositional thinking exemplified by contractarian accounts of how pre-social individuals come to constitute community, and on the other hand, of conventional communitarian understandings of community deriving from, and constituted around, an essence (be this nation, language, religion, etc.). It can, moreover, be essential for thinking beyond the reduction of community to the nation-state and tackling more empirical concerns surrounding the expansion or broadening of community with which we are currently faced (see also Campbell 1998, Linklater 1998, Archibugi *et al.* 1998).

The chapter proceeds by, first, outlining the main concerns raised about Heidegger's politics, as specifically relating to the issue of community. Out of this discussion it, second, proposes an account of community constitution through a critical process of mimesis and identification. This almost paradoxical kind of identification leads to what the chapter calls 'critical belonging', delineating a relationship to the community that is marked not by acquiescence but, rather, by resistance. The final part concludes by reflecting further on the implications of this retrieval on the theorisation of community for political thought and on the continuing debate about Heidegger's politics.

Heidegger's politics and the thought of community

The suggestion that one could think together Martin Heidegger's thought and the constitution of political community might be met with surprise, at best, and recoiling horror, at worst. This is because such a proposal necessarily takes place within a still-raging debate fuelled by increased acknowledgement within the fields of philosophy and politics of his deplorable engagement with National Socialism, which is now familiarly captured by the term 'Heidegger's politics'.[5] This debate has taken place both at the level of historiography as well as political philosophy, with the result of calling into question whether it is, in fact, still possible to put Heidegger's thought to political use; and, even if it is possible, whether it is desirable to use his thought politically. In other words, is not any political thought of community derived from, or associated with, the thought of Martin Heidegger immediately tainted by his commitment to National Socialism in the 1930s, when he assumed the rectorship of the University of Freiburg in 1933, and his subsequent failure to apologize for, or even discuss, this involvement in the post-war years (see, most prominently, Ott 1993, Farias 1987, Heidegger 1985)? Heidegger's many critics might accept that his thought assists in the deconstructive enterprise of political and social philosophy, questioning its reliance on modern subjectivity; they might easily acknowledge that it can call liberal-proceduralist accounts of community constitution into question by 'unworking' the sovereign, pre-social and individualist subject on which they rely. But they are likely to also regard that his politics, if not his *thought*, compromises these deconstructive insights by determining community according to a nationalist essence, resulting in the valorisation of the communal historical tradition.

In this section, I examine the debate on Heidegger's politics,[6] which has had a serious impact on our ability to usefully utilise Heidegger's *Daseinanalytik* for a political thought of community. In particular, I examine a prominent objection which (re)reads *Being and Time* in light of Heidegger's involvement with the Nazis, deeming it to be at best politically vague, and thus open to conservative revolutionism, and at worst as determining community along 'nationalistic' and 'racist' lines, and thus wholly inappropriate for a progressive and critical thought of community.

A Nazi thought? Mapping the debate on Heidegger's politics

The major objection to using Heidegger's existential analysis[7] for political thought asks whether the possibility for articulating a *political* account of community is impaired both by the apparent determination of authentic 'Being-with' according to 'a people' within the analysis of *Being and Time* and also by the political interpretation of the overall project of fundamental ontology given to it by Heidegger's own subsequent engagement with National Socialism.

Let us briefly consider what Heidegger means by 'Being-with' (*Mitsein*). For Heidegger, human being 'is essentially Being-with' – Being-with is an existential attribute of human existence (*Dasein*, or There-Being). By this Heidegger means that the term 'with' cannot be seen:

as designating a relationship that can be noted once there are more than two terms. Rather we have to think of *Mit-sein*, of *Being-with*, or more exactly of the very Being *of* with, of witness. There can be two terms that can encounter one another only if first *there is* witness. That is, only if first there is a primordial structure of commonness, of a with relationship, can a specific type of relationship be instituted (emphasis in original).

(Georgopoulos 1994: 91)

To say that Dasein is Being-with has little to do with the actual presence of one or multiple others, because 'with' is not about spatial proximity: it is not merely a description that 'I am not present-at-hand alone, and that Others of my kind occur', nor that 'I am currently with others' (Heidegger 1962: 156). 'Being-with is an existential characteristic of Dasein even when factically no Other is present-at-hand or perceived' (Heidegger 1962: 156). Even when no Others are present, Dasein is Being-with. Being-alone is possible only for an entity who has Being-with as its Being (Heidegger 1962: 157). 'Withness', Heidegger suggests, is the existential commonness that makes all actual interactions with, and experiences of, others possible. This 'sharing' of the world is a 'prior capacity', which Dasein possesses; it is the capacity to-be-with (*mit-sein*) that makes any consideration of, and relationship with, others possible. Coexistence, as well as community, and their multifaceted dimensions rest on this existential structure of Being-with. As Michael Gelven (1970: 67–8) notes '[t]o say that Being-with (or to-be-with) is an *a priori* existential of Dasein means that one cannot be a self unless it is within one's possibilities to relate in a unique way to other Daseins. Hence, to be Dasein at all means to-be-with'. Human being is 'with' to such an extent, Heidegger's analysis suggests, that the legacy of the philosophy of the subject whereby human being is understood as an individual, as an 'I', can no longer be sustained. Not only is human being *not* an individual but the appropriate answer to the question 'who is Dasein?' is not the 'I' but the 'they' (*das Man*, see Heidegger 1962: ¶27).[8] The 'they', or the 'one' as it is also sometimes referred to, is part of Dasein's constitution. Dasein belongs to others 'who proximally and for the most part "are there" in everyday Being-with-one-another' (1962: 164). 'The "they", ... which we all are, though not as the sum, prescribes the kind of Being of everydayness', notes Heidegger (1962).

What does it mean to suggest that the answer to the question of 'who' is the 'they' signify, however? From the perspective of everydayness, human existence is heteronomously constituted and manifested not as the 'I' assumed by accounts of modern subjectivity, but as 'anyone'. The 'they', it can be argued, rescinds any priority of the self and affirms the primacy of sociality and relationality:

[w]e live in the midst of others with their beliefs and values, fears and conflicts already so deeply embedded in us that the initial experience of reflection is the shock of discovering how utterly the voice of the other comes pouring forth whenever I, the sovereign individual, speak, feel, think, or act.

(Davis 1989: 115)

This brief discussion of Being-with allows us to presently return to the charge that Heidegger determines Being-with, described as an existential attribute of Dasein in Division I of *Being and Time*, according to a 'people' in the more contentious Division II (Heidegger 1962: ¶74). At the most obvious level, such a nationalist determination can be seen in Heidegger's comments on history and 'historising'. For Heidegger, the self is historical in the sense that it exists 'between' birth and death. Its existence unfolds between the two, and this unfolding he calls 'historis-ing'. Historising, moreover, refers to the self's relationship with its 'historical background', what we commonly refer to as the 'tradition' or 'historical heritage' in which the self is 'thrown'. Since human being is Being-with, Heidegger claims, its historising is *co-historising* (Heidegger 1962: 347 and 435ff).

Specifically, Heidegger appears to determine Dasein's co-historising in a nationalist manner when authentic Being-with is attached to the 'community' and the 'people' in paragraph 74 of *Being and Time*. Let us quote extensively from this crucial and contentious paragraph, where Heidegger writes that:

> if fateful Dasein, as Being-in-the-world, exists essentially in Being-with Others, its historizing is a co-historizing (*Mitgeschehen*) and is determinative for it as *destiny* [*Geschick*]. This is how we designate the historizing of the community, of a people. Destiny is not something that puts itself together out of individual fates, any more than Being-with-one-another can be conceived as the occurring together of several Subjects. Our fates have already been guided in advance, in our Being with one another in the same world and in our res-oluteness for definite possibilities. Only in communicating and in struggling does the power of destiny become free. (Italics in original)

(1962: 436)[9]

Why should Heidegger specifically determine Being-with in terms of a 'people', why does he emphasize such terms as 'community', 'fate', 'destiny' and the histor-ical tradition? And, more importantly, should this discussion about 'a people' be read, in light of Heidegger's subsequent involvement with Nazism, as the emer-gence of nationalism in his thought? These two questions require greater examina-tion and the response to them is decisive for a critical account of *political* co-existence and community.

Let us take the second question first, which must be discussed within the context of the continuing debate about the 'case of Heidegger'.[10] Although few scholars would ignore or excuse Heidegger's involvement with the Nazis, three distinct positions seem to exist as to how this affects our consideration of *Being and Time* and his earlier thought more generally. A first group of scholars has argued that Heidegger's thought is inseparable from his politics and even *Being and Time*, which chronologically predates his rectorship, should be read as a response to National Socialism, as some kind of proto-fascist text in which the very origins of his politics can be traced (Wolin 1990, 1991). Johannes Fritsche (1999: xv), for example, has provided a rich textual discussion of paragraph 74 of *Being and Time*, which leads him to argue that 'the soil of *Being and Time* is völkisch'. He castigates most (left-leaning)[11] Heideggerians for having cultivated this ignorance [of the völkisch character of *Being and Time*] by making procedures of decontextualization their primary tool, and they have been harvesting the sweet grapes of postmetaphysical plurality and recognition of the other as irreducible other from the notion of historicality in *Being and Time*.

(Fritsche 1999: xiii).

Fritsche maintains that it is challenging for non-Germans and especially Americans (where the Heidegger controversy is still raging)

to understand Heidegger's notion of historicality and authentic Dasein. For there could not be a more marked difference than the one between the 'German' rightist notions of *Held* and fate on the one hand and the 'American' understanding of what it means to be authentic on the other

(1999: xiii).

Fritsche argues that if *Being and Time* is read as Heidegger *intended*, by responding to his own (and Germany's) specific historical situation, it becomes immediately apparent that '*Being and Time* was a highly political and ethical work, that it belonged to the revolutionary Right, and that it contained an argument for the most radical group on the revolutionary Right, namely the National Socialists' (1999: xv): as such, he regards the usage of Heidegger's thought to be itself reactionary and right-wing. The language of *Being and Time* would have been recognisable to all Germans of the Weimar and Nazi eras who would have recognised in it the Nazi agenda, he argues further. Therefore, '[t]he phenomenology in *Being and Time* can scarcely be saved by screening the nuggets of gold and throwing away the dirt' (Neaman 2001: 148–9).

A less extreme position is put forward by a second group of authors who acknowledge that there is an ambiguity and vagueness within Heidegger's discussion of these core concepts, which may leave them open to a political determination. They, nevertheless, argue that it is Heidegger himself who later infuses the analysis of *Being and Time* with political motifs. For example, Philippe Lacoue-Labarthe (1998: 286), calls the communal determination of authentic Being-with 'an ontic preference' of Heidegger's, arising presumably from his own conservative revolutionist political persuasions, but not made inevitable by the ontological discussion in *Being and Time*. Miguel de Beistegui (1997: 19) adds that the concept of historicality (*Geschichtlichkeit, Geschehen*) is ontologically vague within *Being and Time*, which allows it to be 'from the start politically oriented'. Jürgen Habermas, moreover, regards the communal determination of *Mitsein* to be a consequence of the way 'understanding' and 'sense' are connected to disclosure, which is, of course, collective. He considers (1987: 132) that 'the historical destiny of a culture or society is determined by a collectively binding pre-understanding of the things and events that can appear in the world at all'. Habermas (1989: 439 and 441) dates the turn to Nazism, however, to 1929 arguing that 'from around 1929 on, Heidegger's thought exhibits a *conflation* of philosophical theory and ideological motifs' which amounts, for Habermas, to 'the invasion of the philosophy of *Being and Time* by ideology', made possible by Heidegger's own re-reading of his thought. More critically, Simon Critchley calls this communal determination of Being-with the 'political fate of fundamental ontology and the *Dasein*-analytic'; for Critchley, thinking about politics and coexistence in the space opened by *Being and Time* would have to avoid the 'autarchic telos and tragic-heroic pathos of the thematics of authenticity, where in Paragraph 74, *Mitsein* is determined in terms of "the people" and its "destiny"' (1999: 240, cf. Adorno 1973). Yet Critchley, unlike Fritsche above, does allow for the possibility that alternative readings of Being-with may be possible.

There is a third group of scholars who, while still condemning Heidegger's politics as one cannot fail to do, seek to situate his discussion of community and historicality within his broader philosophical preoccupations with the predominance of modern subjectivism. R.N. Newell, for example, suggests that the apparent political orientation of Being-with in the language of the 'people' comes from Heidegger's philosophic 'concern of how to achieve a cohesive community in a world increasingly dominated by the values of liberal individualism' (1984: 783). It is important to highlight that Heidegger avoided any references to 'society' (*Gesellschaft*) because he believed that 'society today is only the absolutization of modern subjectivity' (cited in Harries 1978: 304). Indeed, de Beistegui (1997: 22, first emphasis added) also argues that the usage of the term 'community' (*Gemeinschaft*) by Heidegger is made 'as much in favour of a specific understanding of the nature of our being-in-common as it is made *against* the view – associated with liberalism, capitalism and intellectualism – which articulates the meaning of communal life in terms of *Gesellschaft* and *Staat*'. This is a point developed further by David Wood (1993: 151), who argues that '[t]he distinctive function played by destiny ... is to provide a way of transcending the mere arithmetic addition of individual fates'.[12] And indeed, as was quoted above, the sentence which follows the reference to 'community' and 'people' reads: '[d]estiny is not something that puts itself together out of individual fates, any more than Being-with-one-another can be conceived as the occurring together of several Subjects' (Heidegger 1962: 436).

Yet, does linking the discussion of 'the co-historizing of Dasein' to this philosophic concern with liberal understandings of *Gesellschaft* settle the question of 'community', as well as its relation to 'destiny'? Hardly, for even de Beistegui (1997: 20) notes that the identification with community is what 'gives a political orientation to Heidegger's discussion'. Lacoue-Labarthe best articulates the centrality of the issue of community and identification when he argues (1998: 297) that the concept of 'mimesis' is the 'formidable unanswered, or unformulated, question that continually haunts Heideggerian thought'. Heidegger refuses, according to Lacoue-Labarthe (1998: 299), to examine the problem of identification, which is the 'German political problem par excellence'.[13] A return to the first question is called for, therefore, of why Heidegger discusses Dasein's co-historising in terms of *community*, and how to understand this discourse of Dasein's historical happening, its co-historising, in terms of the historical past of the 'community'. Is it necessarily the emergence of nationalism in his thought, as Karl Löwith insisted (1994: 38), seen in the 'passage from a particular and individual *Dasein* to one that is general, no less particular by virtue of its generality – namely, one of German *Dasein*'? The crucial question here has to be, therefore: is the communal determination of Being-with inevitably nationalistic ('*German* Dasein'), embedded, as Fritsche suggested earlier, in a *völkisch* rhetoric and the 'political and ethical' programme of National Socialism? An interpretation of this is essential in order to assess whether the thought of Being-with binds the discussion of tradition and community, when seen in light of the horror of the 1930s and 1940s, to a nationalistic determination. But the question of community is not a problem for Heidegger *alone* but, indeed, a central problem of political thought and practice in general. As Lacoue-Labarthe (1998: 300) asks emphatically: '[w]hy would the problem of identification not be, in general, the essential problem of the political?'

For the present discussion on the constitution of political community – which this chapter understands to involve divorcing community from exclusionary nationalism and its practices, but at the same time to avoid the pitfalls of pure proceduralism and its assumptions about the pre-social nature of selves – this question of identification and its relationship with 'destiny' and 'the historical past' cannot be ignored. It has to be discussed directly and alongside the related question of whether a non-nationalist, critical reading of authentic Being-with can be given and justified. Therefore, the chapter examines this fundamental question of identification in *Being and Time* below, in an attempt to retrieve out of Heidegger's discussion an account of how community is constituted without being bound to a homogeneous totality determined 'biologically', 'ethnically' or according to other modes of (as)sociation tied to an essence, while at the same time, avoiding the determination of community according to an additive impulse, which assumes already constituted selves prior to community, and which I have called elsewhere the logic of composition (cf. Odysseos 2007). The interpretation which appears below would, almost certainly, be castigated by the first group of scholars, who purport that there exists only *one* historically accurate reading of *Being and Time*, one tied to a nationalist agenda. Yet what is offered below is not a misreading of *Being and Time*, but must be understood as a critical appropriation of Heidegger's thought. Such appropriation is not misplaced, naïve or erroneous; it exists, arguably, within the phenomenology of *Being and Time* as a possibility, and can be uncovered and restructured for a political thought of community.

Mimesis, community and critical belonging

This section discusses the emergence of Dasein's historicality within its manifested public group ('community'). In particular, the notion of identification, or *mimesis*, is examined, enabling the recasting of Dasein's co-historising away from a nationalist determination. Heidegger's discussion of Dasein's attitude towards its historical tradition contains within it, it is argued, the possibility of a critical and productive relationship with the community. Indeed, Dasein's relationship with its tradition displays an agonistic sensibility toward the historical tradition, a sensibility which maintains a critical, one might say, resisting relationship towards the tradition's past historical possibilities, uncovering those that can be 'repeated' in Dasein's contemporary concrete situation, disavowing and discarding others which are not deemed appropriate or productive. Dasein's agonistic attitude recovers 'repeatable possibilities', possibilities which are worth recasting, in other words, through a mode of deconstruction parallel to that which Heidegger had himself employed towards the ontological tradition in philosophy.

Interpreting Heidegger's discussion of Dasein's 'repetition of past historical possibilities' in a critical and agonistic manner provides a *productive* conception of identification, where the mimetic process contains *also* an element of critique, resistance and displacement towards the community's historical tradition, and particularly, the community's past *possibilities*. Such a displacing and resisting towards the community's past possibilities forms the contours of a practice through which community itself is constituted outside of conventional modes of belonging and association. Such a discussion is useful both for international political theory engaged in serious discussions on the constitution and future of political community but also for illustrating that Heidegger's communal determination of Being-with need not be inevitably nationalistic or *völkisch*, regardless of Heidegger's own political commitments. In other words, Heidegger's text contains within it critical possibilities that belie the historical juncture of its writing, as well as Heidegger's discernible authorial intentions. As such, it can be productive for theorising community in the midst of contemporary political challenges.

'Critical belonging': tradition, repetition, destructive retrieve

Contentiously, in paragraph 74 Heidegger discusses Dasein's relationship to the heritage and tradition of the public group in which it is historically manifested. While this has been cast as part of a conservative agenda, it is also open to alternative readings and crucially, this section proposes, it can be made a central part of the theorisation of the constitution of community. Let us return to Heidegger's text, where he writes that, the

> resoluteness in which Dasein comes back to itself discloses current factical possibilities of authentic existing, and discloses them *in terms of the heritage* which that resoluteness, as thrown, *takes over.*
> (Heidegger 1962: 435, emphasis in original)

Dasein, in other words, in acknowledging and resolutely grasping that it is a being defined by the finitude of its existence, is able to 'take over' particular possibilities that are handed down to it by the historical tradition of the public group in which it finds itself (or, is 'thrown'). 'Taking over' is, moreover, associated with a process Heidegger calls 'repetition', further examined later in the section. Let us first discuss the usage of 'heritage' and 'tradition'.

The discussion of 'tradition' is part of the overall 'determination' of historical being-there, which is embedded in a historically situated public group, or community.

Stated otherwise, Dasein is radically embedded (*thrown*) in its world and this world is manifested publicly and historically; when Dasein resolutely projects itself upon possibilities (1962: ¶31), it must do so in terms of those possibilities that are publicly and historically available to it as part of the historical tradition of its community. However, the discussion of the historical tradition is also part of Heidegger's attempts to distinguish between history and his own claim that Dasein is *historical*.

As Heidegger suggests, history is commonly understood as 'something past', as 'that belonging to an earlier time', as 'context of events', and as 'the transformations and vicissitudes of man, of human groupings and the "cultures" as distinguished from Nature' (1962: 430). He claims, however, that Dasein is *historical* – Heidegger forthrightly asks of his own argument, 'by what right do we call this entity "historical", when it is not yet past?' (1962: 431). According to his account, since Dasein is never merely occurrent (present-at-hand), it can never be past in the sense of 'now *no longer present-at-hand or ready-to-hand*' (emphasis in original) (1962: 432). Dasein's capacity to-be-a-whole (to be self-constant) 'is the movement of Dasein as it stretches itself through time and is called Dasein's happening or *Geschehen*' (Hoy 1978: 338). David Couzens Hoy (336) argues that 'Dasein becomes aware of how it *is* its past (the past of its generation, i.e., its tradition) insofar as the past is an essential part of the *constitution* of Dasein's understanding of its futural possibility'. As Heidegger argues, Dasein projects itself futurally onto the possibilities available to it as a radically embedded self, a *thrown* being. Its projection must take place within, and is shaped by, this 'heritage', understood as 'that in which *Dasein* is always immersed and implicated: its historical possibilities' (Birmingham 1991: 29).

In light of this, Hoy (1978: 340) further suggests that the notion of 'taking over' inherited possibilities has to be interpreted as 'a recognition of the compelling situation of the actual historical world' but one that can lead Dasein 'to an urgent commitment to what is most unique and individual about one's way of being-there'. This urgent commitment is what has been called 'resoluteness', understood as Dasein's readiness for anxiety in light of its finitude; in its resolute response to its finitude and in recognition of its heteronomy, Dasein plunges itself towards the factical world, rather than remain lost in the comfort of the 'they'. This is paramount for Heidegger, because '[t]hrough anticipatory resoluteness, the "there" or the situation of Dasein is made transparent to Dasein' (de Beistegui 1997: 15); the actual choices or options which Dasein can resolutely make about its possibilities, however, are intentionally *not* discussed by Heidegger. Neither is speculation about them entertained, because a consideration of actual factical possibilities is not *possible* in the abstract: they can only be thought through by each particular Dasein finding itself in a uniquely different factical situation and thrown in a distinct public group. Therefore, de Beistegui argues '[i]f an ethics or a politics could indeed unfold from this fundamental existential constitution, Heidegger refuses to consider it. Dasein's resoluteness remains empty' (de Beistegui:15).[14]

But as was noted earlier, the emptiness of resoluteness is but a step away from 'the abyss of steely and *völkish* rhetoric' (de Beistegui: 16). A step which apparently Heidegger takes when he asserts, as was already quoted in the preceding discussion, that 'our' heritage and tradition guide our projection upon possibilities:

> [o]ur fates have already been guided in advance, in our Being with one another in the same world and in our resoluteness for definite possibilities. Only in communicating and in struggling does the power of destiny become free. Dasein's fateful destiny in and with its 'generation' goes to make up the full authentic historizing of Dasein.
>
> (Heidegger 1962: 436)

This can be, and has been, read as the emergence of a conservative nationalism in Heidegger, where the struggle of the community in its self-determination leads to a process of repetition and, hence, identification and mimesis.[15] Such a reading would concur with Lacoue-Labarthe's assessment (1998: 300) of the unstated identificatory process at play in *Being and Time* and justify his concern that '[a]n unacknowledged mimetology seems to overdetermine the thought of Heidegger politically'.

Can 'repetition', 'fate' and 'destiny' avoid a nationalist communal specification, however? Hoy suggests (1978: 340–341) that in the discussion of historicality, '[d]estiny (*Geschick*) and fate (*Schicksal*) are technical terms for Heidegger' where 'fate represents the way Dasein becomes definite and actual through its relation to events in the world' and destiny 'involves the essential connection of the individual to the *community* or a *people*'.[16] One could suggest, following this, that it is possible to consider the determination of the 'with' in terms of a community's tradition or heritage to be a technical matter, a *repercussion*, so to speak, of the primacy of relationality, which dictates that 'since Dasein is essentially in the world with others … and since Dasein is essentially fateful or historical it follows that Dasein's fate is a co-fate and its history a co-history' (de Beistegui 1997: 17).[17]

But it is not until the conception of 'repetition' is examined more closely that the general discussion of the historical tradition can be better located. Heidegger (1962: 437) suggests that the relationship of Dasein towards the tradition can be understood as *repetition* and that '[r]epeating is handing down (*Überlieferung*) explicitly* – that is to say, going back to the possibilities of the Dasein that has-been there'. For Lacoue-Labarthe, as was noted earlier, this discussion of Dasein repeating the tradition's possibilities as part of its 'historising' reveals the troubling presence of a nationalist or 'communitarian' identification process, which nevertheless remains 'unthought' by Heidegger himself. Yet, we must bear in mind that 'repetition' is a particular kind of 'taking over' possibilities which belies its immediate association with nationalist identification. Heidegger is explicit that 'the Dasein that has-been-there is not disclosed in order to be actualized over again … repetition does not let itself be persuaded of something by what is "past", just in order that this, as something which was formerly actual, may recur' (1962: 437–38).[18] Therefore, it would be wrong to assume that repetition implies the blind re-enactment of what has occurred in the past. As Derrida was to later argue (1972: 40) with respect to 'iteration', this sort of repeating also 'alters, something new takes place'. Repetition takes place, each time, in a unique historical and socio-political context ('factical situation'): in typical polysemic fashion (Bourdieu 1991: 57), the Heideggerian text makes difficult the understanding of repetition as mere replication of what had previously occurred in and to the 'community' in which Dasein is thrown, or a reiteration of the community's values and ideas.

For Heidegger, then, repetition 'is an attempt to retrieve a more original, a more positive and hence *constructive* comportment towards one's history' (de Beistegui 1997: 25). Yet, constructive engagement might well take an agonistic and critical form. To explore this element further, Peg Birmingham has developed a notion of 'critical mimesis' by examining specifically the *response* towards the heritage which resolute Dasein takes over (see Heidegger 1962: 435). She explores the possibilities contained within Heidegger's discussion of repetition, in order to elucidate Dasein's agonistic relationship toward the tradition. According to her analysis, Dasein's is a *critical* process of identification and this calls into question Lacoue-Labarthe's claim that in Heidegger's discussion of historicity there is a process of nationalist or 'communitarian' mimesis at play. She asserts (1991: 25) that 'Lacoue-Labarthe overlooks a crucial aspect of the discussion of destiny and historicity in *Being and Time*, namely, Heidegger's discussion of *Erwidert*: *Dasein's* response to its repeatable possibilities'. Birmingham joins commentators such as David Wood and de Beistegui in noting that Heidegger expands the meaning of repetition beyond its casual connotations and in highlighting that, remarkably, 'the repetition of tradition opens up our destiny' (Wood 1993: 150) and affords a '"go[ing] back" to a given situation, but in such a way that this situation is thus disclosed, illuminated in a new way, revealed as a unique historical possibility' (de Beistegui 1997: 25). Once this occurs, Dasein 'takes over' its communal historical heritage, *responds* to it, in a specific way: it comports itself towards the past historical possibilities of its tradition in the manner of *erwidern*.

What does it mean to respond by way of *Erwiderung*? Macquarrie and Robinson's translation of *Being and Time* rendered *Erwiderung* as a 'reciprocative rejoinder' to correspond to the normal usage of *erwidern* in the sense of 'to reply' (Heidegger 1962: 438). This, however, fails to clearly indicate its full implications, and those of the root *wider*, which include strife and which in casual discourse mean 'contrary to or against' (Birmingham 1991: 31). To emphasize this particular aspect of repetition, Birmingham argues (31) that '[t]he response to repeatable his-torical possibilities is one which disavows any notion of continuity or identity with the past'. Therefore, when the concrete situation is 'illuminated', there is no guar-antee that Dasein will accept the tradition's possibilities uncritically or allow itself to be submerged in what is 'past' so that it can make it occur all over again. On the contrary, the disclosure of the tradition may well lead Dasein to attempt 'to *over-come* the way the tradition conditions or limits its possibilities' (Hoy 1978: 336–7). It can, in other words, 'take over', or 'repeat', its inherited possibilities by engaging in critical mimesis: a 'repetition' which practices critique and retrieval with respect to the possibilities available to it within its heritage. The notion of 'destructive retrieve', put to use by Heidegger with respect to the ontological tradition of philosophy, here comes to describe Dasein's very response to the heritage and tradition in which it is thrown.

De Beistegui concurs with such an assessment, asking in addition:

> Is it not in the context of such a strifely or adverse attitude of Dasein in the face of its own historical situation that we must understand the use that Heidegger makes of the word *Kampf*? Does the 'struggle' not refer to Dasein's ability to engage with its own time in a strifely dialogue ...?
>
> (de Beistegui 1997: 25).[19]

When Heidegger states (1962: 436) that '[o]nly in *communicating* and in *struggling* does the power of destiny become free',[20] 'communication' (*Mitteilung*) and 'struggle' must be evaluated as part of this agonistic attitude and disposition which Dasein displays towards the tradition. *Mit-teilung* communicates that which is shared, which is itself 'communicated through the sharing (*Teilung*)' (de Beistegui 1997: 23; cf. Derrida 1993). The contentious reference to 'struggling' and 'communicating' thus performs two functions: first, to initiate the internal contestation of community by its own members, in order to counteract the account of 'idle talk' (*Gerede*) with which the 'they' drown all communication (Heidegger 1962: ¶35 and ¶27); and second, to indicate the way in which Dasein's historicality unfolds as a critically disposed repetition of the past repeatable possibilities of the community's tradition (de Beistegui 1997: 168, n.32).[21]

This kind of agonistic repetition, in the manner of *erwidern*, 'does not abandon itself to that which is past, nor does it aim at progress' (Heidegger 1962: 438). In this way, it neither lends itself to 'reactionism' as a political modality which 'is nourished by a thinking of the return (to the origins, God, to values, to meaning, etc.)' and nor does it support a teleological understanding of politics and history as 'the arche-teleological unfolding of a meaningful process in a certain appropriation of the philosophy of the Enlightenment' (de Beistegui 1997: 29). Heidegger's analytic, therefore, is as suspicious of the conservative alternative as of the liberal political understanding. The future does not unfold according to a teleology: it is perhaps best imagined (as an extrapolation from Heidegger's work) in the sense of 'engender[ing] a collective field of imaginable possibilities ... a restricted array of plausible scenarios of how the future can or cannot be changed' (Cruz 2000: 277). The future is critically projected upon past possibilities, which *become* 'imaginable' in a factical situation through the very process of critical mimesis.

Such a response to Dasein's historical being-there participates in a critical engagement with the customary practices of its historical tradition in order to reveal the positive possibilities it inherits and to recover a constructive way of relating to this heritage without blindly re-enacting it. This movement of a factical 'destructive retrieve' enables Birmingham (1991: 25) to suggest that the concern regarding the nationalist identification entailed in Dasein's co-historising must be reinterpreted on the basis of *Erwiderung*, namely, as 'displacement and disruption'. Employed in this disruptive mode, mimesis encourages a radical rethinking of the determination of Being-with in terms of a 'people' and also of the understanding of community as such, because Heidegger's articulation of mimesis is 'not based on a classical model of identification' of part to whole (Birmingham 1991: 25).[22]

If Dasein's response is understood as a critical, rather than a 'reciprocative', rejoinder with respect to its tradition and more generally to the social context in which it is thrown, there ought to be more than one possibility in which to think its co-historising. The suggestion that Being-with becomes historical by way of a *critical* mimetic response to the historically manifested tradition and 'people' – a response whose manifold meanings include *struggle*, strife or agonism, even a certain betrayal towards the tradition (cf. de Beistegui 1997, Derrida 1993, Cavell 1979) – accommodates *both* Dasein's radical embeddeness within the tradition seen in its indistinguishability from the 'they' and *also* Dasein's struggle against prevalent understandings of the tradition's possibilities. Moreover, it leaves open the space to think about tradition or heritage not only in terms of a people and a national or local community but as a 'group-in-becoming', a group that can be inclusive in its practice of critical belonging (cf. Connolly 1996). As Slavoj Žižek (2001: 93) notes in this regard, there is a certain 'trangression' constitutive of the community which points to the 'way we are allowed/expected to violate its explicit rules', to the extent that a subject which closely follows the explicit rules of a community will never be accepted its members 'as one of us'. In this way,

> we are 'in', integrated, perceived by the other members as 'one of us', only when we succeed in practicing this unfathomable DISTANCE from the symbolic rules. It is ultimately only this distance, which exhibits our identity, our belonging to the culture in question.
>
> (Žižek 2001: 93)

In sum, Dasein's identification might be always already embedded in a historical tradition, and thus part of a 'thicker' understanding of community, but if authentic, it ought to be critical, disruptive and, at the same time, productively applied to the specific historical ('factical') situation. It is in this sense that the constitution of community can be seen as an instance of critical mimesis, and coexistence can be understood as constituted through the practice of critique against the background of repeatable historical possibilities. The notion of *critical* mimesis, therefore, provides a response to the question of political identification, an identificatory response already infused with critique, rather than the mere unproblematic replication of the historical heritage.

The discussion of Dasein's historicality and co-historising, then, need not be immediately thrust aside as the premonition of a conservative agenda, tied to a racist or biological understanding of the community and the tradition; rather, it is open to alternative readings, ones that are useful for a theoretical account of a critical practice of identification or mimesis and ultimately for the theorisation of a thick and yet non-essentialising conception of community. The notion of 'critical mimesis', in this sense, can lead not only to the constitution of community through a response that has the disposition of critique towards its past possibilities, but also a community in which the mode of belonging is itself critical. 'Critical belonging' makes concrete Dasein's primacy of relation – evident in its thrownness – but shows this primacy to be manifest in Dasein's critique, displacement and resistance to the tradition. Critical belonging, therefore, is the mode in which the self makes the community out of her critical and resisting disposition.

In Birmingham's words (1991: 27), '*Dasein* determines itself authentically in a co-determination of being-with wherein the indifferent and efficient mode of solicitude becomes emancipatory'. In this way, the mode of 'critical belonging' also allows solicitude towards others to be 'radically transformed' into a liberating kind of comportment: 'no longer viewed as part of the indifferent emptiness of the crowd, the homogeneous anonymity of the anyone, the other is freed to be who he or she is in his or her potentiality-for-Being' (Birmingham 1991: 27; cf. Odysseos 2003: 199). Rather than being the sign of an essentialist/nationalist determination, the self's being-with others 'now has a sense of a heterogeneous space, a differentiated temporality in which each is grasped in his or her own specificity' (Birmingham 1991: 27). This is a critical activity which rests on the centrality of critique and agonism in social life (cf. Campbell 1998) and one which allows us to recast Dasein's 'agency' as both 'thrown' but also critical, radically embedded but also critically free (cf. Tully 1995: 202–06). Thinking about agency does not have to accommodate belonging and critique: Dasein actively belongs in the mode of critique and resistance.

To conclude this section, the critical mimetic response of the self, understood as a kind of 'critical belonging', refutes the reading of Dasein's co-historising according to a nationalist essence. This allows a return to the question of Heidegger's politics and whether scholars ought to refrain from using his thought for a political thought of community and coexistence. The earlier discussion of critical mimesis and critical belonging is *itself* a practice of disavowal, displacement and resistance. It has disavowed Heidegger's politics and resisted the determination which he imposed on the analysis of *Being and Time* by his political engagement. This is not a case of 'sorting what in his thought may be preserved free of his own Nazified orientation' (Rockmore and Margolis 1992: 1). Discussing the possibility of a critical mimesis according to Birmingham's analysis, and delineating an account of communal constitution through the mode of critical belonging towards the community is akin to undertaking the *destruction* (in the sense of 'destructive retrieve', cf. Kockelmans 1978) of Heidegger's legacy: an act of resistance and critique towards the determination of *Being and Time* given to it by Heidegger's political involvement with the Nazis. What is given herein is not, in other words, a blind reading of *Being and Time*, but constitutes a constructive retrieval of certain unacknowledged insights within the text. This is tantamount to releasing the past possibilities of that text. The present discussion, thus, disrupts and displaces Heidegger's 'ontic' determination of the thought of Being-with and resists his politics. This, arguably, is the Heideggerian gesture *par excellence*, which he undertook towards the ontological tradition, and which has been employed here in order to retrieve from his thought a critical account of community constitution today.

Conclusion: poiesis, praxis and politics

This chapter addressed the question of whether, and how, the thought of *Being and Time* might aid us in rethinking political community. It examined the concern, articulated within the context of the debate on Heidegger's politics, that any conception of community derived from Heidegger's thought inevitably falls into the trap of an essentialist and exclusionary nationalist determination of community. In response, the chapter engaged in a re-reading of the contentious paragraph 74 of *Being and Time* which enabled a critical appropriation of the process of 'repetition' described by Heidegger. Rather than necessarily falling prey to an essentialist mimetology, as argued by Lacoue-Labarthe, it was suggested that the very constitution of community can be understood as taking place through a process of 'critical mimesis'. Peg Birmingham's analysis in this regard illustrated how Dasein can comport itself towards the 'past possibilities' of the historical tradition, in which it is thrown, with an agonistic and resisting attitude. The radically embedded self *identifies* with the community by critically repeating certain past possibilities of its tradition, in the sense given to repetition by Heidegger, which entails the retrieving of *repeatable* possibilities. Those productive possibilities found within the tradition's past are emphasised and re-articulated within the political space opened up by the very act of critical engagement; others regarded as not wholly expressive of the tradition's historical potential are abandoned. Such a relationship towards the tradition does not refute the radical embeddedness (thrownness) of the self in the community. But it does suggest that this kind of political self *belongs* by exercising critique, resistance and displacement towards the tradition's past possibilities, and that community itself is constituted through such critical belonging.

The self's continuous practice of 'critical mimesis' is useful for international political theory because it incorporates a critical and agonistic attitude which enables a movement towards a subject, and a politics, of non-essentialist and non-exclusionary community. The discussion of how the community is constituted through the self's critical mimetic response to its historical tradition, which might be called in shorthand 'community through critique', not only displaces Heidegger's *own* determination of the phenomenology of *Being and Time*, but, moreover, offers an understanding of communal constitution that is inclusive of others and otherness. This is because others, who are not embedded in the specific historical public group in question according to conventional modes of belonging and association, are hereby acknowledged by the self as having a voice[23]; the questioning kind of belonging, which retrieves from those possibilities 'inherited' by the tradition those worth 'repeating', is open to everyone engaging in practices of critique towards the tradition's heritage. Others who wish to critically 'repeat' possibilities in a community where they might not be members under more commonplace criteria, such as the figurations of language, nation, ethnicity, or religion (cf. Nancy 1991b), may too engender critique and thus participate in the 'critical mimesis' of possibilities of the group in which they envision their future projection. Critical belonging notes only the desire to engage in a critique of the possibilities handed down to the group to which one *wishes* to belong (as in the case of migrants, for example, see Žižek 2001: 93).

The 'praxeological' character of this critique entails the endless critical engagement with the repeatable possibilities of the tradition and constitutes 'membership' as such. Although any understanding of a community would be exclusionary in some formal sense, the notion of a 'critical mimesis' as the mode of constitution of the community may be so in ways which are not arbitrary. When *critique* becomes the mode of belonging, the community is not arbitrarily excluding others because of race, religion, colour, birthplace, etc. The critical mimetic process does not limit belonging to territorial or other identity-related criteria (cf. O'Sullivan 1997) and, as such, can reinvigorate existing discussions of 'multiculturalism' and of the extension of the community (Tully 1995, Taylor, 1992; see Cochran 2000 on 'extending the "we"').

Moreover, the mode of 'critical belonging' discussed earlier makes two further contributions to international political theory. First, it enables the discussion of community constitution outside of the dichotomy of proceduralist composition and essence. The understanding of community constitution provided earlier acknowledges 'thickness' in the sense that it is based on Dasein's thrownness in a historical tradition but in no way constrains the 'opening up' of the tradition. The tradition is historical, in the sense of the location of the ideas, projects and practices which it comprises in a specific public group; membership to it, however, is not to be restricted to those who 'inherit' it in a conventional sense (as might be the case with other immutable characteristics). This is because membership and belonging are based on a substantially different understanding of 'tradition' as such, where community is conceived not only as *open* to critique, but as *constituted* by the self's very act of critically engaging with the past possibilities of the tradition in which one wishes to locate oneself.

Second, 'critical belonging' is essential for international political theory in an era of globalisation, precisely because of its focus on otherness. It invites others outside of the particular historical tradition to enter the critical mimetic process because it acknowledges:

> the claim of others who, from beyond 'our' horizon, call into question the parochialism of our tradition insofar as it does not speak for them and who demand that we include their perspectives in the effort to understand ourselves.

> (Vogel 1994: 70)

The multiplicity of perspectives that globalisation involves, referred to as the intensification of 'value pluralism' in the IR literature (cf. Lensu and Fritz 1999), does not negate this process. On the contrary, plurality *assists* the forcefulness of critique by re-articulating and re-imagining the repeatable possibilities of the tradition by bringing difference to bear on them productively. Therefore, critical belonging, open to all those who wish to critique and retrieve a tradition's possibilities, constructively theorises the 'friendly struggle' (cf. Derrida 1993, Coole 2001) of the negotiations of multiple perspectives in an era of global transformations. Most significantly, it illustrates that plurality is to be found *within* the tradition. This enables a movement away from the community's conceptualisation as uniform and essentialist, towards its diversification, both from inside and from an outside that is already within.

Notes

1 See, for example, Nancy 1991a, Linklater 1998, Odysseos 2007, Brown 1992, Miami Theory Collective 1991, Archibugi *et al.* 1998, Tully 1995, and Walzer 1994.
2 'Unlikely' for a number of reasons: first, because of Heidegger's involvement with the Nazis, discussed later; second, because the nature of his thought is regarded as essentially a-, non- or pre-political (see Janicaud 1996: 39, de Beistegui 1997: 11 and 2007: 88; cf. also Ward 1995) and third, because of the need to distinguish between ontic and ontological discussions of community, with Heidegger's work falling within the latter (Heidegger 1962: 31).
3 I use the term 'heteronomous' in the sense of the primacy of relation and the self's constitution by otherness (see, Odysseos 2007, Chapter 1), contrary to the meaning of heteronomy as the 'abandonment' of the self to 'the despotic rule of nameless, higher powers' and a subsequent relinquishment of responsibility (Wolin 1990: 150) or the meaning associated with 'paternalism' (Salem-Wiseman 2003: 550).
4 'Being-there' or 'There-being'; for Heidegger's particular use of the German term Dasein (conventionally understood as 'existence'), see Richardson 1963: 44–46.
5 And indeed, this is a continuing debate; see for example, the special issue on Heidegger's politics in the *European Journal of Political Theory* 6(1) January 2007.
6 See de Beistegui 1997, Bourdieu 1991, Caputo 1991, Derrida 1989, Fritsche 1999, Habermas 1989, Ijsseling 1992, Janicaud, 1996, Levinas1990, Rockmore and Margolis 1992, Sluga 1993, and Wolin 1990, 1991.
7 *Daseinanalytik*, or the analysis of There-being. Also invoked in this term is the distinction between existential and existentielle analysis (see Heidegger 1962: 31–35, as well as ¶9–10).
8 The 'they' is the somewhat unfortunate and misleading translation of Heidegger's term 'das Man' and it should not lead one to one assume that Dasein is distinct from the 'they' on the basis of this translation.
9 Parenthesis for (*Mitgeschehen*) added, square brackets [*Geschick*] in the original Macquarrie and Robinson translation. In German the first sentence reads: 'Wenn aber das schicksalhafte Dasein als In-derWelt-sein wesenhaft im Mitsein mit Anderen existiert, ist sein Geschehen ein Mitgeschehen und bestimmt als *Geschick*. Damit bezeichnen wir das Geschehen der Gemeinschaft, des Volkes' (Heidegger 1993: 384).
10 '*Der Fall Heidegger*', the German term *Fall* meaning both the 'case' of and the 'fall' of Heidegger (cf. Rockmore and Margolis, 1992).
11 Thomas Sheehan (2001) calls them 'self-hating Heideggerians'.
12 This entails transcending the determination of community (and coexistence) according to a compositional, additive logic, which I have elsewhere analysed as the 'logic of composition' (Odysseos 2007).
13 With regards to the manifestation of this problem in the 1930s in the form of National Socialism, Lacoue-Labarthe and Nancy argue that there is a complicity or responsibility of 'German thought' in the continued mythic response to this problem of identification:

> [t]here incontestably has been and there still is perhaps a German problem; Nazi ideology was a specifically political response to this problem; and there is no doubt whatsoever that the German tradition, and in particular the tradition of German thought, is not at all foreign to this ideology.
>
> (Lacoue-Labarthe and Nancy 1990: 295)

Also,

> it is because the German problem is fundamentally a problem of *identity* that the German figure of totalitarianism is racism ... It is because myth can be defined as an *identificatory mechanism* that racist ideology became bound up in the construction of a myth, (emphasis in original).
>
> (Lacoue-Labarthe and Nancy 1990: 296)

See also, the discussion of Nazism's revival and production of mythic identification (296–312).

14 Because of the emptiness of anticipatory resoluteness de Beistegui refuses to identify it 'with the heroism and decisionism with which it has been often charged' by authors such as Karl Löwith (1994, 1995) and Richard Wolin (1990, 1991).

15 Moreover, is there not the danger, as has been argued by Karl Löwith, that the reference to the struggle of the collective entity (especially in the context of Being-toward-death) entails the very constitution of the 'we' through the assumed or posited threat to its continued existence by an 'enemy' – much like in Carl Schmitt's *Concept of the Political*? Dasein's co-historising might manifest itself as the collective confrontation with an enemy. Indeed, Löwith suggests that there is a correspondence between Heidegger's being-toward-death and '[Carl] Schmitt's "sacrifice of life" in the politically paramount case of war' (Löwith 1994: 32; see also Löwith 1995: 160–61 and Schmitt 1996: 33).

16 Yet this distinction between 'fate' and 'destiny' is not sustained in the work of the later Heidegger (Inwood 1999: 68).

17 The reference to community may not be, in this understanding, a theoretical commitment to a (necessarily right-wing) understanding of community (*Gemeinschaft*) but might be, rather, a reminder of the *historical manifestation* of the worldliness of being-there. As Fritsche rightly reminds us, in Heidegger's case the historical situation would have been the post-WWI Weimar Republic, with its economic uncertainty and the emergent political rise of both communism and fascism.

18 In Joan Stambaugh's translation: 'The handing down of a possibility that has been in retrieving it, however, does not disclose the Da-sein that has been there in order to actualize it again' (Heidegger 1996: 352).

19 De Beistegui rightly points out that the best example of this *Erwiderung* is none other than Heidegger's method of *Destruktion* or 'destructive retrieve' through which he engages with traditional ontology in order to be able to restate anew the question of Being. Naturally, this point is rejected by those who suggest that only one reading of paragraph 74 is possible (see, for instance, Fritsche 1999: 1–28, and in particular his refutation of such critical readings of 'repetition' and 'critical rejoinder': 7–28 and pp. 251–53).

20 The sentence reads in German: *In der Mitteilung und im Kampf wird die Macht des Geschickes erst frei* (Hedegger 1993: 384).

21 The reference to the 'they' and 'idle talk' could be understood, moreover, as an explicit stance against a subjectivist conception of *Gesellschaft*, where community is invoked to contest and problematise the 'absolutization of subjectivity'.

22 Regarding Heidegger's involvement with the National Socialists Birmingham argues (1991: 44) that at the time of the 'turn' Heidegger 'begins to think that the Dasein's destiny can be given a *topos*'. See also the discussion of 'ontopology' (Campbell 1998: 33–81).

23 In the sense of the voice that Dasein carries within (cf. Odysseos 2003; Derrida 1993).

Bibliography

Adorno, T.W. (1973) *The Jargon of Authenticity*, trans. K. Tarnowski and F. Will. London: Routledge and Kegan Paul.

Archibugi, D., Held, D. and Köhler, M. (eds) (1998) *Re-imagining Political Community: studies in cosmopolitan democracy*, Cambridge: Polity and Blackwell Publishers.

Birmingham, P. (1991) 'The time of the political', *Graduate Faculty Philosophy Journal*, 14(2) -15(1): 25–45.

Bourdieu, P. (1991) *The Political Ontology of Martin Heidegger*, trans. P. Collier. Oxford: Polity Press.

Brown, C. (1992) *International Relations Theory: new normative approaches*, London: Harvester Wheatsheaf.

Campbell, D. (1998) *National Deconstruction: violence, identity, and justice in Bosnia*, Minneapolis: University of Minnesota Press.

Caputo, J.D. (1991) 'Heidegger's *Kampf*', *Graduate Faculty Philosophy Journal*, 14(2)-15(1): 61–83.

Cavell, S. (1979) *The Claim of Reason: Wittgenstein, skepticism, morality, and tragedy*. New York: Oxford University Press.

Cochran, M. (2000) *Normative Theory in International Relations: a pragmatic approach*, Cambridge: Cambridge University Press.

Connolly, W.E. (1996) 'Suffering, Justice, and the Politics of Becoming', *Culture, Medicine, and Psychiatry*, 20(3): 251–77.

Coole, D. (2001) 'Thinking Politically with Merleau-Ponty', *Radical Philosophy*, 108: 17–28.

Critchley, S. (1999) *Ethics – Politics – Subjectivity: essays on Derrida, Levinas, and contemporary French thought*, London: Verso.

Cruz, C. (2000) 'Identity and Persuasion: how nations remember their pasts and make their futures', *World Politics*, 52: 275–312.

Davis, W.A. (1989) *Inwardness and Existence: subjectivity in/and Hegel, Heidegger, Marx, and Freud*, Madison, WI: The University of Wisconsin Press.

de Beistegui, M. (1997), *Heidegger and the Political: dystopias*, London: Routledge.

—— (2007), 'Questioning Politics, or Beyond Power', *European Journal of Political Theory*, 6(1): 87–103.

Derrida, J. (1972), *Limited Inc*, trans. J. Mehlman and S. Weber. Chicago: Northwestern University Press.

—— (1989) *Of Spirit: Heidegger and the question*, trans. G. Bennington and R. Bowlby. Chicago: The University of Chicago Press.

—— (1992) *The Other Heading: reflections on today's Europe*, trans. P.-A. Brault and M.B. Naas. Bloomington: Indiana University Press.

—— (1993) Heidegger's Ear: philopolemology (*Geschlecht* IV), in J. Sallis (ed.), *Reading Heidegger: commemorations*, Bloomington: Indiana University Press: 163–218.

Farias, V. (1987) *Heidegger and Nazism*, trans. P. Burrell and G.R. Ricci: Philadelphia: Temple University Press.

Fritsche, J. (1999) *Historical Destiny and National Socialism in Heidegger's Being and Time*, Berkeley: University of California Press.

Gelven, M. (1970) *A Commentary on Heidegger's Being and Time*, New York: Harper and Row.

Georgopoulos, N. (1994) *The Structures of Existence: a reading of Heidegger's* Being and Time, University Park, PA: The Dialogue Press of Man and World.

Habermas, J. (1987) 'The Undermining of Western Rationalism Through the Critique of Metaphysics: Martin Heidegger', in J. Habermas, *The Philosophical Discourse of Modernity: twelve lectures*, trans. F.G. Lawrence, Cambridge: Polity Press: 131–60.

—— (1989) Work and *Weltanschauung*: The Heidegger controversy from a German perspective, trans. J. McCumber, *Critical Inquiry*, 15: 431–56.

Harries, K. (1978) 'Heidegger as a Political Thinker', in M. Murray (ed.), *Heidegger and Modern Philosophy: critical essays*, New Haven: Yale University Press: 304–28.

Heidegger, M. (1962) *Being and Time*, trans. J. Macquarrie and E. Robinson, Oxford: Blackwell.

—— (1985) 'The Self-Assertion of the German University', trans. K. Harries, *Review of Metaphysics*, 38: 470–80.

—— (1993) *Sein und Zeit*, Tübingen, Germany: Max Niemeyer Verlag.

—— (1996) *Being and Time: a translation of Sein und Zeit*, trans. J. Stambaugh, Albany: State University of New York Press.

Hoy, D.C. (1978) 'History, Historicity, and Historiography in *Being and Time*', in M. Murray (ed.), *Heidegger and Modern Philosophy: critical essays*. New Haven: Yale University Press: 329–53.

Ijsseling, S. (1992) 'Heidegger and Politics', in A.B. Dallery and C.E. Scott (eds), *Ethics and Danger: essays on Heidegger and continental thought*, Albany: State University of New York Press: 3–10.

Inwood, M. (1999) *A Heidegger Dictionary*, Oxford: Blackwell.

Janicaud, D. (1996) *The Shadow of that Thought: Heidegger and the question of politics*, trans. M. Gendre, Evanston. IL: Northwestern University Press.

Kockelmans, J.J. (1978) 'Destructive Retrieve and Hermeneutic Phenomenology in *Being and Time*', in J. Sallis (ed.), *Radical Phenomenology: essays in honor of Martin Heidegger*, Atlantic Highlands, NJ: Humanities Press: 106–37.

Lacoue-Labarthe, P. (1990) *Heidegger, Art and Politics: the fiction of the political*, trans. C. Turner, Oxford: Blackwell.

—— (1998) *Typography: Mimesis, Philosophy, Politics*, trans. C. Fynsk; Stanford: Stanford University Press.

Lacoue-Labarthe , P. and Nancy, J.-L. (1990) 'The Nazi Myth', trans. B. Holmes; *Critical Inquiry*, 16(2): 291–312.

Lensu, M. and Fritz, J.-S., (eds), (1999) *Value Pluralism, Normative Theory and International Relations*, Basingstoke: Macmillan.

Levinas, E. (1990) 'Reflections on the Philosophy of Hitlerism', trans. S. Hand, *Critical Inquiry*, 17(1): 63–71.

Linklater, A. (1998) *The Transformation of Political Community: ethical foundations of the post-Westphalian era*, Cambridge: Polity Press.

Löwith, K. (1994) *My Life in Germany Before and After 1933: a report*, trans. E. King. Urbana, IL: University of Illinois Press.

—— (1995) *Martin Heidegger and European Nihilism*, trans. G. Steiner. New York: Columbia University Press.

Miami Theory Collective (ed.) (1991) *Community at Loose Ends*, Minneapolis: University of Minnesota Press.

Nancy, J.-L. (1991a) *The Inoperative Community*, trans. P. Connor, L. Garbus, M. Holland and S. Sawhney. Minneapolis: University of Minnesota Press.

—— (1991b) 'Of Being-in-Common', trans. J. Creech. in: Miami Theory Collective (ed.), *Community at Loose Ends*, Minneapolis: University of Minnesota Press: 1–12.

Neaman, E. (2001) 'Review of *Historical Destiny and National Socialism in Heidegger's Being and Time by Johannes Fritsche*', *Constellations*, 8(1): 148–49.

Newell, R. N. (1984) 'Heidegger on Freedom and Community: some political implications of his early thought', *American Political Science Review*, 78(3): 775–84.

Odysseos, L. (2002) 'Radical Phenomenology, Ontology and International Political Theory', *Alternatives*, 27(3): 373–405.

—— (2003) 'On the Way to Global Ethics? Cosmopolitanism, "ethical" selfhood and otherness', *European Journal of Political Theory*, 2(2): 183–207.

—— (2007) *The Subject of Coexistence: otherness in international relations*. Minneapolis: University of Minnesota Press.

Ott, H. (1993) *Martin Heidegger: a political life*, trans. A. Blunden. New York: Basic Books.

O'Sullivan, N. (1997) 'Postmodernism and the Politics of Identity', in K. Dean (ed.), *Politics and the End of Identity*. Aldershot: Ashgate: 234–64.

Richardson, W.J. (1963) *Heidegger: through phenomenology to thought*, the Hague, Netherlands: Martinus Nijhoff.

Rockmore, T. and Margolis, J. (1992) 'Introduction', in Rockmore, T. and Margolis, J., (eds), *The Heidegger Case: on philosophy and politics*, Philadelphia: Temple University Press.

Salem-Wiseman, J. (2003) 'Heidegger's Dasein and the Liberal Conception of the Self', *Political Theory*, 31(4): 533–57.

Schmitt, C. (1996) *The Concept of the Political*, trans. G. Schwab. Chicago: The University of Chicago Press.

Sheehan, T. (2001) 'A Paradigm Shift in Heidegger Research', *Continental Philosophy Review*, 34: 183–202.

Sluga, H. (1993) *Heidegger's Crisis: philosophy and politics in Nazi Germany*, Cambridge: Harvard University Press.

Taylor, C. (1992) *Multiculturalism and the Politics of Recognition: an essay*, A. Gutmann (ed.), Princeton: Princeton University Press.

Tully, J. (1995) *Strange Multiplicity: constitutionalism in an age of diversity*, Cambridge: Cambridge University Press.

Vogel, L. (1994) *The Fragile "We": ethical implications of Heidegger's Being and Time*, Evanston, IL: Northwestern University Press.

Walzer, M. (1994) *Thick and Thin: moral argument at home and abroad*, Notre Dame, IN: University of Notre Dame Press.

Ward, J.F. (1995) *Heidegger's Political Thinking*, Amherst: The University of Massachusetts Press.

Wolin, R. (1990) *The Politics of Being: the political thought of Martin Heidegger*, New York: Columbia University Press.

—— (ed.) (1991) *The Heidegger Controversy: a critical reader*, New York: Columbia University Press.

Wood, D. (1993) 'Reiterating the Temporal: toward a rethinking of Heidegger on time', in J. Sallis (ed.), *Reading Heidegger: commemorations*, Bloomington: Indiana University Press: 136–59.

Žižek, S. (2001), 'The Feminine Excess: can women who hear divine voices find a new social link?', *Millennium: Journal of International Studies*, 30(1): 93–109.

6 The limits of post-territorial political community

From the cosmopolitan politics of global civil society to the biopolitics of the multitude

David Chandler

For many critical theorists it is clear that the era of territorialized political community is over. We appear to have no greater sense of political connection to our fellow citizens than we do to the activities and struggles of people elsewhere in the world. In Britain, where I live and work, my colleagues are much more likely to take an interest in or express concern over the political process of the United States, Kenya or Zimbabwe than to become engaged in domestic political contestation. It would appear that even governing elites can muster little interest in traditional territorial politics with little to distinguish the main parties and the business of government increasingly reduced to technocratic administration and managerialism. Even for governing classes it appears that what happens elsewhere, in Africa, the Balkans or the Middle East, is what really matters, or that key policy issues are ones which necessitate new institutional frameworks of post-territorial co-operation, such as the dangers of global warming or the war on terror. Domestic or territorial politics appears to have been reduced to an empty shell, with little meaning or importance attached to traditional contests of political representation.

The death or hollowing out of territorial politics has created a crisis of traditional frameworks of political community. Territorially-defined and constructed political communities are suffering from a generic lack of cohering values and sentiments, expressed in regular discussions of the meaning and relevance of different national values, symbols and traditions. Governments have great difficulty in legitimating themselves in traditional ways. With the decline in party membership and voting, even holding elections every five years does little to legitimate governing elites or to cohere political programmes for which they can be held to account. Traditional framings of foreign policy in terms of the national interest appear problematic and are often buttressed with claims of ethical or values-based foreign policy which seek to secure the interests of people elsewhere rather than collectively expressing the interests of their citizens. In the face of this crisis in and transformation of traditional ways of understanding and participating in politics it is of little surprise that discussion of the possibilities of post-territorial political community has taken centre stage.

Today there is a growing consensus that expressing political community in territorially-bounded terms is inherently problematic because of its narrow, self-interested and divisive framework, in which radical politics are sidelined. Perhaps even more problematically, territorial political allegiances are held to be the product of uncritical and unreflective understandings of the role of state-based political communities in interpolating subjects which are submissive and uncritical. As the theoretical engagement with the problems or the failure of territorial politics develops, increasingly counterposed to this hollowed out, exclusivist and hierarchical framework are new possibilities of being political and of doing and participating in politics. These possibilities are to be opening up with global interconnectedness and new forms of media and communications. While the traditional state arena, in which modern liberal frameworks of political community first appeared, is now considered to be much less relevant it seems that the possibilities of post-territorial political community are only now about to be realized.

Critical theorists seemingly agree that post-territorial political community is the only possibility for the reconstruction of meaningful political practice in today's globalized world. The possibilities of post-territorial politics became increasingly articulated in the 1990s, mainly by theorists who argued that liberal democratic politics could no longer be practiced meaningfully within the confines of the nation state. Liberal cosmopolitan theorists, such as Mary Kaldor, David Held, Andrew Linklater, Richard Falk and Daniele Archibugi argued for the need for a new cosmopolitan political order, based on the extension of political community beyond the nation state (for example, Archibugi, Held and Köhler 1998). For liberal cosmopolitans, the power of the state was undermined both from above and below: from above it was undermined by globalization, which weakened the controlling capacity of the nation state to both shape policy and to control and marshal resources; from below it was undermined by new expressions of post-territorial political community, organizing and communicating in post-territorialized global space. This new arising political subject was global civil society (Kaldor 1999; Baker 2002; Keane 2003; Chandler 2004a; Baker and Chandler 2005).

The 1990s was the high point for liberal cosmopolitanism as a radical critique of traditional territorially-bound political community which suggested that we were witnessing a progressive transformation of both domestic and international relations. There was an assumption that the forces of immanent cosmopolitan change would be able to challenge the reactionary, exclusivist and divisive domination of the international agenda by nation states, creating a new cosmopolitical era. For many of these advocates the war over Kosovo in 1999 was held to mark the birth of the new cosmopolitan order (Habermas 1999). However, for others the resort to militarism – and the connection between humanitarianism and human rights and a war not sanctioned by the UN Security Council and fought in such as way as to minimize Western casualties – signalled problems in the cosmopolitan agenda being used to legitimize the exercise of Western power and a new interventionist order (Booth 2001). However, it was 9/11 and the birth of the global war on terror which saw a shift towards the critical affirmation of an immanent post-territorial community in opposition to the claims of a new cosmopolitan global order.

The development of academic perspectives of post-territorial political community in opposition to those of liberal cosmopolitanism pre-dated 9/11 and were shaped by the development of anti-globalization campaigns and environmental protests. A radical alternative vision of post-territorial community was formulated by Michael Hardt and Antonio Negri, first in *Empire* (2001) and later in *Multitude* (2006). For Hardt and Negri, post-territorial political community is derived from the shared desires of the 'multitude', the universal people united in struggle against domination:

> The virtuality of world space constitutes the first determination of the movements of the multitude … [which] must achieve a global citizenship. The multitude's resistance to bondage – the struggle against the slavery of belonging to a nation, an identity, and a people, and thus the desertion from sovereignty and the limits it places on subjectivity – is entirely positive.
>
> (2001: 361–2)

Since 2000, the radical critique of liberal cosmopolitan frameworks has been enhanced by the translations into English of Michel Foucault's lectures at the Collège de France (2003; 2007) and the critical work of post-Foucaultian theorists such as Giorgio Agamben (1998; 2005). For these critics, the Westphalian or UN-based international order based on the sovereign equality of nation states has been challenged both from above and below: above by the shifting needs of post-material or biopolitical processes of production (Hardt and Negri 2006; Virno 2004) cohered through the networked power of Empire (Hardt and Negri 2001); and below by the resistance to neoliberal biopolitical global governance, through the multitude.

In this chapter, I seek to draw out the similarities in approach to post-territorial political community as expressed by both the 1990s liberal cosmopolitans and the 2000s radical post-structuralists. First, that both approaches derive their strengths from their rejection of state-based political community rather than from their capacity to demonstrate the existence or strength of alternative post-territorial political community. Second, that key to both approaches is the degradation of modern liberal conceptions of the rights-bearing subjects: once the connection between citizenship and political community is broken then political community lacks any objective conceptional grounding. Third, the chapter seeks to highlight that discussions about post-territorial political community fail to recognize that particular individuals or struggles appear to directly confront power – either in the form of elite advocacy or oppositional protest – precisely because the mediating links of political community are so attenuated.

My conclusion is that the death of politics and hollowing out of the meaningful nature of representation constitutes the death of political community. In the 1990s the discourse of liberal cosmopolitanism sought to redefine the modern liberal frameworks of rights, democracy and the rule of law to rescue a legitimizing liberal discourse despite the lack of mediating links between governing elites and society. The was a discourse which sought to respond to the death of political community rather than one which reflected the birth of a newer or more expansive one at a global level. In the 2000s the hollow nature of liberal cosmopolitan claims stood clearly exposed in the new hierarchies of power and domination. The radical discourse of post-structuralist, post-territorial political community sought to critique the international order as a product of global liberalism, however the nature of the critique, I suggest, is in content and form little different from that of 1990s cosmopolitanism.

Regarding the potential of post-territorial political community, it will be argued that there is little difference between the frameworks of the post-structuralist critics and the liberal cosmopolitans because the groundwork of the critique was already laid by the crisis within liberal thinking. It was the self-proclaimed liberal cosmopolitan theorists who fundamentally challenged the foundational liberal ontology which established the modern liberal order through deriving political legitimacy from the rights of autonomous individual subjects. The liberal basis of political order and of political community on the basis of shared rights and duties had already corroded from within. In the 1990s this was given clear political expression in the liberal critique of the division between the domestic and the international and the desire to 'domesticate' the international order, reconstituting political community on the basis of the human rather than the citizen. As we shall see, the post-structuralist critique of this order has tended to buttress the claims made in this ideological framing of post-territorial political community rather than challenging them.

The political project of post-territorial political community

The debates around the constitution of cosmopolitan political community in the 1990s and 2000s revolve around different understandings of the emergence of an immanent universalizing political community, capable of overcoming exclusion and hierarchy in international relations. For the 1990s critics, this universalizing power which sought to undermine the power of state sovereignty and privilege the rights of cosmopolitan individuals was often termed global civil society. This universal was grounded in a view of an emerging cosmopolitan or universalist or global consciousness in the wake of the ending of the Cold War (for example, Shaw 1994). The discourse of universal rights challenged the prerogatives of state sovereignty; therefore it was assumed that states were not capable of originating and bearing this discourse. The leading agents of cosmopolitan political approaches were assumed to be non-state actors, primarily NGOs, often described as 'norm entrepreneurs' (Finnemore and Sikkink 1998). The rise of this universalist discourse was often understood in a social constructivist framework, based on the 'power of ideas' and the importance of global information networks (Risse, Ropp and Sikkink 1999). For liberal cosmopolitans such as Mary Kaldor, since the end of the Cold War we have been witnessing a fundamental political struggle between global civil society and state-based approaches (Kaldor 2003; 2007).

For the 1990s critics, the universal discourse was driven by progressive agency 'from below' and therefore was a challenge to power. In our more disillusioned 2000s, particularly since 9/11, there has arisen an alternative critical reading of the discourse of cosmopolitan universality and the nature of post-territorial political community. Often a starting point for these critics is the work of German legal

theorist Carl Schmitt, who, writing in the mid Twentieth Century was highly critical of US claims to uphold universal cosmopolitan rights in opposition to what he
saw as the European view of international law which privileged sovereign rights
(see Schmitt 2003). Schmitt claimed famously that 'whoever invokes humanity
wants to cheat' (Schmitt 1996: 54). Rather than a new progressive liberal universal
subject arising from below, critical theorists in the 2000s saw the dangers of the liberal discourse as one which uncritically legitimated new totalizing mechanisms of
intervention and regulation from above. Michael Hardt and Antonio Negri in their
path-breaking book *Empire* (2001, first published in 2000) saw global neo-liberal
governance as superseding the state-based international system, with the US no
longer viewed in traditional terms of state-based imperialist power but as a representative of the universalizing power of Empire.

In a direct challenge to the advocates of liberal cosmopolitan approaches, these
critical approaches have been primarily constructed within post-structuralist
frameworks; drawing on theorists such as Carl Schmitt, Michel Foucault and
Giorgio Agamben and suggesting that a new universal subject may be emerging
from below, but in opposition to the cosmopolitan discourse of power promoted by
the liberal advocates of the 1990s. In the recent work of Mark Duffield (2007)
Vivienne Jabri (2007a) and Costas Douzinas (2007) this framework is melded
with post-Foucauldian readings of cosmopolitan rights as an exclusionary and
hierarchical exercise of biopower and the constitution of an alternative political
community in the struggle against the universalizing power of biopolitical
global governance. In this framework, new global governmental practices are highlighted which are legitimized through the privileging of declarations of the rights of
the human over and above the formal rights framework of sovereignty and non-
intervention. For Duffield, the focus on cosmopolitan human rights, expressed in
the discourses of state failure and the merging of security and development, creates
a biopolitical blank cheque to override the formal rights of sovereignty on the
basis of the needs of securing the human. For Jabri, the recasting of military
intervention in terms of the human undermines the state-based order and the line
between domestic and global politics, constituting a new global biopolitical
order. For Douzinas, human rights discourses undermine territorial forms of
sovereignty but enable the emergence of a new 'super-sovereign' of global hegemonic power.

Here, the universalism of liberal cosmopolitan theorists is 'stood on its head' to
argue that it is the universalizing interests of power, understood in vague terms of
biopolitical neo-liberal global governance, rather than the genuinely cosmopolitan
ethics of empowerment, which drives the discursive practices of regimes of global
governance. As the 1990s liberal discourse has been challenged by the 2000s post-
structuralist discourse, we seem to be caught up in a contestation over which academics have the most progressive or radical understandings: of hierarchies of
power – as a product of 'statist' exercises of national self-interest or as a product of
new global governmentalities; and of post-territorial political community – as a
response and opposition to these hierarchies, either in the form of global civil society or multitude.

However, it is not clear whether this contestation in terms of ontological framings of the relations and dynamics of power or of alternative political subjects of post-territorial political community reflect much more than the starting positions of the critical academic theorists engaged in this contestation. It seems that the radical differences between those who espouse and critique global liberal ontologies, and thereby read post-territorial community in liberal or post-structuralist framings, are derived less from empirical investigations than from their own normative aspirations. For cosmopolitan theorists, their normative aspirations for a more ethical and engaged foreign policy agenda were given added legitimacy through linking their demands with those of activist NGOs and assertions of global civil society's imminent existence. As liberal cosmopolitan Mary Kaldor asserts, the concept of global or transnational civil society is on the one hand an analytical device, but on the other hand, and more importantly, 'a political project' (1999: 195).

Similarly, for post-structuralist critics, the struggle against Empire is alleged to be more than philosophical idealism on the basis of the immanent existence of the multitude. Just as with the concept of global civil society, Hardt and Negri's multitude is partly framed as an abstract heuristic device (2006: 221). But more importantly it is a normative project, in that it requires a political project to bring it into being, rather than merely being 'latent and implicit in our social being' (2006: 221). Hardt and Negri describe this mixture of abstraction and normative wish as illustrating that multitude 'has a strange double temporality: always-already and not-yet' (2006: 222). It appears that the new post-territorial political communities held to be coming into existence conflate empirical and normative aspirations in the critique of the perceived hierarchies of power: either being seen as constituted against state-based domination of the international or against the biopolitics of Empire.

At the level of discursive analysis (as we shall see) the choice between these two approaches can easily appear to be a purely subjective one. Neither one satisfactorily grounds the existence of a new emerging universal subject capable of constituting post-territorial political community as the agent of cosmopolitical regimes or of post-cosmopolitical resistance to these regimes. In both, the subject which demonstrated the existence of and creates or produces post-territorial political community is grounded in a way which confuses normative political critique with empirical analysis. Both approaches suggest that traditional territorial political communities have been fundamentally undermined by the changing nature of social relations – by globalization or by biopolitical production processes. These changing social relations are held to have undermined territorial political community through the deconstruction of the unitary assumptions involved in modern liberal democratic political theory. However, they have been much less successful in demonstrating that new post-territorial forms of political community have been constructed in their stead.

What is clear is that in the name of post-territorial political community liberal and radical critics have sought to represent the crisis of legitimacy of representative political bodies as a product of political contestation emerging from post-territorial actors. The claims of the critics have been bolstered by the fact that they argue they are made on behalf of the excluded and marginalized, and thereby express both a moral and political challenge to power. Both the advocates of global civil society and the radical critics who counterpose the struggles of the multitude express their views on the possibility of post-territorial community in terms which privilege advocacy over representation. The fact that both global civil society and the multitude are immanent rather than existing enables the radical academic to speak on their behalf in the framework of advocacy, despite arguments which emphasize the autonomy and independence of the actors about to be constituted in new post-territorial framings of political community.

Political community without political subjects

Neither the liberal nor the post-structuralist visions of post-territorial community contain modern liberal rights-bearing subjects. For neither is there a universalizing sphere of legal or political equality constituted by autonomous rights-bearing subjects. The liberal cosmopolitical critique of liberal democratic frameworks of political community is precisely that they are not able to empower and protect minorities and the marginal or excluded and that therefore there needs to be an external level of regulatory enforcement of cosmopolitan rights. The biopolitical critique of the discourse of cosmopolitan rights is that rather than a mechanism of empowerment it is an exercise of power. Rather than critique cosmopolitan rights for their fictitious equality (Chandler 2003), the post-structuralists wish to portray all rights constructions – whether posed in terms of the citizen or the human – as equally oppressive and hierarchical.

The post-structuralist critique in fact reflects a very similar view of citizen rights to the liberal cosmopolitan vision: expressing a similar aspiration to evade the problematic question of political representation and the constitution of political community. For cosmopolitan human rights advocates there is no distinct difference between human rights and democratic and civil rights. All rights claims are seen to be equally empowering and able to tame power in the name of ethics and equality. Here, the extension of cosmopolitan frameworks of global governance is read to be the extension of the realm of freedom and a restriction on state sovereign power. The post-structuralist response is to argue that the liberal discourse reveals the truth in its blurring of the relationship between democracy and dictatorship, law as *ad hoc* and arbitrary power and law as a reflection of the autonomy and agency of legally constituted subjects (Agamben 1998: 10).

For the critics of cosmopolitan rights regimes, the extension of a discourse of rights and law merely enhances the power of liberal governance. Indeed, Giorgio Agamben has captured well the ethico-juridical blurring of human rights regimes as a 'state of exception', by which he means not a dictatorship but a hollowing out or emptying of the content of law:

> the state of exception has today reached its maximum worldwide deployment. The normative aspect of law can thus be obliterated and contradicted with impunity by a governmental violence that – while ignoring international law

externally and producing a permanent state of exception internally – nevertheless still claims to be applying the law.

(Agamben 2005: 87)

However, in reading the state of exception as the essential nature of the sovereign state and law, Agamben argues that the lesson is that progressive politics can never operate within the modern state form: 'Politics has suffered a lasting eclipse because it has been contaminated by law, seeing itself, at best, as constituent power (that is violence that makes law), when it is not reduced to merely the power to negotiate with the law' (2005: 88). In his earlier work, *Homo Sacer*, he argued:

> It is almost as if ... every decisive political event were double-sided: the spaces, the liberties, and the rights won by individuals in their conflicts with central powers always simultaneously prepared a tacit but increasing inscription of the individual's lives within the state order, thus offering a new and more dreadful foundation for the very sovereign power from which they wanted to liberate themselves.
>
> (1998: 121)

For both the liberal cosmopolitan advocates of human rights and the radical post-structuralist critics there is no specific understanding of the problem of cosmopolitan rights as based on non-socially constituted legal subjects (Lewis 1998). For both liberal cosmopolitan theorists and post-structuralists, rights regimes are understood to be independent and prior to rights subjects. For liberal advocates, it is precisely because the poor and excluded cannot autonomously enforce their rights that an external agency needs to step in to empower them. For post-structuralists this is clear in the view that the declaration of rights constitutes the subject; rights precede and interpolate the subject (Douzinas 2007: 92). Douzinas stresses the darker side of rights; 'the inexorable rise of registration, classification and control of individuals and populations' (2007: 129). Post-structuralist critics exaggerate the claims of rights as independent from subjects to view all rights claims as representing not citizens but non-subjects (Agamben's 'bare life').

For radical post-structuralists, the ambiguity of cosmopolitan frameworks of political community – which can only empower those who decide on the content and *ad hoc* implementation – are read to be, not an attack on modern liberal democratic frameworks of rights and law, but instead essentialized as the key to understanding the modern state as a biopolitical power. The radical critics critique the claims of the liberal cosmopolitans by essentializing them as modern liberal rights claims per se. This one-sided understanding of rights, through breaking their connection to rights subjects, produces in an exaggerated form the cosmopolitan critique of the political sphere of representation. For liberal advocates of cosmopolitan rights, representational claims are problematic because they may undermine rights protections and regulatory power needs to exist above the nation state; for post-structuralists any participation in the political sphere of the territorial state is inherently disempowering.

The understanding of rights in both liberal cosmopolitan and post-structuralist frameworks is crucial to enable the move from territorialized understandings of political community to post-territorial constructions. For modern liberal political theory it was the rights framework which reflected and institutionalized the existence of a political community of equal rights-bearing subjects. The liberal political ontology has the autonomous rights-bearing individual as the foundational subject of law and politics as a universal sphere of formal equality. The rule of law and the legitimacy of government was derived from the consent and accountability of rights-holding citizens.

In the frameworks of cosmopolitan and biopolitical framings of post-territorial political community, political community is no longer constituted on the basis of a rights framework of autonomous subjects. Formal frameworks of politics and law are held to come prior to the political subject (which is reinterpreted as the object of administration and regulation rather than as a rights subject). For liberal cosmopolitans, the existence of rights (law) prior to and independently of political subjects is held to legitimize regimes of international intervention and regulation, while for post-structuralists the autonomy of law is read as the autonomy of power to interpolate and create the ruled subject. In both frameworks, by theoretical construction, there is no longer a distinction between the citizen and the non-citizen as rights claims are merely a reflection of the claims of rule made by power.

Once the construction of political community is freed from political and legal frameworks of rights, both liberal and post-structural approaches are free to establish the existence of political community at the global level, as a post-territorial construction. The only problem with this construction is the question of how political community can be constituted without the rights and duties of citizenship. The approaches to this problem will be briefly addressed in the next section.

Individuals and the 'community'

In modern liberal theorizing it is the rights and duties of citizenship which constitute the shared bonds of political community. The political sphere is clearly distinct as the public sphere of law and politics from the private sphere of particularist identities, hobbies and interests. Political community is therefore distinct from the bonds of family, friendship or groupings of special interests. What makes political community distinct is its public nature, which forces people to engage with others whom they do not necessarily know or agree with in order to contest representational alternatives. It seems clear that the attenuation of political contestation, of the struggle between Left and Right, has meant that political community has less meaning for many of us than other (non-political) communities with which we may participate or identify.

The dismissal of the bonds of citizenship constituted by modern liberal rights frameworks, based on the autonomous rights-bearing subject, by the advocates of post-territorial political community means that the bonds which are constitutive of post-territorial community are much more difficult to locate. For cosmopolitan theorist John Keane, global civil society, constituted by networked actors, constitutes a form of political community, albeit a 'paradoxical' one:

It refers to a vast, sprawling non-governmental constellation of many institutionalized structures, associations and networks within which individual and group actors are interrelated and functionally interdependent. As a society of societies, it is 'bigger' and 'weightier' than any individual actor or organization or combined sum of its thousands of constituent parts – most of whom, paradoxically, neither 'know' each other nor have any chance of ever meeting each other face-to-face.

(2003: 11)

The question of engagement and interconnection between the multitude of networked actors constituting the alternative framework for post-territorial political community is a problematic one, which reveals the lack of mediation between the particular and the 'community' or the 'many'. This lack of mediation is highlighted in Hardt and Negri's description of the multitude as neither one nor many. They assert that the multitude 'violates all such numerical distinctions. It is both one and many' thereby allegedly threatening all the principles of order (2006: 139). They assert that if the multitude were a unified political movement 'then it could be known, confronted and defeated' and if instead it were 'many separate, isolated social threats, they too could be managed' (2006: 140). The threat of the multitude is held to stem from the fact that: 'it is composed of innumerable elements that remain different, one from the other, and yet communicate, collaborate, and act in common' (2006: 140). Hardt and Negri seek to celebrate the lack of mediating links by insisting against any collapse of the particular into the universal.

The multitude does not, in fact, constitute a political community anymore than liberal cosmopolitan constructions of global civil society (Chandler 2004b; 2007). Hardt and Negri merely 'seek to demonstrate that there exist sufficient common bases, interaction, and communication among the various singular figures of production to *make possible* the construction of the multitude' (2006: 158) and that, in their understanding, biopolitical production 'has *the potential* to create a new, alternative society' (2006: 159, emphasis added). There is no mediation between the particular, at the level of the individual or the particular struggle and any collective political subject. This lack of mediation is given a radical content in the poststructuralist desire to critique and deconstruct the cosmopolitan universals used to justify new regimes of global intervention. Post-territorial political community is constructed precisely on the basis of preserving the individual and the particular. This makes any declaration of 'community' a highly abstract one. As Vivienne Jabri argues in expressing the post-territorial alternative of 'political cosmopolitanism', the alternative is 'a conception of solidarity without community'; one which does not assume any shared vision or views but in fact seeks to deconstruct universal perspectives as merely the project of hegemony (2007b: 728).

It is not clear what the theorists of post-territorial political community – whether in its liberal cosmopolitan or post-liberal post-cosmopolitan forms – have to offer in terms of any convincing thesis that new forms of political community are in the process of emerging. Political community necessarily takes a territorial form at the level of the organization for political representation on the basis of the nation state (in a world without a world government), but has a post- or non-territorial content at the level of ideological and political affiliation. This has meant that support and solidarity could be offered for numerous struggles taking place on an international level (given formal frameworks in the nineteenth and twentieth century of internationals of anarchists, workers, women and nationalists) (see, for example, Colas 2000).

For the content of territorial political community to be meaningful does not mean that politics can be confined to territorial boundaries: the contestation of ideologies, ideas and practices has never been a purely national endeavour. However, without a formal focal point of accountability – of government – there can be no political community, no framework binding and subordinating individuals as political subjects. The critique of territorial political community and assertion of the birth of post-territorial political community in fact seeks to evade the problem of the implosion of political community in terms of collective engagement in social change. The death of politics and with it the death of political community is thereby over politicized by both 1990s liberals and 2000s radicals.

Without the death of political community there would be little discussion of the meaning of post-territorial politics. Hardt and Negri highlight this when they counterpose post-territorial networked struggles of the multitude to territorial struggles, revealing that: 'Many of these [territorial] movements, especially when they are defeated, begin to transform and take on [post-territorial] network characteristics'. (2006: 83) So, for example, it was the defeat of the Zapatistas which freed them to take up life as a virtual internet struggle. It was political defeat and marginalization which meant that they could take up an even more radical challenge than confronting the Mexican government, that of the postmodern subject, attempting to 'change the world without taking power' (2006: 85). The failure of modernist political projects based on the collective subject is clear; as Hardt and Negri observe: 'The people is missing'. (2006: 191) But unlike Paolo Virno's theorizing of the multitude (2004) as reflecting merely the crisis of the state form in terms of the plurality and incommensurability of political experiences – i.e., the lack of political community – Hardt and Negri seek to see the multitude as the constitutive agent of the postmodern and post-territorial political world.

Many authors have understood the rejection of territorial politics as the rejection of the ontological privileging of state power. Fewer have understood that this implies the rejection of political engagement itself. Politics without the goal of power would be purely performative or an expression of individual opinions. Politics has been considered important because community was constituted not through the private sphere, but through the public sphere in which shared interests and perspectives were generated through engagement and debate with the goal of building and creating collective expressions of interests. Without the goal of power, i.e. the capacity to shape decision-making, political engagement would be a private expression rather than a public one. There would be no need to attempt to convince another person in an argument or to persuade someone why one policy was better than another. In fact in rejecting territorial politics it is not power or the state which is problematized – power will still exist and states are still seen as important actors even in post-territorial frameworks. The essential target of these critical theorists is political engagement with citizens, i.e., the necessity to legit-imize one's views and aspirations through the struggle for representation. For both liberal and radical views of post-territorial political community political contesta-tion is unnecessary. Political views are considered self-legitimating without the need to engage in politics – i.e., bypassing society or the masses – and directly expressing the claims to power.

This evasion of society, this retreat from political community, is expressed in radical terms as the need to maintain difference. Yet political community is only constituted on the basis of the potential to agree on the basis of shared, collective interests. The refusal to subordinate difference to unity is merely another expres-sion of the rejection of political engagement. Political community cannot be con-stituted on the basis of post-territorial politics in which there is no central authority and no subordination to any agreed programme. For Hardt and Negri: 'The multi-tude is an irreducible multiplicity; the singular social differences that constitute the multitude must always be expressed and can never be flattened into sameness, unity, identity, or indifference' (2006: 105).

The missing essence of political community constitutes post-territorial political community: the lack of common aims in terms of practice (the ontological primacy of state power) and the lack of common aspirations or goals on a broader ideologi-cal level (political or philosophical agreement). All that is left is networked com-munication. For Hardt and Negri: 'The common does not refer to traditional notions of either the community or the public; it is based on the communication among singularities' (2006: 204). While communication is important there is little point in communication without purpose, what the multitude lacks is precisely this subjective purpose which could bind them and constitute political community. As Hardt and Negri note: 'The multitude needs a political project to bring it into exis-tence' (2006: 212).

In the absence of popular engagement in politics it could be argued that Jean Baudrillard's warning *In the Shadow of the Silent Majorities* (1983) of the simu-lacrum of the contestation over political power is being fully realized:

> [Out of the disengagement of the masses] some would like to make a new source of revolutionary energy … They would like to give it meaning and to reinstate it in its very banality, as historical negativity … Final somersault of the intellectuals to exalt insignificance, to promote non-sense into the order of sense. Banality, inertia, apoliticism used to be fascist; they are now in the process of becoming revolutionary – without changing meaning … .
>
> (1983: 40)

The demise of political community reflecting the attenuation of political contesta-tion has been reinterpreted by theorists of post-territorial community in ways which over-politicize the death of politics by constructing fictional forms of community alleged to articulate particular theorists own normative beliefs (whether liberal or post-structuralist). This is done through, first, dismissing the idea of political community as one based on rights of equality and representation, thus blurring the meaning of the political. Second, dismissing the idea of community as one based on mediating links of engagement in a common political project, thus blurring the meaning of community.

Cosmopolitan theorists remove the distinction between the citizen and the non-citizen to constitute a political engagement based on the inequalities of advocacy. However, the post-structuralists argue that even engagement at the level of advocacy is impossible and that awareness of the Other is all that political engagement can constitute without becoming oppressive. Mark Duffield, for example, suggests that the only alternative to the hierarchies of liberal advocacy is to assert that we are all victims of governmentalism: 'we are all governed and therefore in solidarity' (2007: 232). Apparently we should focus on what we share with post-colonial societies, not offering the hierarchical 'solidarity' of development or political autonomy but instead the solidarity of learning from the poor and being marginalized as equals; once humbled: 'through a practical politics based on the solidarity of the governed we can aspire to opening ourselves to the spontaneity of unpredictable encounters' (2007: 234).

Vivienne Jabri argues that we need a new cosmopolitanism, but one that reflectively recognizes that 'any discourses that view their worth in universal terms, are but expressions of "forces of domination" based upon explicit principles of exclusion' (2007a: 177). Instead, the *'politics* of peace' [emphasis in original] emphasizes a solidarity which:

> makes no claim to universality, nor is it teleological in outlook... Rather, the politics of peace expresses local and often rather invisible acts, expressions of solidarity that are neither hierarchically defined nor suggestive of any claim to universality.
>
> (2007: 177)

For Costas Douzinas, political opposition has to take the form of a 'cosmopolitanism to come' of individualized protest:

> Dissatisfaction with nation, state, the international comes from a bond between singularities. What binds me to an Iraqi or a Palestinian is not membership of humanity, citizenship of the world or of a community but a protest against citizenship, against nationality and thick community. This bond cannot be contained in traditional concepts of community and cosmos or of polis and state. What binds my world to that of others is our absolute singularity and total responsibility beyond citizen and human, beyond national and international. The cosmos to come is the world of each unique one, of whoever or anyone; the polis, the infinite number of encounters of singularities.
>
> (2007: 295)

Post-structuralist constructions of post-territorial political community celebrate the atomization and dislocation of the individual with the implosion of political community. But what connects atomized individuals is merely the lack of political community. The cosmopolitanism 'to come' looks rather like the world we are already living in. Post-territorial political community is the world which exists but radically reinterpreted. This is why global civil society is both a descriptive and normative concept and why multitude 'has a strange double temporality: always-already and not-yet' (Hardt and Negri 2006: 222). As Baudrillard presciently noted, once the political subject, the people, are disengaged from politics, the vacuum left can be reinterpreted by radical academics to suit their predilections without reality changing.

Conclusion

Despite the differences in their views of whether the development of cosmopolitan political regimes are to be welcomed or criticized, both liberal advocates and post-structuralist critics seek to ground their position of critique on the basis of their 'global solidarity' with the non-Western poor and marginalized. Both seek a vicarious radicalism or legitimacy in their distancing from representational demands and their ability to stand outside of politics seen as an instrumental aspiration for power.

The rejection of political representation by the advocates and the critics of cosmopolitan community demonstrates the ideological nature of radical discourse today. The further radical political claims shift from engagement with the society the more radical they become. The advocates of cosmopolitan political community in the 1990s were the first to distance themselves from state-based politics, finding a freedom in the free-floating rights of global advocacy. The post-structuralist critics of the 2000s exaggerate this rejection of society, finding an even more radical way to express their subjectivity and at the same time a more radical critique of the prison or 'concentration camp' of state-based politics.

In the 1990s the implosion of political community was evaded by liberal cosmopolitans claiming the elite rights of advocacy on behalf of the excluded and marginal. In the 2000s the radical critique of this bifurcated framing of political community (which empowered Western elites at the expense of denying the subjectivity and autonomy of the non-Western Other) was critiqued by the radical theorists of multitude or post-cosmopolitanism. However, in the absence of a political subject constituting a new framework of political community, the result is one of rejection of the political sphere and political engagement under the banner, not of advocacy on behalf of the Other, but of respect for and awareness of the Other.

Bibliography

Agamben, G. (1998) *Homo Sacer: sovereign power and bare life*, Stanford: Stanford University Press.
—— (2005) *State of Exception*, Chicago: University of Chicago Press.
Archibugi, D., Held, D. and Köhler, M. (eds) (1998) *Re-Imagining Political Community: studies in cosmopolitan democracy*, Cambridge: Polity Press.
Baker, G. (2002) *Civil Society and Democratic Theory: alternative voices*, London: Routledge.
Baker, G. and Chandler D. (eds) (2005) *Global Civil Society: contested futures*, London: Routledge.

Baudrillard, J. (1983) *In the Shadow of the Silent Majorities*, New York: Semiotext(e).
—— (1987) *Forget Foucault*, New York: Semiotext(e).
Booth, K. (2001) 'Ten Flaws of Just Wars', in K. Booth (ed.) *The Kosovo Tragedy: the human rights Dimensions*, London: Frank Cass.
Chandler, D. (2003) 'New Rights for Old? Cosmopolitan citizenship and the critique of state sovereignty', *Political Studies*, 51(2), 2003: 339–56.
—— (2004a) *Constructing Global Civil Society: morality and power in international relations*, Basingstoke: Palgrave.
—— (2004b) 'Building Global Civil Society "From Below"', *Millennium: Journal of International Studies*, 33(2): 313–39.
—— (2007) 'Deriving Norms from "Global Space": the limits of cosmopolitan approaches to global civil society theorizing', *Globalizations*, 4(2): 283–98.
Colas, A. (2002) *International Civil Society: social movements in world politics*, Cambridge: Polity.
Douzinas, C. (2007) *Human Rights and Empire: the political philosophy of cosmopolitanism*, London: Routledge Cavendish.
Duffield, M. (2007) *Development, Security and Unending War: governing the world of peoples*, Cambridge: Polity.
Finnemore, M. and Sikkink, K. (1998) 'International Norm Dynamics and Political Change', *International Organization*, 52(4): 887–917.
Foucault, M. (2003) *"Society Must Be Defended": lectures at the Collège de France 1975–1976*, London: Allen Lane/Penguin.
—— (2007) *Security, Territory, Population: lectures at the Collège de France 1977–1978*, Basingstoke: Palgrave.
Habermas, J. (1999) '*Bestialität und Humanität*', *Die Zeit*, 54:18, 29 April. Franz Solms-Laubach; trans. available at: http://www.theglobalsite.ac.uk/press/011habermas.htm.
Hardt, M. and Negri, A. (2001) *Empire*, New York: Harvard University Press.
—— (2006) *Multitude: war and democracy in the age of empire*, London: Penguin.
Jabri, V. (2007a) *War and the Transformation of Global Politics*, Basingstoke: Palgrave.
—— (2007b) 'Solidarity and Spheres of Culture: the cosmopolitan and the postcolonial', *Review of International Studies*, 33: 715–28.
Kaldor, M. (1999) 'Transnational Civil Society', in T. Dunne and N. J. Wheeler (eds) *Human Rights in Global Politics*, Cambridge: Cambridge University Press.
—— (2003) *Global Civil Society: an answer to war*, Cambridge: Polity.
—— (2007) *Human Security*, Cambridge: Polity.
Keane, J. (2003) *Global Civil Society?*, Cambridge: Polity.
Lewis, N. (1998) 'Human Rights, Law and Democracy in an Unfree World', in T. Evans (ed.) *Human Rights Fifty Years On: a reappraisal*, Manchester: Manchester University Press.
Risse, T., Ropp, S.C. and Sikkink, K. (eds) (1999) *The Power of Human Rights: international norms and domestic change*, Cambridge: Cambridge University Press.
Schmitt, C. (1996) *The Concept of the Political*, Chicago: University of Chicago Press.
—— (2003) *The Nomos of the Earth: in the international law of the Jus Publicum Europaeum*, New York: Telos Press.
Selby, J. (2007) 'Engaging Foucault: discourse, liberal governance, and the limits of Foucauldian IR', *International Relations*, 21(3): 324–45.
Shaw, M. (1994) *Global Society and International Relations: sociological concepts and political perspectives*, Cambridge: Polity.
Virno, P. (2004) *A Grammar of the Multitude*, New York: Semiotext(e).

Part III

Learning from the past and understanding future transformations

7 Rethinking political community from neglected places

Giuseppe Ballacci

According to the tradition of rhetoric one of the most important moments in the composition of discourse was that of *inventio*, that is, the ingenious and creative finding of the 'places', or *loci*, from where to draw all the relevant arguments about the particular subject matter in question (Cicero 1949a: I.7; 1949b: 6 ff). This search required the ability to move along all the different points of view and to judge their pertinence and verisimilitude, to find the right ideas in each particular case (Quintilian 1920: III.3 5–7). This particular aspect of rhetoric was known as *ars topica*. The great Humanist Giambattista Vico, one of the canonical authors of this tradition, thought of it as a sort of first operation of the mind. Indeed, Vico considered *topica*:

> an art of regulating well the primary operation of our mind, by noting the commonplaces that must all be gone over in order to know all there is in a thing that one desires to know well; that is, completely.
>
> (Vico 1948: ¶497)

It was therefore an operation fundamental to making a sound judgment: 'For one can not form a sound judgment of a thing without having complete knowledge of it; and topics is the art of finding in anything all that is in it' (Vico 1994: 124).

This effort to find all the 'places' of a subject, all the points of view, in authors such as Vico, became a formidable art in making 'minds inventive' and consequently discourse eloquent and copious (Vico 1948: ¶498). From his rhetorical education, in the midst of the Cartesian rationalist revolution, Vico reminded his contemporaries that along with critique (the art of making arguments exact), philosophy is made of fantasy: not only is it necessary to establish the coherence of a particular argument, but also at the same time to find new ways of looking at it. This creative endeavor is led by the faculties of *ingenium* and *fantasia* that permit perception of the common nature of apparently distant phenomena, establishing meaningful connections between them (Vico 1953: 294, 303).

I believe that contemporary political theory should listen to and take notice of this old rhetorical lesson. Political theory can be conceived in the manner of Sheldon Wolin as a tradition of thought about some central questions regarding life in community. Through their imaginative and speculative genius, great authors constantly re-signify and re-interpret this area of human existence, leaving behind them something like a tradition: that is, a common field of inquiry, a subject-matter, and a certain common language to deal with it. In times of crisis, the contours and main features of this tradition start to vanish and to lose coherence, with the consequence that dialogue becomes more and more difficult, but also with the opportunity for opening a range of possibilities for the creation of new meanings and interpretations (Wolin 2004: 4–23).

Nowadays we probably find ourselves in one of these situations. The questioning of the great Enlightened political projects, which by now has reached the status of a new paradigm, has raised the necessity of reconsidering the basic concepts in political theory, of reformulating its vocabulary. Some fundamental political topics such as the meanings of democracy, the interrelation between inclusion and exclusion in the creation and maintenance of political community, the limits and possibilities of dialogue, and so on, have been under scrutiny by thinkers with a new momentum. However, I have the impression that this theoretical effort is in a certain measure deficient in *ars topica*, being almost exclusively moved by the critique impulse. What is missing, in my view, is that imaginative capacity Vico was reclaiming for his contemporaries – consideration of a topic from different points of view.

Indeed, even if one considers the postmodern moment as a real point of inflection with respect to Enlightenment, it is evident that both share at their roots the same basic philosophical impulse: that of critique. One of the most emblematic postmodern authors, Michel Foucault, in his famous essay about Enlightenment, 'what is Enlightenment' (Focucault 1981), tries to define the spirit of that period by commenting on that other famous text where the Enlightened philosopher *par excellence*, Kant, answered this same question. In a quite unexpected move, more than questioning filiations, interrupting traditions, and marking differences, Foucault evokes a deep commonality between that way of philosophizing and his own. That commonality does not lie in some shared theoretical views, but, deeper, in what he calls an attitude and an ethos (in the Greek conception of the term):

> I have been seeking, on the one hand, to emphasize the extent to which a type of philosophical interrogation – one that simultaneously problematizes man's relation to the present, man's historical mode of being, and the constitution of the self as an autonomous subject – is rooted in the Enlightenment. On the other hand, I have been seeking to stress that the thread that may connect us with the Enlightenment is not faithfulness to doctrinal elements, but rather the permanent reactivation of an attitude – that is, of a *philosophical ethos* that could be described as a *permanent critique of our historical era*.
> (Foucault 1984: 42; emphasis added)

This 'philosophical ethos' defined as 'a permanent critique of our historical era' is at the roots of Foucault's philosophical effort as it was for Kant's. It is the basic drive that moves them both.

Critique is of course a fundamental activity because of its striving for truthfulness.

One of its limitations though is its dependence and subordination to the position it wants to criticize, which forces thought to move in a direction partially decided from the start. Obviously this is well known, and Foucault for one recognized it, but its consequences are rarely explored (Foucault 1990). In rhetoric, complementing critique (*iudicium*) with *inventio* was so important that the latter constituted the subject of a specific art (the *ars topica*), and Vico even considered it, as we have seen, a sort of first and fundamental operation of thought. The training in *ars topica* required from the orator a particular curriculum of studies and the proper exercise of *ingenium* and fantasy.[1]

In the general climate of reformulation, reinvention and reconsideration of basic political concepts, political community is one of the topics that have drawn more attention. It is also a good example of the lack of *ars topica*. Thinking about political community, one of the first and most important questions one comes upon is that of exclusion and inclusion. Indeed, in contemporary political theory there has been wide interest in this theme, whose most interesting result has been the denunciation of the exclusionary consequences of the modern and liberal cosmopolitan conception of community. Roberto Esposito, for instance, has pointed out that the mythification of democracy through its total identification with the Good, and the consequent pretension of the democratic community to represent a whole without division, risks eliminating difference (Esposito 1993). In similar terms, William Connolly has shown the incapacity of liberal thought to recognize and deal with the exclusionary consequences of what he has called the 'paradox of difference', that is, the suppression of difference implied by each attempt to constitute and maintain an identity, such as that of a political community (Connolly 1991: 92).[2] It is possible to find similar accents in other important thinkers such as Giorgio Agamben, Jacques Derrida, Chantal Mouffe, and so on.

Now, the question of inclusion and exclusion is of course of great relevance, and it cannot be overestimated. The reaction against the universalistic and homogenizing modern project is indeed very necessary and to be welcomed. Nevertheless, this dialectic movement risks obscuring other essential aspects of political community that should be considered. I am thinking, for example, of such questions as: What is the bond unifying a political community? How and why is dialogue important? What is necessary to make dialogue effective? Trying to exercise *ars topica*, I will propose some reflections on these topics, drawing from some neglected but worthy places in the tradition of political philosophy such as the rhetorical thinking of classic authors, specifically Aristotle and Quintilian. From there it should be possible to propose some original considerations about the general theme of political community.

Rhetoric, of course, attributed a great power to eloquence. Cicero, for instance, told us in a mythical rendering of the origins of civilization that only through eloquence was it possible to uproot humans from their uncivilized state of nature and to establish and maintain cities in peace and justice:

> For there was a time when men wandered at random over the fields, after the fashion of beasts ... At this time a man, a great and a wise man, ... laying down

a regular system, collected men, who were previously dispersed over the fields and hidden in habitations in the woods, into one place, and united them, and lead them on to every useful and honourable pursuit; though, at first, from not being used to it they raised an outcry against it. Gradually, as they became more eager to listen to him on account of his wisdom and eloquence, he made them gentle and civilized from having been savage and brutal. And it certainly seems to me that no wisdom which was silent and destitute of skill in speaking could have had such power as to turn men suddenly from their previous customs, and to lead them to the adoption of a different system of life. And, moreover, after cities had been established how could men possibly have been induced to learn to cultivate integrity and to maintain justice, and to be accustomed willingly to obey others, and to think it right not only to encounter toil for the sake of the general advantage, but even to run the risk of losing their lives, if men had not been able to persuade them by eloquence of the truth of those principles which they had discovered by philosophy? Undoubtedly no one, if it had not been that he was influenced by dignified and sweet eloquence, would ever have chosen to condescend to appeal to law without violence.

(Cicero 1949a: I. 2–3)

This enormous political potentiality granted to eloquence an almost divine status, since Cicero believed that the human condition knows no other activity closer to divinity than that of establishing and maintaining cities in peace and justice (Cicero 1998: I.14). This should give an idea of the role rhetoric was attributed to in antiquity, compared to the current judgment that reduces it to a mere technique for manipulating discourse. In fact, this is an accusation that rhetoric has had to rebut since its beginnings, when in the battle with philosophy it shows all its political value. I am referring to the famous diatribe Plato, through Socrates, held with the Sophists. In his *Gorgias*, Socrates accused rhetoric of being an art concerned only with persuasion and opinion (or belief) and not with the transmission of real knowledge, and for this reason to be a perilous technique potentially at the service of the powerful for their own private ends (Plato 1985: 454e ff).

The attack against rhetoric came from the very heart of Plato's philosophy. There we can find an inherent dichotomy between truth and opinion, which is a constant in all his political dialogues. This irreducible gap corresponds to that between philosophy and politics, a gap that, according to Arendt, opened up irremediably in Plato's mind as a result of the trial and condemnation of Socrates (Arendt 1990: 73).[3] Socrates' inability to convince the judges and his consequent death made Plato suspect of persuasion as a form of speech and pushed him to consider opinion, *doxa*, as antithetical to truth.[4] To be sure, in another dialogue, the *Phaedrus*, Plato would have his conception of rhetoric refined and improved; even though in some manner he kept humiliating it. Rhetoric was accepted as the art (therefore legitimate and positive) of persuading the soul, but located under the hegemony of philosophy. It was asked to abandon the field of contingency and opinion for that of truth and knowledge, and to subsume its interests to those of philosophy (Plato 1993: 259e ff, 270b-c). Plato's disavowal of *doxa* was embedded in him; a position whose significance was political, beyond philosophical. For him, indeed, the supreme and eternal Good towards which the philosophers strive was the moral standard for the city; hence the philosophers, instead of the prudent men, should be its governors (Arendt 1990: 76). So Terry Eagleton is right when he underlines that behind the struggle between Plato and the Sophists lay a political question, urgent and crucial: Is ethics universal and communicable in an objective way, or, on the contrary, is it contingent in its contents and representations through discourse (Eagleton 1998: 88)?

The dispute between philosophy and rhetoric we are evoking is a dispute that, as Stanley Fish noted, has been told and retold countless times without producing a lasting point except for the irreducible difference between the two points of view (Fish 1989: 484, 502). My purpose here is obviously not to suggest some definitive solution, but rather to show how through its reconsideration it is possible to draw some original considerations on the theme of the community.

Now I want to return to the dichotomy between knowledge and truth, on the one hand, and opinion and verisimilitude, on the other, that Socrates evokes in those passages we have referred to in the *Gorgias* and the *Phaedrus*. The first pole, the subject of philosophy (and of its dialectic form), is the realm of inherence and reality; while the second, the subject of rhetoric (and persuasion), is that of contingency and appearance (Arendt 1990: 79). This is a dichotomy recurring in all philosophical tradition since Plato, one that, in the name of epistemological consistency and ontological stability, condemns without appeal as a public peril contingency, verisimilitude, opinion and therefore rhetoric (Gaonkar 2004: 5).

This was the first and indeed enduring critique against rhetoric and Aristotle, the first author to have written a systematic treatise on rhetoric, was also the first to reply to it. As is well known, in the Nicomachean Ethics, Aristotle differentiated between the field of the necessary and that of the contingent. The necessary regards that which cannot be otherwise than it is. The contingent, on the other hand, regards things that can be different. To the learning of the first realm is devoted that rational part of man able to apprehend eternal things, which produces *episteme*. To the second, instead, is devoted the other rational part, that part able to engage in practical thinking and to deliberate on different courses of action (of course it is possible to deliberate only about things that are not necessary) (Aristotle 1984: 1139a 5 ff). With Aristotle, as Dilip Gaonkar has argued, rhetoric was established firmly in this second realm, that of contingency and moral choice. However, not every kind of contingency is relevant for rhetoric, because this class also includes things that occur naturally or by accident, therefore independently from human will. The contingency rhetoric is concerned with is dependent on human choice and one connected with the probable, which means occurring with some regularity. The connection with the probable implies that it can be an object of that particular kind of syllogism, called *enthymeme* or rhetorical syllogism, which is about verisimilar arguments. Aristotle delineated in this way the space for deliberation and persuasion (Gaonkar 2004: 6–8; Aristotle 1984b: 1357a 1 ff, 1359a 30 ff). Firmly established in this realm of moral action, rhetoric was finally redeemed.

We know that for Aristotle *logos*, that is speech and reason, is the specifically human capacity to set forth the advantageous, the just and the good, and what renders humans the only political animal. Through it, men are able to deliberate and to constitute themselves into a political community (Aristotle 1995: 1253a 7–18). Rhetoric, which was defined by Aristotle as 'the faculty of observing in any given case the available means of persuasion', was strictly connected to political science; more precisely, it was defined as one of its branches (Aristotle 1984b: I.2 1355b 26, I.4 1359b 9–11). It was an ability, or a practical faculty, to construct persuasive arguments in those situations where, due to their contingent nature, deliberation is possible. It deals with argumentations only usually true, or verisimilar, while dialectics engages with demonstrations always true (Aristotle 1984b: I.2 1357a 1–7, I.3 1359a 10–17, I.4 1359b 9–17).[5] Matching rhetoric with persuasion, Aristotle was somehow reducing its potentiality. In any case he was also starting to unfold its substance as that practice involved with the activity of conveying and receiving meanings where no clear and definite truth exists, but only consensus. This was reached thanks to Aristotle's association of rhetoric with contingency and politics and by way of his dialogic understanding of the latter. If politics is the construction of the human world *dia-logos*, i.e. via dialogue, then rhetoric, responsible for finding the ways to persuasion, was at the heart of this process.

Aristotle's treatise is crucial because it gave dignity to the realms of contingency and verisimilitude. It is therefore a primary contribution to understanding the practice of public discourse in its own terms. From here, Aristotle could give significant insights about human communication and in particular political communication, such as the necessity of taking into consideration, beyond the subject matter of the discourse, the moral character of the speaker and the disposition of the listeners. In order for an argument to be persuasive, first it is essential that the orator transmits prestige and authority to his audience. Second, he must take into consideration and mold his speech according to the frame of mind and moods of his listeners, which change according to time and location (Aristotle 1984b: I.2 1356a 1 ff; II.1 1377b 21–4).[6] In this manner Aristotle was suggesting that for *logos* to be effective it must be accompanied by *ethos* and *pathos*. In sum, he located discourse and endowed it with anthropological profundity, giving substance to the Platonic suggestion according to which a good rhetor should be expert in the nature of the soul, exactly as the doctor is an expert in the nature of the body (Plato 1993: 270b 1 ff). Through the unity of *logos, pathos*, and *ethos*, Aristotle produced an understanding of political dialogue whose comprehensiveness remains a point of reference in comparison with current theories of communicative action (Ramírez 1999).

I consider the rhetoric of Aristotle as one of those *loci* of philosophic discourse which in the framework of his political thought should be revisited by current political theory. One contemporary author who grasped this potentiality was Heidegger. From his conception of language as the medium for disclosure of the world, he understood the importance of Aristotelian rhetoric. For him the Aristotelian *logos* was to be interpreted first of all as 'speaking' and not as 'reason', and moreover as everyday speaking instead of theoretical discourse (dialectic). This everyday speech, a speaking and listening to others, was in Heidegger's terms the essential

human way of being in the world, in the sense that it is how humans constitute themselves reciprocally in the most basic sense (Elden 2005: 290). In his first work
Being and Time, indeed, Heidegger referred to Aristotle's rhetoric as 'the first systematic hermeneutic of the everydayness of Being with one another' (Heidegger
1962: ¶138).

The reading of rhetoric offered by Heidegger is important because it put to the
fore the constitutive role of dialogue for humans and specifically the intersubjective and contingent nature of meaning and comprehension, which is the subject of
hermeneutic. Hans Gadamer, who deepened the hermeneutic account of
Heidegger, pointed out on several occasions the links between rhetoric and
hermeneutic, underlining their commonality and complementarity.[7] However,
there is a nuanced although significant difference between rhetoric and hermeneutic (at least understood in Gadamer's terms) noticed by Gadamer: if the latter was
conceived in its origin to deal with the remoteness of written texts from the past
with which it was necessary to establish a bridge, rhetoric was born in the immedi-
ateness of the action of public speech (Gadamer 2002a: 228–29). In a word, what
differentiates rhetoric from hermeneutic is the unequivocally political nature of the
former. To put it differently, although it is of course true that hermeneutic too has
an important political significance to the extent that its scope is 'to recuperate the
natural capacity to communicate with others, and this means to recover that fundamental consensus that gives sense to the fact that someone is speaking with someone else' (Gadamer 2002b: 116, my translation), it is important to keep in mind that
rhetoric is thoroughly devoted to the realm of politics where the task of listening, of
understanding, of reaching out, is, so to speak, more immediate and urgent.[8]

To understand this further, we now turn to Quintilian. His view on rhetoric is
indebted in several aspects to Aristotle and above all to Cicero. Within the tradition
of Roman thought, Quintilian succeeded in fully developing the political significance of the question of rhetoric. The Spanish scholar of rhetoric, José Luis
Ramírez, synthesized in this way the contribution of this author:

> If the Aristotelian conception granted to Rhetoric an anthropological founda-
> tion, Quintilian's conception of Rhetoric as *ars bene dicendi*, as the art of edu-
> cating the human being in virtue through the grasp of language (*vir
> bonus dicendi peritus*), gave to it the meaning of the foundation of all human
> education.
>
> (Ramírez 2001: 73, my translation)

Quintilian famously defined rhetoric as the *ars bene dicendi*, the art of speaking
well, i.e. of using the correct words in every situation (Quintilian 1920: II.15 34,
II.17 35). This compelling formula is fascinating because it suggests that rhetoric is
not only a question of persuasion, much less a technique of manipulation, but the
praxis of employing language eloquently for the common good. Understood in this
way, rhetoric manifests its political nature and its character of practical wisdom.
However, the contours of this *prudentia* are vast. In order to be able to speak well,
an orator has to rely not only on his personal qualities, like honesty, intelligence and

sensibility, but also on a broad education, from minor arts to that of eternal things, i.e. philosophy. His eloquence should tend toward perfection; it should be considered as a whole that is complete only if including each one of its parts. The formation of the orator should start from his youth and continue till his maturity and everything important to it should be considered relevant for rhetoric (Quintilian 1920: I.Preface 5, 13, I.10 3–9).

If Aristotle had revalued rhetoric by connecting it with the dialogical nature of man, Quintilian, as Cicero before him, broadened its scope in such a way as to render the art of eloquence one of the highest human virtues (Quintilian 1920: II.20 9). Indeed:

> Reason then was the greatest gift of the Almighty, who willed that we should share its possession with the immortal gods. But reason by itself would help us but little and would be far less evident in us, had we not the power to express our thoughts in speech; for it is the lack of this power rather than thought and understanding, which they do to a certain extent possess, that is the great defect in other living things.
>
> (Quintilian 1920: II.16 14–15)

It is therefore the union of *ratio* and *oratio* (in Cicero's words), instead of reason alone, that renders man unique and rhetoric the fundamental art where this union is reached. Through his intelligence man makes sense of the world. Nevertheless this meaning bestowed on the world must become common in speech through eloquence, allowing thereby the completion of man's political nature. It should be evident by this point how wrong is the reduction of rhetoric to a technique for the treatment of language, including persuasion. The political philosopher Javier Roiz maintains very compellingly that the accusation of 'verbalism' is the most violent accusation that rhetoric as *ars bene dicendi* has had to face (Roiz 2003: 318). This is a very important point, because it is this common misunderstanding that has often prevented a proper consideration of the tradition of rhetoric. The question is not only that for rhetoric a reason that is silent is somehow incomplete, but also, and more fundamentally, that eloquence as the unifying substance of the community has to count on a vast range of human capacities, such as intelligence, honesty, bravery, imagination, sensibility, and so on; indeed on the human in its best manifestation. From this view, Quintilian develops his comprehensive approach to rhetoric as the practice of formation of the perfect orator:

> the art of oratory includes all that is essential for the training of an orator, and it is impossible to reach the summit in any subject unless we have first passed through all the elementary stages. I shall not therefore refuse to stoop to the consideration of those minor details, neglect of which may result in there being no opportunity for more important things, and propose to mold the studies of my orator from infancy on the assumption that his whole education has been entrusted to my charge.
>
> (Quintilian 1920: I. Preface 5–6)

The education of the orator is consequently the main topic of Quintilian's treatise. Following the tradition of Cato's *vir bonus dicendi peritus*, he tried to mold the figure of an honest and wise man striving towards perfection in the practice of oratory (Quintilian 1920: XII.1 1). Being a virtuous activity, rhetoric can only originate from a natural talent, but must be brought to perfection through practice and education in different disciplines (Quintilian 1920: II.17 9). In the same way as an antidote is a mix of different and even contrasting ingredients, so eloquence must be sustained by various arts, each of them giving its own breeding to the mind of the orator (Quintilian 1920: I.10 2–7; Roiz 2003: 39–40).

The idea of education as an antidote reveals how distant was Quintilian's conception of the formation of citizens from the learning of technical knowledge. It was rather a process of the constitution of the self. The rhetor is not expected to apply mechanically a set of instructions, but his education must guide and inspire him in the practice of politics. He must apprehend the capacity to adapt discourse to different circumstances, times and people, in order to be able to move not only through 'narrow paths', but to 'range at large over the open fields' (Quintilian 1920: V.14 31, II.5 13–16, II.6 6, VI.5 11). To sum up, the formation of the rhetor was a demanding practice of cultivation of intelligence, deepening of moral feelings and strengthening of the capacity to judge. It was a process of self-formation wherein the rhetor constituted himself as a good man no less than as a good citizen. Indeed, 'assuredly the man who will best inspire such feelings in others is he who has first inspired them in himself', so that this process of self-formation, not solipsistic but always devoted to public life, was the real 'gift' the good rhetor had to offer to his community (Quintilian 1920: XII.1 25, 29, XII.1 3–4).

The standard required by rhetoric was extremely demanding and in fact the ideal of the best orator remains something 'eternally absent': it was a regulative ideal, coming from the awareness of the fragility of the moral links unifying a political community and of the great potentiality of eloquence in society (Connolly 2007: 14). No other thing is more difficult, Cicero said, than to find what is convenient to say, when you know that from the speech of a good orator may depend peace or war (Cicero 1934: 70; 1934b: 7). Rhetoric aims to maintain this fragile community of speech, where through *isegoria* politics instead of violence can occur. For Hannah Arendt, being excluded from this community and falling into isolation is tantamount to being deprived of an essential human possibility: the possibility to act politically (Arendt 1973: 297, 474–75). This is exactly what rhetoric can help to overcome.

To understand how it can do this and thus conclude this chapter, we need to come back once again to the theme of opinion and truth. In the essay 'Philosophy and Politics' referred to earlier, Arendt reconstructs the meaning of the term *doxa* according to Socrates. She notices that *doxa* was not connected to the verisimilar, but rather to the exposition through speech of the first opening of the world to an individual. It was hence something common to everybody, because everybody has his own opening of the world; and at the same time different to everybody, because this opening depends on the position one has in the world (Arendt 1990: 80). The great mission Socrates wanted to accomplish was to find the truth present in every opinion and in this way to make the city more truthful. The method he invented was what he called maieutic and Plato dialectic. In the dialogue between two, through an exhaustive discussion, the truth inherent in every opinion is eventually revealed. This was the political task of the philosopher (Arendt 1990: 81). Such a form of dialogue was also a way to create friendship in the city, because the ongoing questioning is the typical form of talking among friends about an argument they share. The agonistic spirit of the Greek polis, always on the verge of tearing apart the community, was to be tamed by friendship. Aristotle indeed considered friendship more than justice to be the real bond of a community. Its political component, Arendt underlines, lies in the truthfulness at which friends aim through dialogue. It permits understanding of 'how and in what specific articulateness the common world appears to the other', and indeed it is this capacity to see through the other's eyes and to communicate these different perspectives, which constitutes the quintessential political capacity (Arendt 1990: 82–4).

By now it should be clear that this task of comprehension and communication is also common to rhetoric. Likewise that the bond Socrates and Aristotle found in friendship can not sustain itself only through dialectic dialogue but also needs rhetoric. If we recall the hermeneutic nature of rhetoric underlined by Heidegger and Gadamer, for example, and the high standards the perfect orator and good citizen should reach in intelligence and moral sensibility, this looks persuasive. Yet Arendt, despite her extraordinary openness to the complexity of the human soul, does not refer to rhetoric. Why? She continues her essay by observing that the main criterion Socrates determined for speaking truthfully was to be in agreement with oneself. This is indeed the necessary condition by which the internal dialogue with oneself, i.e. thought, can happen. It is also an essential condition for friendship. If in the internal dialogue the self shows its dual plurality, contradicting oneself would be tantamount with the splitting up of the self into many pieces. This is why, Arendt says, the principle of no contradiction has become the rule of thought and, we may add, the fear of contradiction so pervasive in western philosophy (Arendt 1990: 85–6). Moreover, coherence with oneself is necessary from an ethical point of view in a world such as the Greek one where appearance and essence coincide at the level of politics. Hence, the Socratic command to 'be as you would like to appear' (Arendt 1990: 87).

We find here the typical philosophic bias towards the visual and the assumption that everything must be in the light in order to be good. This is an assumption and a bias that rhetoric does not share: it dwells instead in the realm of the auditory and it is nurtured by silence. We may recall the young Nietzsche inveighing against the ingenuous request of Socrates and his follower Euripides that everything has to be conscious to be beautiful and everything known to be good, reclaiming in the process the unconscious wisdom of the Dionysian (Nietzsche 2004: 108–10). But rhetoric moves rather in another direction. As we have seen, one of its classic teachings is that every speech must be responsive to the specificities of the moment. The rhetoric concept of *kairós* signifies exactly the necessary responsiveness of discourse to contingency: the character of the orator, the disposition of the audience, the specificity of the time and place. All these variables are included in the silence that precedes the speech of the orator. It is therefore a silence charged with mean-ings (Ramírez 1992).[9] Indeed, silence has a sort of founding function for rhetorical speech, because in it there is a call for contingent necessities to be interpreted and attended to.[10] The silence we are talking about, however, is of a kind that in some measure would remain mute even if manifested in speech. In the depth of our being, indeed, there are many parts whose significance can be at most only remotely evoked by speech, but which are nevertheless fundamental. Vico called these parts '*mutoli*', affirming thereafter that only through a metaphorical language can they somehow find expression.[11] The good orator, as with the good citizen, needs there-fore to interpret and give expression to them by using his knowledge of the 'human soul' and his culture, his wisdom and eloquence.[12] The central teaching of rhetoric is perhaps exactly this: that communication cannot be understood without a prior immersion into our *foro interno*, a realm where the principle of no contradiction is not always pertinent, and where the logical coherence of dialectics not always appropriate. The insistence of rhetoric on *paideia* as the only way of endowing citizens with the necessary capacities for intercourse with their fellows, and its account of dialogue from the union of *logos-pathos-ethos*, encompass this teaching.

The thought of Giambattista Vico is one of the most emblematic instances of this kind of rhetorical wisdom. In one of his early writings, he emphatically summed up the reasons for undertaking a broad humanistic education (which includes all the liberal arts and natural sciences), aiming at the ideal of perfect wisdom and elo-quence. He wrote:

> And if I say that each of you must search within himself in order to consider carefully his human nature, he will in truth see himself to be nothing but mind, spirit, and capacity of language … From this he will note that man is thor-oughly corrupted, first by the inadequacy of language, then by a mind cluttered with opinions, and finally a spirit polluted by vice. He will observe that these are the divine punishments by which the Supreme Will punished the sin of the first parent so that humankind who descended from him will become sepa-rated, scattered, and dispersed …
>
> (Vico 1993: 127)

These divine 'punishments' represent human imperfection from which derives the eternal risk of falling into isolation: Because basic human nature has been changed by sin, assemblies of men may appear to be societies, but the truth is that isolation of spirits is greatest where many bodies come together (Vico 1993: 128).

However, this risk can be exorcized, and humanity can find its way towards happiness:

> I have enumerated as the punishments for corrupted human nature the inade-quacy of language, the opinions of the mind, and the passions of the soul. Therefore, the remedies are eloquence, knowledge, and virtue … Three are the very duties of wisdom – with eloquence to tame the impetuousness of the fools, with prudence to lead them out of error, with virtue toward them to earn their

goodwill, and in these ways, each according to his ability, to foster with zeal the society of men.

(Vico 1993: 129–30)

Because our human condition is essentially linked to plurality, as Arendt said, politics dwells in the field of contingency, where more than the principle of Truth reigns that of the verisimilar. Hence opinions, and even more beliefs, are intrinsic to it. They are connected both with the fact that, as we have seen, to each of us the world opens up differently according to our position in it, and with the lack of an eternal Truth. The consequence is that in politics not only critique and the search for the truth is important; also essential is the capacity of rhetoric to comprehend and communicate the complex occurrences of the mind. William James once wrote that the biggest breach in nature is that between two different minds.[13] This may or may not be correct. In any case, opinions and beliefs are certainly very varied and often so rooted in our minds, because of the complex mental processes experience puts in motion, that the hope off reducing them to truth through dialectical dialogue is often in vain. The anthropological insightfulness of the classic and humanist rhetoric tradition is in this sense a lesson contemporary political philosophy should listen to.[14] Its teachings represent *loci* of the discourse that have to be recovered.

Notes

1　See, for instance, the pedagogical considerations Vico (1990) formulated in his work *De Nostri Temporis Studiorum Ratione*.

2　See also Connolly (1999).

3　On this question, see also Arendt (2003:168–83).

4　The question of the consideration of *doxa* by Plato is much more complex, but here we cannot go into it. Particularly interesting is the important role myth plays in his dialogues, which seems at least to problematize the schematic dichotomy *doxa*/truth. See, for instance Voegelin (1957); Havelock (1963); and Baracchi (2002). The same position of Plato towards rhetoric should be reconsidered if one reflects on the fact that he wrote on philosophy in the dramatic form of the dialogue. On the dialogical form of Plato's philosophy see for instance Strauss (1978: 50 ff) and Sallis (1996).

5　Aristotle associated and differentiated rhetoric and dialectic. Both are concerned with argumentation, but while the first is about probable argumentation, the second is about true argumentation (that is, philosophical). He defined rhetoric either as the 'counterpart of dialectic' or as 'its branch' (Aristotle 1984b: I.1 1354a 1 ff; I.2 1356a 30).

6　Aristotle noticed that many authors before him gave much space to the role of passions in persuasion, but none of them did so while taking into consideration the role of the enthymema (the rhetorical argument) and that of *ethos* (the character of the orator) (Aristotle 1984b: I.1 1354a 12–14).

7　See, for instance Gadamer (1996: 49 ff, 242–243; 2002b: 112; and 2002c). For the relations between rhetoric and hermeneutic see also Jost and Hyde (1997).

8　The difference between rhetoric and hermeneutic can be seen also from the point of view of the privileged relation of the first with oral discourse and of the latter with written text. An essential consequence is that the hermeneutic (in Gadamer's version at least) considers dialectic and Socratic dialogue to be the best forms of communication, without considering the rhetorical approach. On the relation between orality and literacy (and rhetoric) see the classic work by Ong (2002).

9　On the significance of 'silence' for rhetoric see also Valesio 1986: Ch. 5.
10　Maybe Heidegger referred to something similar when he wrote: 'Perhaps, then, language requires much less precipitate expression than proper silence' (Heidegger 1993: 246).
11　I am referring to Vico's famous account of the origins of language. The first people were initially mute, '*mutoli*', because devoid of language. Through the power of their imagination they began to create a poetic language charged with metaphors that would be developed successively through reason in a more articulated way. This narrative is also a fascinating metaphor about the mute zones of human being and the power of poetry to make contact with them (Vico 1948: ¶34, 149, 198, 204–10, 225, 403).
12　We are touching here on an essential topic. This is the question of the relation between thought and language. The finitude of language in relation to the infinitude of thought implies that its tropological aspect (the use of rhetorical figures) is something inherent in it, as well as that speech (the concrete and empirical use of language) is irreducible to language (the abstract systematic principles of a language). The literature on this theme is too extensive to be synthesized here. I have advanced some reflections about it, in particular from the perspective of political theory in Giambattista Vico's and Eric Voegelin's works, in '*Giambattista Vico y Eric Voegelin: fundamentos y lenguaje simbólico*' (Ballacci forthcoming).
13　'Neither contemporaneity, nor proximity in space, nor similarity of quality and content are able to fuse thoughts together which are sundered by this barrier of belonging to different personal minds. The breaches between such thoughts are the most absolute breaches in nature' (James 1890: 226). I am grateful to Javier Roiz for drawing my attention to this passage.
14　In a certain sense, this is particularly true for those authors such as Jacques Derrida, Richard Rorty and Stanley Fish, who have shown a keen rhetorical sensibility in their compelling accounts of the linguistic construction of society. This sensibility, however, has not been enriched by the same anthropological depth as that of classical and humanist rhetoric.

Bibliography

Arendt, H. (1973) *The Origins of Totalitarianism*, New York: Harcourt.
—— (1990) 'Philosophy and Politics', *Social Research*, 57(1): 73–103.
—— (2003) 'Que es la autoridad?', in *Entre pasado y futuro: ocho ejercicios sobre la reflexión política*, trans. A. Poljak, Barcelona: Península.
Aristotle (1984a) 'Nicomachean Ethics', in J. Barnes (ed.) *The Complete Works of Aristotle*, Princeton: Princeton University Press.
—— (1984b) 'Rhetoric', in *The Rhetoric and the Poetic of Aristotle*, trans. W.R. Roberts and I. Bywater, New York: Modern Library.
—— (1995) *Politics*, trans. E. Barker, Oxford: Oxford University Press.
Ballacci, G. (forthcoming), 'Giambattista Vico y Eric Voegelin: fundamentos y lenguaje simbólico', in B. Hammar (ed.) *Democracia y retórica*, Madrid: Editorial Complutense.
Baracchi, C. (2002) *Of Myth, Life, and War in Plato's Republic*, Bloomington: Indiana University Press.
Cicero (1934) 'Orator', in *Brutus, Orator*, trans. G.L. Hendrickson and H.M. Hubbell, Cambridge MA: Harvard University Press.
—— (1934b) 'Brutus', in *Brutus, Orator*, trans. G.L. Hendrickson and H.M. Hubbell, Cambridge MA: Harvard University Press.
—— (1949a) 'De Inventione', in M. Hubbell (trans. and ed.) *De inventione, De optimo genere oratorum, Topica*, Cambridge MA: Harvard University Press.

—— (1949b) 'Topica', in M. Hubbell (trans. and ed.) *De inventione, De optimo genere oratorum, Topica*, Cambridge MA: Harvard University Press..

—— (1998) 'The Republic', in *The Republic and The Laws*, trans. N. Rudd, Oxford: Oxford University Press.

Connolly, W. (1991) *Identity/Difference: democratic negotiations of political paradox*, Ithaca: Cornell University Press.

—— (1999) 'Suffering, Justice, and the Politics of Becoming', in D. Campbell and M.J. Shapiro (eds) *Moral Spaces: rethinking ethics and world politics*, Minneapolis: University of Minnesota Press.

—— (2007) *The State of Speech: rhetoric & political thought in ancient Rome*, Princeton: Princeton University Press.

Eagleton, T. (1998) 'A Short History of Rhetoric', in M. Bernard-Donals and R. Glejzer (eds) *Rhetoric in an Antifoundational World*, New Haven: Yale University Press.

Elden, S. (2005) 'Reading Logos as Speech: Heidegger, Aristotle and rhetorical politics', *Philosophy and Rhetoric*, 38(4): 281–301.

Esposito, R. (1993) 'Democrazia', in *Nove pensieri sulla politica*, Bologna: Il Mulino.

Fish, S. (1989) 'Rhetoric', in *Doing What Comes Naturally: change, rhetoric, and the practice of theory in literary and legal studies*, Durham: Duke University Press.

Foucault, M. (1984) 'What is Enlightenment?', in P. Rabinow (ed.) *The Foucault Reader*, New York: Pantheon Books.

—— (1990) 'Qu'est-ce que la critique? Critique et *Aufklärung*', *Bulletin de la Société française de philosophie*, vol. 82(2): 35–63.

Gadamer, H. (1996) *Verdad y Método*, vol. I, trans. A. Agud Aparicio and R. de Aagapito, Salamanca: Ediciones Sígueme.

—— (2002a) 'Retórica, hermenéutica y crítica de la ideología. Comentarios metacríticos a Verdad y método I (1967)', in *Verdad y Método*, vol. II.

—— (2002b) 'Hermenéutica clásica y hermenéutica filosófica', in *Verdad y Método*, vol. II, trans. M. Olasagasti, Salamanca: Ediciones Sígueme.

—— (2002c) 'Retórica y hermenéutica', in *Verdad y Método*, vol. II.

Gaonkar, D.P. (2004) 'Introduction: contingency and probability', in W. Jost and W. Olmsted (eds) *A Companion to Rhetoric and Rhetorical Criticism*, Malden MA: Blackwell.

Havelock, E.A. (1963) *Preface to Plato*, Cambridge: Belknap Press of Harvard University Press.

Heidegger, M. (1890), *The Principles of Psychology*, vol. I, New York: H. Holt and Company.

—— (1962) *Being and Time*, trans. J. Macquarrie and E. Robinson, London: S.C.M. Press.

—— (1993) 'Letter on Humanism', in D. Farrell Krell (ed.) *Basic Writings*, London: Routledge.

Jost, W. and Hyde, M.J. (eds) (1997), *Rhetoric and Hermeneutics in Our Time: a reader*, New Haven: Yale University Press.

Nietzsche, F. (2004) 'Socrates y la tragedía', in A. Sánchez Pascual (trans. and ed.), *Escritos póstumos 1870–1871*, Madrid: Biblioteca Nueva.

Ong W.J. (2002) *Onality and Literacy: The Technoligizing of the Word*, 2nd edition London: Routledge

Plato (1985) *Gorgias*, trans. W.C. Helmbold, Indianapolis: The Bobbs-Merrill Company.

—— (1993) 'Phaedrus', in W.S. Cobb (trans. and ed.), *The Symposium and The Phaedrus: Plato's erotic dialogues*, New York: State University of New York Press.

Quintilian, M.F. (1920) *Institutio Oratoria*, trans. H.E. Butler, Cambridge MA: Harvard University Press.

Ramírez, J.L. (1992) 'El significado del silencio y el silencio del significdo', in C. Castilla Del Pino (ed.), *El silencio*, Madrid: Alianza Editorial.

—— (1999) 'Arte de hablar y arte de decir. Una excursion botánica en la pradera de la retórica', *RELEA*, 8: 61–79.

—— (2001) 'El retorno de la retórica', *Foro Interno: anuario de teoría política*, 1: 65–73.

Roiz, J. (2003) *La recuperación del buen juicio: teoría política en el siglo veinte*, Madrid: Editorial Foro Interno.

Sallis, J. (1996) *Being and Logos: reading the Platonic dialogue*, Bloomington: Indiana University Press.

Strauss, L. (1978), *The City and Man*, Chicago: University of Chicago Press.

Valesio, P. (1986) *Ascoltare il silenzio: la retorica come teoria*, Bologna: Il Mulino.

Vico, G. (1948) *The New Science of Giambattista Vico: unabridged translation of the third edition (1744)*, trans. T. Goddard Bergin and M. Harold Fish, Ithaca: Cornell University Press.

—— (1953) 'L'antichissima sapienza degli italici', in F. Nicolini (ed.), *Opere*, Milano: Riccardo Ricciardi Editore.

—— (1990) *On the Study Methods of Our Time*, trans. E. Gianturco, Ithaca: Cornell University Press.

—— (1993), 'On the Proper Order of Studies. Oration VI', in *On Humanistic Education (Six Inaugural Orations, 1699–1707)*, trans. by G.A. Pinton and A.W. Shippee, Ithaca: Cornell University Press.

—— (1994) *The Autobiography of Giambattista Vico*, trans. M. Harold Fish and T. Goddard Bergin, Ithaca: Cornell University Press.

Voegelin, E. (1957) 'Plato and Aristotle', in *Order and History*, vol. 3, Baton Rouge: Louisiana State University Press.

Wolin, S. (2004) *Politics and Vision: continuity and innovation in western political thought*, Princeton: Princeton University Press.

8 Homer, Virgil and identity in international relations

Richard Ned Lebow

> Then first in Delos Homer and I, the singers,
> stitching together our song in novel hymns,
> glorified Phoibos Apollo, gold-sworded,
> Leto's child.
>
> (in Herington 1985: 173)

Some philosophers (Kant, Hegel) consider creation of 'others' a necessary adjunct to state formation and national solidarity, and one (Schmitt) even welcomes it. Others (e.g., Nietzsche, Habermas) hope to transcend this dangerous binary through dialogue. This debate, like so many in moral philosophy, takes place in an empirical vacuum. I attempt to offer a more complex understanding of identity and the diverse roles that 'others' play in its construction and maintenance. To do so, I draw on empirical evidence from surveys and laboratory research. I then turn to Homer's *Iliad*, the founding text of a literary tradition, and Virgil's *Aeneid*, its Roman successor. They frame the problem of identity and 'others' differently from Kant, Hegel and their successors. Their approach is more consistent with the findings of modern psychology. I conclude with a comparative analysis of Homer and Virgil in the light of modern psychology and discuss some of the links between this literary tradition and modern political practice.

The philosophy of identity

Identity is one of those concepts whose meaning was always fluid but in recent years has become stretched to avoid the charge of 'essentialism'. Rogers Brubaker and Frederick Cooper identify five key uses for the term. Identity can be understood as a ground or basis for social or political action, a collective phenomenon denoting some degree of sameness among members of a group or category, a core aspect of individual or collective 'selfhood', a product of social or political action, or as the product of multiple and competing discourses. They note the irony that constructivist notions of identity now so much in vogue provide no insight into the process by which coercion is used to compel identification. Their recognition of multiple, fluid identities also stands in sharp contrast to 'the terrible singularity that is often striven for – and sometimes realized – by politicians seeking to transform mere categories into unitary and exclusive groups' (Brubaker and Cooper 2000: 2).

In philosophy, political science and politics, identity construction has routinely been assumed to require the creation of 'others', if not their demonization. The most extreme formulation of the claim is Carl Schmitt's assertion (1976) that political identities can best be formed in the course of violent struggles against adversaries. There is considerable historical evidence for such a claim, beginning with the ancient Israelites (Colley 1992a and 1992b; Said 1978).[1] In modern times politicians and intellectuals have routinely created or exploited dichotomies between 'us' and 'others' to advance racist and authoritarian political agendas. A recent and prominent example is Samuel Huntington's *Clash of Civilizations* which constructs Latin immigrants as an unassimilatable 'other' and Islam as an external 'other' that threatens our economic primacy and physical security. Following 9/11, the Bush administration had notable success in mobilizing support for its 'war on terror' and invasions of Afghanistan and Iraq by convincing many Americans that the world was divided into good 'freedom loving peoples' and evil 'cowardly terrorists'.

The 'us' and 'other' binary has a long and distinguished lineage. It was first conceptualized in the eighteenth century in response to efforts by Western European governments to promote domestic cohesion and development by means of foreign conflict. Immanuel Kant theorized that the 'unsocial sociability' of people draws them together into societies, but leads them to act in ways that threaten their dissolution. He considered this antagonism innate to our species and an underlying cause of the development of the state. Warfare drove people apart, but their need to defend themselves against each other compelled them to band together and submit to the rule of law. Each political unit has unrestricted freedom in the same way individuals did before the creation of societies, and hence is in a constant state of war. The price of order at home is conflict among societies. The 'us' is maintained at the expense of 'others' (Kant 1991: 41–53 and 93–130).

Hegel built on this formulation, and brought to it his understanding that modern states differed from their predecessors in that cohesion does not rest so much on pre-existing cultural, religious or linguistic identities as it does on the allegiance of their citizens to central authorities who provide for the common defense. Citizens develop a collective identity through the external conflicts of their state and the sacrifices it demands of them. 'States', he writes in the *German Constitution*, 'stand to one another in a relation of might', a relationship that 'has been universally revealed and made to prevail'. In contrast to Kant, who considers this situation tragic, Hegel rhapsodizes about the life of states as active and creative agents who play a critical role in the unfolding development of the spirit and humankind. Conflict among states, he contends, helps each to become aware of itself by encouraging self-knowledge among citizens. It can serve an ethical end by uniting subjectivity and objectivity and resolving the tension between particularity and universality. After Hegel, peace came to be seen as a negotiated agreement between and among European states, and not the result of some civilizing process (Hegel 1991 and 1999).

International relations as a zone of conflict and war was further legitimized by the gradual development of international law and its conceptualization of international relations as intercourse among sovereign states. In the seventeenth century, Grotius, Hobbes and Pufendorf endowed states with moral personalities and sought to constrain them through a reciprocal set of rights and duties. In the eighteenth century, the state was further embedded in a law of nations by Vattel. The concept of sovereignty created the legal basis for the state and the nearly unrestricted right of its leaders to act as they wish within its borders. It also justified the pursuit of national interests by force beyond those borders so long as it was in accord with the laws of war. Sovereignty is a concept with diverse and even murky origins, that was first popularized in the sixteenth century. At that time, more importance was placed on its domestic than international implications. Nineteenth- and twentieth-century jurists and historians, many of them Germans influenced by Kant and Hegel (e.g., Heeren, Clausewitz, Ranke, Treitschke) developed a narrative about sovereignty that legitimized the accumulation of power of central governments and portrayed the state as the sole focus of a people's economic, political and social life. The ideology of sovereignty neatly divided actors from one another, and made the binary of 'us' and 'others' appear a natural, if not progressive, development, as did rule-based warfare among states (Kant 1991: 44–7 and 112; Bartelson 1995: 220–9; Osiander 2001; Schmidt 1998).

This binary also found expression in the concept of a European or Christian society, which initially excluded Russia and the Ottoman Empire as political and cultural 'others'. There was no conception of the 'international' until the late eighteenth century, and its development reflected and hastened the transformation of European society into an international system in the course of the next century (Bartelson 1995: Ch. 5; Halliday 1994: 6). New standards of legitimacy enlarged the boundaries of the community of nations following the Napoleonic War (Clark 1989: Ch. 6). By 1900, non-Western states were being admitted to the community, and the number of such units burgeoned with decolonization in the late 1950s and 1960s. In recent decades, non-governmental organizations (NGOs) and diverse social movements have pushed a more cosmopolitan notion of democracy that extends to units beyond states and challenges the legitimacy of many recognized international organizations (Held 1995).

Efforts to expand the conception of self and community always meet strong opposition. In 1859, John Stuart Mill held that it was a 'grave error' to 'suppose that the same international customs, and the same rules of international morality, can obtain between one civilized nation and another, and between civilized nations and barbarians' (Mill 1964–7: vol. 3; Onuf 1998: 250; Jahn 2006: 178–206). Huntington's *The Clash of Civilizations* makes the same kind of invidious distinctions (1996: 21; 29). Basing their claims on Kant, but really acting in the tradition of Mill, liberal advocates of the Democratic Peace update his dichotomy to divide the world into liberal states and authoritarian 'others'. In sharp contradiction of Kant's categorical imperative, some liberals justify economic penetration or military intervention to bring the benefits of democracy to these states and their peoples (Doyle 1983).[2] American domestic and foreign policy since 9/11 indicate how easy it remains for political leaders to exploit fear of 'others' to create solidarity at home (Campbell 1998).

The self-other binary also draws support from Foucault's assertion that order and identity are created and maintained through discourses of deviance. Building on this formulation, William Connolly argues in a thoughtful and influential study of identity that it requires 'the conversion of some differences into otherness, into evil, or one of its numerous surrogates'. Identity for Connolly is 'a slippery, insecure experience, dependent on its ability to define difference and vulnerable to the tendency of entities it would so define to counter, resist, overturn, or subvert definitions applied to them' (Connolly 1991: 64). Power is therefore essential to maintain, even impose, identity and gives rise to hierarchies whose primary function is to safeguard and propagate sanctioned discourses of identity while suppressing or marginalizing those who question these secular truths. Connolly extends the parallel between identity and religion in his contention that concepts of good and evil are central to both and find expression in the demonization and exclusion, rather than toleration and dialogue, with those who dissent. He sees this response as a 'temptation' for human beings, not something they are hard-wired to do, and remains hopeful that we will one day become capable of feeling secure in our identities without demonizing others (1991: 4–9, 64–81 and 124).

Not all philosophers and international relations scholars have accepted the need for stereotyped 'others', although there is widespread agreement that every identity and culture is surrounded, even penetrated, by constitutive others. Johann Herder thought that each individual and culture had a unique way of being human, and that we in turn become more human by understanding and appreciating this variety (Herder 1877–1913: 291). Drawing on Herder, Friedrich Nietzsche offered the general proposition that the good human life is fundamentally dialogical in character. Such dialogue rests on the premise that interlocutors embrace opposing metaphysical truths, but affirm the contestable and uncertain nature of these truths. 'Noble' adversaries learn to practice 'forbearance' and 'thoughtfulness' in their relations with others (Connolly 2000). Nietzsche's understanding of dialogue in turn influenced Jürgen Habermas, for whom ethics and truth can only arise through meaningful interactions with others based on the principle and practice of equality (Habermas 1984–87; 1990). John Rawls also argues that justice can only arise from dialogue and compromise among interlocutors. While his *Theory of Justice* is a monological thought experiment, he nevertheless contends that liberalism can only work in practice as a dialogue among people with opposing points of view and metaphysical commitments. The influence of Habermas and Rawls is such that finding the conditions for open and meaningful dialogue has become a central project of contemporary moral philosophy.

Despite their numerous differences, the principal focus of Kant, Hegel and Schmitt is on the construction of one's own national identity. Historians and psychologists have also investigated the consequences of such projects on 'others' and have documented or demonstrated the negative consequences of exclusion and stereotypy for their development and self-esteem (Allport 1954; Jordan 1968; Lebow 1976). Neither Kant nor Hegel were unidimensional thinkers and they framed identity not only as the construction of difference, but as an encounter with a pre-existing difference. Underneath cultural and other differences lay a common humanity, which might allow the dichotomy between 'us' and 'other' to be over-come through a process of mutual recognition by individuals and their collectivi-ties. Such a reading of Kant and Hegel, and of Herder as well, surfaces in Mead and Pizzorno and helped to inspire the projects of Gadamer and Levinas.

Some late twentieth century philosophers – who also draw on Hegel – adopt this perspective and stress the needs of 'others' for recognition and inclusion. According to Charles Taylor, identity

> is partly shaped by recognition or its absence, often by the *mis*recognition of others, and so a person or group of people can suffer real damage, real distor-tion, if the people or society around them mirror back to them a confining or demeaning or contemptible picture of themselves.
>
> (Taylor 1992: 73)

Axel Honneth makes a parallel case in the domain of international relations for non- and mis-recognition as a basis of social and interpersonal conflict (Honneth 1996; Fraser and Honneth 2003). Drawing on Aristotle's notion of friendship and Heidegger's notion of anxiety, Felix Berenskoetter (2007) contends that the friend as the 'significant other' is capable, even at the international level, of reducing anx-iety and creating the framework for moral authenticity and recognition.

In recent years, right and left have intersected in what many consider an alarm-ing way (Brown 2007). Since the near collapse of communist regimes, or their evo-lution into something else, Marxist writings are no longer a credible vehicle to *épater le bourgeoisie*. Toward this end, some radical critics of liberalism have turned to the arguments of radical anti-Semite, Nazi theoretician and active collab-orator Carl Schmitt to criticize liberal conceptions of identity. Chantal Mouffe deploys his understanding of the political to expose what she considers the arbitrary exclusion and violence in the liberal philosophy of John Rawls. She maintains that society inevitably entails 'a fundamental antagonism in every associational form, a division internal to the construction of every social identity that enables it to func-tion while simultaneously defeating its ability to realize itself as a rational, cooper-ative, unified or non-antagonistic whole' (Mouffe 1993: 141).

For modern thinkers, the question of identity has been framed with the back-ground understanding that there are no demonstrable metaphysical truths. William Connolly notes that Nietzsche and Schmitt – who provide opposing foundational texts in the debate about the 'other' – respond in diametrically opposed ways to this philosophical reality. Nietzsche attempts to transcend it through dialogue that builds understanding and community among those who adhere to competing truths and cultural orientations. Schmitt turns to the state for certainty and the artificial unity it can enforce through an exclusionary ideology and policies. If Nietzsche identifies the beautiful with individual freedom and creativity, Schmitt sees it in homogeneity, unity and strength (Connolly 2000).

These opposing orientations and projects cannot be overcome by Nietzschean dialogue or Schmittian repression. They rest on different philosophical foundations and empirical assumptions, and the latter can be evaluated by social science. In the next section I will review some of the key findings of psychology in this regard and show how the consensus in the field has evolved away from the view that ingroup solidarity inevitably necessitates the creation of stereotyped outgroups and toward acceptance of the idea that ingroup and outgroup creation are the products of separate dynamics. I then turn to the texts of Homer and Virgil to show that many of the insights of modern psychology are implicit in their narratives.

Ingroups and outgroups

Even in psychology, Marilynn Brewer (1999) laments, it was long conventional wisdom that ingroup solidarity and outgroup hostility were flip sides of a coin. This belief dates back to the early twentieth century and William Graham Sumner's foundational treatment (1906) of ethnocentrism and stereotypy. Adopting a structural-functional perspective, he reasoned that pride, loyalty and feelings of ingroup superiority were positively correlated with contempt, hatred and hostility toward outgroups. Group formation was a functional response to the struggle for scarce resources and gave rise to hostility, even violence, toward competing groups (1906: 12; see also Sherif and Sherif 1953 and Sherif 1966).

More recent research on 'entiativity' finds the need to construct an 'other' to be endemic at the group level. Henri Tajfel and co-researchers theorize that social identities buffer anxiety and build self-esteem by allowing individuals to bask in the reflected glory of a group's achievements. Ingroup identification leads to a bias in favor of those who are part of the ingroup and prejudice against those who are not. There is compelling evidence that people will allocate resources across groups in response to this bias even when it is disadvantageous to them (Tajfel *et al.* 1971; Tajfel 1978 and 1981; Tajfel and Turner 1986; Brown 2000).

Social identity theory suggests that people join and maintain groups for varied and often reinforcing reasons (Tajfel 1981; Tajfel and Turner 1986; Brown 2000). The evidence for self-esteem as a motive nevertheless remains strong. Research indicates that members of low status groups usually adopt one of two strategies: collective action intended to improve the standing of their group or defection to a group with higher standing. Studies using sports teams as their focus find that people are more likely to identify with highly ranked teams and disassociate themselves from teams that decline in the rankings (Dechesne *et al.* 2000). Cross-cultural research also reveals that people prefer to identify with high-status groups, although patterns of group identification (social versus political) vary across countries (Taylor 1981; Freeman 1981). Group and contextual variables complicate the relationship between self-esteem and group identification, making the choice of identity maintenance strategies extremely sensitive to context (Tajfel 1978; Brown 2000; Abrams and Hogg 1990a). There is growing evidence that similar kinds of preferences are exhibited by state actors (see, for example, Flockhart 2006; Narilkar 2006; Suzuki 2007).

Gordon Allport's pioneering study of prejudice, published in 1954, was the first important work to suggest that ingroup attachment does not require outgroup hostility. Allport reasoned that ingroups are 'psychologically primary' and develop before any conceptions of outgroups. Ingroup solidarity, moreover, is compatible with positive and negative affect toward outgroups. Allport also discovered that the boundaries between in- and outgroups were flexible; ingroup identification becomes more or less inclusive depending on the circumstances. Subsequent laboratory and cross-cultural surveys lend weight to the proposition that ingroup identification is independent of negative affect toward outgroups (Brewer and Campbell 1976; Brewer 1979; Hinkle and Brown 1990; Kloserman and Feshbach 1989). Surveys in particular indicate that patriotism and national pride – both manifestations of ingroup solidarity – are conceptually distinct from stereotypes of outgroups and aggression toward them (Feshbach 1994; Struch and Schwartz 1989). 'Oppositional consciousness', to use Jane Mansbridge's term for identity based on hostility toward outgroups, may be far less common in practice than generally supposed (Mansbridge 2001; see also Hopf 2002).

Summarizing recent research, Brewer finds complicated and still poorly understood patterns among ingroup solidarity, hostility and discrimination (1999). Ingroup bias and outgroup hostility is more closely associated with preferential treatment of ingroup members than it is with discrimination or violence against outgroups (Feshback 1994; Stuch and Schwarts 1989). Even in the absence of strong negative stereotypes, studies of ethnic and racial prejudice in the United States and Western Europe indicate the widespread existence of 'subtle racism', defined as the absence of positive feelings toward minority groups. Subtle racism reinforces the propensity of ingroups to reward their members over those of outgroups (Dovido and Gaertner 1987; Pettigrew and Meertens 1995; Iyengar, Sullivan and Ford 1980). Discrimination in turn does not require ingroup loyalty or attachment or even negative stereotypes of outgroups. Survey and comparative political research indicates that is most pronounced in conditions where groups compete for physical resources or political power (Sherif and Sherif 1953; LeVine and Campbell 1972; Horowitz 1985).

Sherif and Sherif (1953) theorized that loyalties to large collectives like nations, even humankind, were compatible with those to family, religion and region. They reasoned that 'transcendent' identities might actually mute feelings of hostility because they provide some base for common identity and empathy between in- and outgroups. The European project appears to have had this effect in some long-standing national and ethnic conflicts. However, greater interdependence with outgroups can sometimes promote intergroup conflict and hostility. As ingroups become larger and more impersonal, the institutions, rules and customs that maintain ingroup loyalty and co-operation tend to assume the character of moral authority. Outgroups who do not adhere to the same rules and customs are no longer viewed indifferently, but with contempt and hostility (Lebow 1976, Brewer 1999). More inclusive groups, whether sub- or supranational, also threaten the loss of distinctiveness for individuals with strong ingroup identification. In this connection, it is important to note that groups strive for distinctiveness that is considered positive by their members (Turner 1975; Taylor 1981; Freeman 1981; Elmers 2001;

Abrams and Hogg 1990b). When outgroups feel distinctive on dimensions that matter to them, and thus superior, they can tolerate, even acknowledge, ingroup superiority in other domains (Mummendey and Schreiber 1983; Mummendey and Simon 1989). When they hold common standards for worth, the mutual search for positive distinctiveness, and the higher status associated with it, becomes more competitive (Mummendey and Wenzel 1999; Deschamps and Brown 1983). Any of these processes can be intensified or dampened by leaders seeking to exploit or downplay hostile feelings for their own political ends.

In conclusion, there is ample historical evidence that identity construction has often been accompanied by the creation of stereotyped 'others'. However, there is little empirical or laboratory evidence to support the claim that identity or national solidarity requires 'others', let alone their violent exclusion from domestic, regional or international communities.

The *Iliad*

Institutional and collective memory are the principal vehicle of group identity and solidarity. They are sites of contestation, as political authorities, intellectuals and institutions of all kinds attempt to foster memories conducive to their political projects or psychological needs. There is not only conflict about the contents of institutional and collective memories, but also between these forms of memory when they represent different and clashing understandings (see Lebow *et al.* 2006). Intellectuals play critical roles in both kinds of conflict. They create oral and written discourses and counter-discourses that have the potential of shaping collective and institutional memory, although the latter requires the support of those in power.

The text, I am about to examine offers the quintessential example of this process. We know nothing about Homer's intentions – assuming he even existed – or about the bards who shaped or reshaped his poem until it finally assumed written form. Collectively, they established a discourse that taught Greeks who they were. In classical times the sign of an educated man was his ability to recite sections of the *Iliad* and *Odyssey*, and there were people who knew both epics by heart (Xenophon, *Symposium*: 3.5). Greeks assimilated Homeric values to such a degree according to Socrates, that there were Greeks who thought they should mould their lives around the characters and values of the epics (Plato *Republic*: 606e). Homer's poetry shaped not only the collective memory of generations of Greeks, but institutional memory, as the *Iliad* and *Odyssey* became central features of the school curricula of *poleis* stretching from Spain to the Black Sea. Knowledge of Greek language and culture, propagated through these enduring works of literature, helped to create a strong sense of Hellenic community that transcended, but did not supercede, commitments to individual city states.

The *Iliad* is a fictional work that describes a fictional world. Homer, if he actually existed, lived sometime in the ninth or eighth centuries BCE, some three or four hundred years after the Trojan War is supposed to have occurred. It is possible that the *Iliad* portrays a real war on the basis of stories passed down by word of mouth through the Greek Dark Ages. At some stage, bards combined these stories into a larger narrative – the *Iliad* is 15,000 lines – and improvised many lines in retelling them according to a sophisticated set of rules. Improvisation inevitably, perhaps purposefully, introduced some of contemporary society's values, ideals and practices. The bards constructed what Max Weber would call an ideal type: a mental construct that will never be encountered in practice, but nevertheless offers insights into real worlds.

According to Greek myth, the Trojan War is the direct result of Paris's elopement with Helen, wife of King Menelaus of Sparta. This was a violation of Menelaus' honor and of guest friendship (*xenia*), a convention common to most traditional societies.[3] In Greece, the obligation to receive guests was considered so important that hospitality was made one of the epithets of the father of the gods: Zeus Xenios (Finley 1978: 99–101). In return, the guest must not abuse his host's hospitality or overstay his welcome. Menelaus defends his honor by attempting to punish Paris and regain Helen. He is also defending his position, as he would be regarded as weak by rivals and neighbors if he failed to act. He asks Zeus to grant him revenge 'so that any man born hereafter may shrink from wronging a host who has shown him friendship' (*Iliad* Book 3.351–4).[4] Honor requires Greeks connected to Menelaus by ties of obligation, family or guest friendship to come to his aid (Seaford 1994: 13–25; Taplin 1992: 56–8). On the Trojan side, guest friendship moves King Priam to offer refuge to his son Paris and the woman he has run off with even though he and most Trojans thoroughly disapprove of the pair and recognize that their presence is certain to provoke a war with the Greeks.

The principal focus of the *Iliad* is the conflict between Achilles and Agamemnon, which is also driven by honor. In an act of moral blindness (*atē*), the greedy Agamemnon takes a slave girl from Achilles to replace the one he must return to her father. Achilles is furious, withdraws from the struggle, refuses gifts subsequently offered him by Agamemnon and only returns to the fighting to avenge the death of his beloved Patroclus. Homer ends his tale while the war is still raging, but his listeners know that Troy will be captured and its inhabitants slaughtered or enslaved, but not before Achilles, Hector and many other Greek and Trojan heroes die. Menelaus will return home with Helen, but his brother Agamemnon will be murdered by his unfaithful wife Clytemnestra, who has never forgiven him his sacrifice of their daughter.

The Trojans give the superficial appearance of being the principal 'other' for the Greeks. The war against them, already in its tenth year, has rallied Greeks from all over Hellas and helped to build a common Greek identity – just as reading Homer's description of the war would do for later generations of Greeks who considered themselves their linear descendants. Greek warriors are filled with 'hate'(*misei*) for their Trojan adversaries, and Achilles in particular, rages against them – but only after Patroclus is killed by Hector. It is not enough for him to kill Hector in turn, he must disfigure his body, drag him back to camp on his chariot and slaughter 12 young Trojan boys before Patroclus' funeral pyre (*Iliad* Book 23.199–201).

Close listeners or readers of the poem understand hate to be an artifact of a war that has taken Greeks far away from their homes, exposed them to the rigors of camp life and to mounting losses of family and friends through illness and enemy action. Their leader Agamemnon is a greedy and authoritarian bastard whose behavior makes a mockery of the values that led Greeks to follow him to Troy. Achilles is absolutely explicit about the focus of his hatred: 'The Trojans never did *me* damage, not in the least, they never stole my cattle or my horses, never in Phthia where the rich soils breeds strong men did they lay waste my crops'. Furious at Agamemnon for taking his slave girl Briseis for himself, he exclaims: 'No you colossal, shameless – we all followed you, to please you, to fight for you, to win your honor back from the Trojans – Menelaus and you, you dog-face!' (1.180–92). After this incident Achilles and his Myrmidons withdraw from the fighting. Achilles has the standing to do this. Other warriors cannot just sulk in their tents or pack up as go home without being denounced as cowards and deserters. Nor can they complain openly like Thersites, the only common soldier with a voice in the poem, and he is beaten into a pulp by Odysseus for speaking out (2.246–324). Aristocratic warriors must repress and redirect outwards against the Trojans their pain, suffering, anxiety, anger and fear. Given this situation, what is truly remarkable about the *Iliad* is its portrayal of Greeks and Trojans as fundamentally similar and equally worthy peoples, a characterization that reveals Greek hate as the psychological defense it is and gives additional poignancy to the war and its unrelieved slaughter. Listeners and readers grieve equally for death of heroes on both sides, an emotional response that generates strong dissonance with the initial binary the poem appears to set up.

This dissonance is enhanced in the portrayal of individual Trojans, Greek–Trojan behavior on and off the battlefield, the many parallels and few differences the poem draws between the two sides and divine intervention, which suggests that Greeks and Trojans alike are the playthings of gods motivated by ego, passion and jealousy. The dissonance is partially resolved in the penultimate scene, one of the most moving in Western literature, in which emotion and reason come together to create a precarious reconciliation between Priam and Achilles. Homer is telling us that Greeks become Greeks through their engagement with Trojans, and that their most distinguished warrior can only regain his humanity through the combined efforts of the gods and the Trojan king. The self does not form so much in opposition to the 'other', but more in conjunction with it. In doing so, the self is not only constructed but stretched. One's identity is defined not just in terms of the family (*oikos*) and ethnic group (Greek) but as part of humanity as a whole. This stretching provides the ethical foundations of identity that make it and human existence ultimately worthwhile.

Let us begin with Homer's depiction of the Trojans. They are the Greeks' enemy, to be sure, but are never portrayed in stereotypic terms by either the poet or Greek warriors. Hector is a warrior and a civilized man. He returns from battle, picks up his son who recoils in terror because he does not recognize his father and sees only a man in a fierce war helmet with a great plume on top. Hector takes off his helmet, laughs, lifts his son up into the air and asks the gods to grant him glory. Andromache, his wife, takes the child from him, presses it to her breast and smiles through her tears (6.556–600). We know that the young Astyanax will be thrown from the walls by victorious Greeks – the very negation of civilized behavior.

Trojan heroes and their allies emerge as men of outstanding character and quality as do their women. King Priam and his son Hector are arguably the most admirable figures in the epic. They are deeply committed to their families and city, but also to the behavioral code, shared by Greeks and Trojans, that brings them *time*, a word used by Homer and later Greeks to signify honor and office. Their unflinching adherence to this code brings war to the city when Priam extends guest friendship to Helen and death to Hector when he refuses the wise advice to retreat inside the wall of Troy and instead allows Achilles to engage him in single combat. He tells Andromache: 'I would die of shame to face the men of Troy and the Trojan women trailing their long robes if I would shrink from the battle now, a coward' (6.523–5). A recent survey of West Point cadets reveals that Achilles – the most skilled, but least disciplined of warriors – is no longer the most admired figure in the epic. Students offer a victorious Hector as their role model, explaining that he is acting in defense of his family and city (Coker 2007). There are striking contrasts between Priam and Agamemnon, whose greed dishonors his office, and Hector and Achilles, who becomes a raging lion without human feelings after Patroclus is killed.

Even more revealing are the contrasts between Greek and Trojan women. Helen, the only Greek woman in the epic, is a self-hating woman of low character who laments the day she was born, but makes every accommodation necessary to stay alive. Priam's queen Hecuba and Hector's wife Andromache, like Penelope in the *Odyssey*, live up to the Greek ideals of womanhood. They are loyal to their husbands, offer them emotional support and sound advice and perform valuable services on the 'home front'. They behave with exceptional restraint and correctness toward Helen, whose presence has caused the war that is likely to kill their husbands and make them widows and slaves.

Helen divides Greeks from Trojans but also unites them. She was married to Agamemnon and is now betrothed to Paris. Standing on the ramparts of Troy she identifies and describes the various Greek warriors and praises their skills and hospitality (3.200–88). Helen is aware of how she brings the two sides together, not only in the action of the poem, but in the 'dark, folding robe' she weaves, 'working into the weft the endless bloody struggles stallion-breaking Trojans and Argives armed in bronze had suffered all for her at the god of battle's demands' (3.150–4).

The text stresses the many similarities between Greeks and Trojans. Book 2, a catalogue of the armies, describes the Greek forces and then the Trojans and their allies. Fewer lines are devoted to the Trojans, but the same positive adjectives are used to describe their leading fighters. Book 3 indicates that Greeks and Trojans worship the same gods and share common values. In Book 4, both sides make sacrifices before the first detailed description of battle and mourn in its aftermath (4.502–517–630).[5] Their warriors display equal bravery and success, with Greeks and Trojans alternating kills. Both sides act in accord with the rules of war, generally giving quarter to disarmed men and showing civility, even kindness, to their opponents. Homer drives home their fundamental sameness in his description of the battleground once the fighters have withdrawn: 'That day ranks of Trojans, ranks of Achaean fighters sprawled there side-by-side, facedown in the dust' (4.629–30). In Book 7, the two sides agree to a truce so they can recover the bodies of the fallen. It is hard to tell who belongs to which side until the bodies are washed and prepared for immolation (7.487–99).

Book 3 foregrounds the two men directly responsible for the war: Paris and Menelaus. Paris is the least admirable man in the epic. He absconded with Menelaus' wife and is a coward to boot, content to let his brothers bear the brunt of the fighting while he dallies with Helen safely within the confines of the palace. Menelaus is forthright if tedious, and committed to getting Helen back and destroying Troy for the succor it has given to Paris and Helen. Upbraided by Hector, Paris agrees to fight Menelaus in a single combat, with the winner to receive Helen and all her possessions. Greeks and Trojans swear by Zeus to live in peace ever afterwards, a recognition that there is no fundamental issue dividing them other than Helen. Even Menelaus agrees to this arrangement, although he proclaims that 'Such limited vengeance hurts me most of all – but I intend that we will part in peace, at last, Trojans and Achaeans' (3.119–21). The two armies come together to sacrifice a white and black ewe to symbolize their agreement, and invoke the gods as guarantors of their promises to live in peace after the combat. The Greeks honor Priam by asking for him to seal the truce, as they do not trust his sons (3.125–35).

Menelaus is the worthier opponent and the better warrior. His spear penetrates Paris's shield, but Paris deftly sidesteps its bronze point. Menelaus rushes forward and is on the verge of cleaving Paris' skull when Aphrodite causes his sword to shatter on his opponent's helmet. She then cuts Paris' helmet strap and snatches him away to prevent Menelaus from dragging him back behind the Greek lines (3.98–42). Paris reappears in the palace and fired up by Aphrodite has an overwhelming need to make love to Helen. But even Helen turns on him, declaring that 'It would be wrong, disgraceful to share that coward's bed once more'. She relents when Aphrodite threatens her: 'I might make you the butt of hard, withering hate from both sides at once. Trojans and Achaeans – then your fate can tread you down to dust' (3.484–6). To make sure the fighting resumes, the gods intervene to break truce. Athena 'fires up the fool's heart' inside of Pandarus, a Trojan archer who then shoots at and wounds Menelaus (4.59–146). Most of these encounters are closely observed by the gods in Olympus who take to their seats to watch the ranging armies fight it out on the plain below (20.181–4).

A second great combat, that between Ajax and Hector, also ends indecisively. It nevertheless reveals the awe with which Greeks regard Hector. Nobody wants to confront him until they are shamed and brought to their feet by wise old Nestor (7.183–201). Hector shows himself to be a fair warrior. He exclaims to Ajax: 'On guard! Big and bluff as you are, I've no desire to hit you sniping in on the sly – I'd strike you out in the open, strike you now!' (7.282–5). The gods keep Hector and Ajax from killing each other and the two exhausted warriors finally agree to a personal truce. Hector tells Ajax: 'Come, let us give each other gifts, unforgettable gifts, so any man may say, Trojan soldier or Argive, "First they fought with heart-devouring hatred, then they parted, bound by pacts of friendship" (7.346–50).

The third and fourth great combats result in kills. Hector bests Patroclus and Achilles kills Hector. The terms of engagement change as does the language used by the warriors. Before striking him down Hector tells Patroclus that 'the vultures will eat your body raw' (16.937). His threat presages the inhuman treatment Achilles has in store for him. After killing Hector, he pierces his ankles, runs rawhide straps through them to his chariot and drags his body back to the Greek camp where he leaves it exposed to the dogs. Learning of her son's death, Hecuba in turn exclaims that she could eat Achilles 'raw!' (24.252). For Greeks, one of the defining conditions of humanity was the preparation and cooking of meat, so both these references to rawness indicate at least a figurative return to an animal state. Achilles' defilement of Hector's body takes this descent another step, alienating himself from his identity, and threatening the honor of the Greek army. The gods intervene to preserve Hector's body, express their disapproval to Achilles and sneak Priam into the Greek camp to ransom back his son. They exclaim that 'Achilles has lost all pity! No shame in the man' (24.252). Pity is another distinguishing feature of humans, and shame a sign of civilization.

Book 24 brings Achilles and Priam together in the culminating and climactic encounter between Greeks and Trojans. The encounter is fraught with danger; Priam must sneak through the Greek lines and camp with his cart and trust in Achilles to receive him properly. Achilles must repress his anger, which threatens to break through and express itself in violence against Priam. Achilles and his retainers are restrained by the sight of Priam: 'Achilles marveled, beholding majestic Priam. His men marveled too, trading startled glances' (24.567–8). Seeing his moment, Priam pours his heart out to Achilles: 'Remember your own father, great godlike Achilles – as old as I am, past the threshold of deadly old age! No doubt the countrymen round him plague him now, with no one there to defend him, beat away disaster' (24.567–73). A few lines later, he attempts to transfer some of Achilles' feelings about his father to himself: 'Revere the gods, Achilles! Pity me in my own right, remember your own father!' (24.588–9). Achilles softens and Priam now suggests: 'Let us put our griefs to rest in our own hearts, rake them up no more, raw as we are with mourning .... So the immortals spun our lives that we, we wretched men live on to bear such torments – the gods live free of sorrows' (24.610–14). Priam, in effect, offers Achilles a chance to honor the gods and cheat them by returning his son and lessening his suffering. Achilles agrees to exchange Hector for the ransom and instructs his retainers to wash and wrap his body for its return journey to Troy. The two men share a meal, the symbolic end to mourning for Greeks. Before they part,

> Priam the son of Dardanus gazed at Achilles, marveling now at the man's beauty, his magnificent build – face-to-face he seemed a deathless god ... and Achilles gazed and marveled at Dardan Priam, beholding his noble looks, listening to his words.
>
> (24.740–5)

The narrator suggests that together, but not individually, they have attained honor and wisdom through Achilles' build and bravery and Priam's noble looks and *logos*, in this instance meaning wisdom. Greeks and Trojans become who they are through their interaction and need each other to realize their human potential.

The encounter between Achilles and Priam does not end the war. Both men grieve for their loved ones, recognize the destructiveness, and even the irrationality of their conflict, but lack a language they could use to construct new identities for themselves that would allow them to terminate the conflict and escape their preordained fates. Priam returns to Troy, knowing that it will be destroyed and he and his family with it. Achilles knows that he must soon die and prepares for his final battle, proleptically brooding about his father mourning his death. The saga ends on a somber note but leaves listeners with the idea that they, unlike Achilles and Priam, can forge new identities and use the text as a vehicle toward this goal. This is precisely what happened in Greece. The Homeric texts – the *Odyssey* as well as the *Iliad* – take shape in repeated performances in which bards competing for honor repeatedly adapt the poems to local conditions and aspirations. The history of these epics reveals a gradual synthesis of diffused traditions and dialects, a stitching together, as suggested by the fragment from Pindar that I quote at the outset. This process stimulated and mediated the project of mutual self-definition by Greeks speaking many different dialects and gave rise to an explicit pan-Hellenic identity and agenda (Nagy 1990 and 1996; Collins 2004; Taplin 2000: 4–39).

The *Aeneid*

The *Aeneid* is a single-authored work by Virgil, modeled on Homer's *Iliad* and *Odyssey*. Virgil had a very specific audience in mind: Augustus. Like the *Iliad*, the *Aeneid* is an epic about victory and empire. An alternative epic form, about the defeated, arose with Lucan (Marcus Annaeus Lucanus, 39–65 CE), but never achieved the same status in Rome or Christian Europe (Quint 1993: 8–9). Epic poetry was the genre of the aristocracy, celebrating their heroic accomplishments, and even downgrading those of kings, as the *Iliad* does in its contrast of Achilles and Agamemnon. It reached its zenith in Europe just as the conditions that gave rise to it were fast disappearing due to the centralizing authority of kings.

Biographical information about Virgil is relatively scant. He was born in 70 BCE. in a small village near Mantua (Mantova) in the Po Valley. Roman citizenship had been extended north to the Po River, but the territory north of it was a *provincia*, and its inhabitants, Virgil among them, did not become citizens until 49 BCE Unlike many landowners in the *provincia*, Virgil's family estate was not confiscated to reward veterans of Octavian and Mark Anthony's campaign against Brutus and Cassius. Virgil was an Italian before he was a Roman and his writings reveal a lifelong identification with Italy and Italians (Miles and Allen 1986: 14–17; Knox 2006). In the *Georgics*, there is a passage vaunting the beauties, riches and people of Italy over those of the East (Virgil *Georgics*, 2.136–69).

The *Ecologues*, Virgil's first great work, was published in 39 or 38 BCE. It was patterned on Greek pastoral poetry that used Homeric hexameter to memorialize rustic rivalries and love affairs. The *Ecologues* nevertheless contains a thinly veiled reference to the confiscation of northern Italian estates and the hardship this created for its former owners and their families. The poem was an instant success, and its rhythmic patterns, modeled on Homer, were widely hailed and imitated, even parodied. It was followed by the *Georgics*, for which Hesiod's *Works and Days* was the model, and appealed to the traditional Roman love of the land and its crops and animals. In 30 BCE, Virgil read it to Octavian (who was voted the title Augustus by the Senate in 27), not long after his victory at Actium over Anthony and Cleopatra and their subsequent suicides in Egypt. Suetonius tells us that Virgil spoke hesitatingly, almost like an uneducated man, but read his poetry in a manner that 'was sweet and wonderfully effective'. When he read the *Aeneid* to Augustus and his sister Octavia, she is supposed to have fainted after listening to his lines about her dead son Marcellus (Suetonius 1920: 467–73).

Virgil's final and most ambitious work is the *Aeneid*, in which he aspires to celebrate 'The fiery fights of Caesar [meaning Octavian], make his name live in the future' (*Georgics* 3.46–47). Its rhythmic pattern is Homeric and there are numerous references to characters and scenes from the *Iliad* and *Odyssey*. Virgil intends the *Aeneid* to become the founding document of *Romanita* as Homer's epics were for Hellas. The central figure of the poem is Aeneas, a Trojan warrior who is the son of Aphrodite and Anchises and survives the sack of his city by the Greeks. He carries his father from the burning city, but is somehow separated from his trailing wife. He returns to Troy desperate to find her and encounters her ghost who tells him that fate has a long exile in store for him until he reaches the Hesperian Land [Italy] where the Lydian Tiber flows through a smooth march with rich loamy fields. 'There great joy and a kingdom are yours to claim, and a queen to make your wife' (*Aeneid* Book 2.967–72).[6] En route his armada is blown by storms on to the African coast, where the Trojans are given refuge by Queen Dido. Aeneas and Dido fall in love, with some help from Juno, who is dead set on keeping him from reaching Italy. Aeneas settles in and helps Dido build Carthage. Jupiter is furious and sends Mercury down to remind Aeneas of his responsibility for founding Rome (2.219–37). In an act of *pietas* (loyalty and duty to the gods, one's family and Rome) and *gravitas* (seriousness in the face of religious and civic responsibilities) Aeneas orders his fleet to set sail. The disconsolate Dido, who has lost her lover and her authority, falls on her sword.

Arriving in Sicily, Aeneas organizes funeral games for Anchises, reminiscent of those Achilles organizes for Patroclus in the *Iliad*. Juno tries and fails to burn his armada. In a dream, his father tells him he must journey to Elysium. Guided through its portals by Sibyl, he meets his father and witnesses a pageant of the Romans who in coming centuries will establish the world's greatest empire and impose peace on the world. Back in the mortal world, Aeneas and his men set off for the Tiber, where they establish a fortified camp on the river's shore. Aeneas sends an emissary to King Latinus asking for land and the hand of his daughter Lavinia. The king is inclined to agree, but Juno sends the fury Allecto to turn Lavinia's mother against the marriage and to inspire outrage in Turnus, the King of Rutulia, daughter of the water nymph Venilia and suitor of Lavinia. The Rutulians declare war on the

Trojans and local leaders and peoples choose sides. The Etruscans come to the aid of the Trojans, in part because their cruel king Mezentius, whom they have expelled, sides with the Rutulians. As in the *Iliad*, the slaughter is unrelenting and hero after hero, or heroine in the case of Camilla, meets a violent and often graphic end.

Venus persuades Vulcan to forge arms and a shield for Aneneas – as he did for Achilles in the *Iliad* – with the story of 'Rome in all her triumphs' blazoned across the face of the shield (8.738–9). Turnus attacks the Trojan camp and wreaks havoc. Jupiter convenes the gods and listens to Venus and Juno plead their respective cases. He decides to let Aeneas and Turnus resolve the affair in a one-on-one combat. After still more bloodshed in which several Trojan champions die, Aeneas kills Mezentius and his son and Camilla is laid low by an Etruscan arrow. In the final book, Turnus challenges Aeneas, but Juno intervenes to save him and Aeneas is wounded by an arrow. Venus supplies a drug to restore him to health and inspires him to burn Latinus's city. Jupiter restrains Juno, but agrees to her request that Latium endure and never adopt the Trojan name, manners or language. Aeneas and Turnus now confront one another, and Turnus, bested by his rival, lies at his feet and pleads for his life. Aeneas spies the sword belt of his boon companion Pallas, son of Evander, whom Turnus has killed and taken from him to wear as a trophy. Enraged, he thrusts his sword deep into Turnus' heart.

Virgil spent the last three years of his life in Greece revising the *Aeneid*, which was never completed to his satisfaction. In 19 BCE, he was persuaded by Augustus, in Greece on his way back from Egypt, to return to Rome with him. On the voyage, Virgil contracted a fever and died on 21 September and was buried near Naples. His *Aeneid* had a long afterlife. It became a standard text in Roman schools and their medieval Christian successors. As Virgil had hoped, his poetry became the point of reference for subsequent Roman writers; Latin poetry and prose quote and makes frequent allusions to his works, as do later writers like Dante, Ariosto, Tasso and Milton (Thomas 2001: 34–40; Quint; 1993). It also achieved oracular status. The emperor Hadrian, like many Romans, sought to learn his future by opening the book at random and reading the first passage that struck his eye (Knox 2006: 36–7).

The *Aeneid* differs from the *Iliad* in many important ways, one of them being the multiplicity of peoples with whom the Trojans interact, ally with and fight. The list of 'others' begins with the Greeks, and their sack of Troy in Book 2. This is the cause of Trojan suffering, the death of Aeneas' wife and his hegira to Italy. Virgil's negative depiction of the Greeks stands in sharp contrast to Homer's largely positive account. They are portrayed as booty-seeking barbarians. In the attack on Troy, Pyrrhus (Neoptolemus), the son of Achilles, 'crazed with carnage', wounds Polites, one of King Priam's sons. He flees to the altar in his parents' house where he vomits out his life blood before their very eyes and before Pyrrhus, his sword drawn, can run him through (*Aeneid* 2.620–59). An enraged Priam denies Pyrrhus' parenthood, reminding him how his father honored a suppliant's rights. Old Priam flings his spear at Pyrrhus, but it fails to penetrate the boss of his shield, and his shameless adversary shouts back: 'Well, then, down you go, a messenger to my father, Peleus' son! Tell him about my vicious work, how Neoptolemus [another name of Pyrrhus] degrades his father's name – don't you forget. Now – die!' He drags Priam to the altar through the blood and guts of his son that litter the floor, 'and twist[ing] Priam's hair in his left hand, his right hand sweeping forth his sword – a flash of steel – he buries it hilt-deep in the king's flank' (2.673–86). The contrast between Priam's encounter with Achilles and his son could not be more striking.

Although writing about the past, Virgil had his eye on the present. His negative portrayal of the Greeks would have resonated with many of his readers. In the second century BCE, Rome had fought a bloody war with Macedonia and other Greek states. Lucius Mummius sacked Corinth in 146 BCE and Aemilius Paullus routed Perseus, the Macedonian king, at Pydna in 168 BCE. The political subjugation of Hellas opened Rome to penetration by Greek culture, a development loathed by conservatives, for whom Greeks became the kind of 'other' they were for the *Aeneid*'s Trojans. Virgil, who drew so heavily on Homer, idolized Greek culture. He nevertheless suggests that Rome's triumph over Greece is justifiable revenge for the sack of Troy. In Book 1, he has Jove announce his proleptic pleasure in the conquest of 'Achilles' homeland, brilliant Mycenae too', by the house of Assaracus [one of Aeneas' descendants], and the enslavement of their peoples (1.338–41).

The next 'other', in order of appearance, is Dido and her Tyrians. They are also émigrés from their homeland, having fled injustice to settle on the northern coast of Africa. Jupiter arranges for Dido to extend hospitality to Aeneas and his followers, although it would have been natural for the Tyrians to do this in accord with the custom of *xenia* and their strategic need for allies against local adversaries (1.297–304). The two peoples get on famously and work together to build the new city of Carthage. We can reasonably assume that Aeneas is not the only Trojan trysting with a local girl. Dido's subsequent suicide is modeled on the *devotio* of a defeated Roman commander who takes his life to commit the gods to take revenge on his adversary. She issues such a curse against the city Aeneas' descendants will found and commits Carthage to no-holds-barred warfare against it:

> This is my prayer, my funeral cry – I pour it out
> with my own lifeblood. And you, my Tyrians,
> harry with hatred all his line, his race to come:
> make that offering to my ashes, send it down below.
> No love between our peoples, ever, no pacts of peace!
> Come rising from my bones, you avenger still unknown,
> to stalk those Trojan settlers, hunt with fire and iron,
> now or in time to come, whenever the power is yours.
> Shore clash with shore, seas against sea and sword
> against sword – this is my curse – war between all
> our people, all their children, endless war!

(4.774–84)

What are we to make of this fabulous tale? The intended reading is undoubtedly the imperial one: Dido and Carthage distractions that keep Aeneas from proceeding to Italy. Erotic involvement threatens to reduce the hero to the status of an ordinary mortal; the same danger Calypso and Circe pose to Odysseus. Like Odysseus, Aeneas must escape from their clutches if he is to fulfill his mission. He must learn to 'love 'em and leave them'. Greek and Tyrian 'others' accordingly represent two different kinds of threats. The masculine Greeks threaten to cut short Trojan lives with their spears and swords, while the 'feminine' Tyrians threaten to deny them their chance of gaining fame as heroes. For Homer and Virgil the latter is by far the greater loss. This is why Homer's Achilles, given the choice of long life or a short one as a hero, does not hesitate to choose the latter (*Iliad* 1.496–8). He recognizes that great deeds bring the only kind of immortality attainable by humans: having their name and accomplishments carried forward by succeeding generations (Lebow 2008: Ch. 3).

In the *Iliad*, Helen corrupts Paris and is ultimately responsible for Troy's destruction. In the *Odyssey*, Odysseus successfully escapes entrapment by Calypso and Circe. In the *Aeneid*, Dido and Cleopatra are set up as parallel temptresses, although the former only behaves this way because of the intervention of Venus. Anthony fails in his efforts to gain Rome because he is in thrall to Cleopatra, while Aeneas succeeds in laying the foundations for Rome because he is able to exercise sufficient *gravitas* to tear himself away from the charms of Dido. Empire building is a male affair. For Virgil, the struggle between masculine and feminine reinforces that between West and East. The 'otherness' of the Easterner merges with the 'otherness' of woman, a theme that would also be pronounced in the Renaissance epics of Ariosto, Tasso and Milton.[7]

David Quint suggests that the feminization of Easterners is most evident in Virgil's account of the Battle of Actium, fought off the coast of Greece in September of 31 BCE. It resulted in a rout of Anthony and Cleopatra's forces and the consolidation of Augustus' authority over the Roman Empire. Barbaric riches – wealth is another source of corruption – pay for Anthony's fleet and armies – as gold from the East underwrote the founding of Dido's Carthage. The West represents order and unity – Augustus (the autocratic *princeps*) is supported by Agrippa, in command of disciplined Roman forces. The East is characterized by disorder; two commanders, Anthony and Cleopatra, lead a rag tag collection of diverse and poorly co-ordinated eastern forces – Egyptians, Indians, Arabs, Sabaeans – none of whom speak mutually intelligible languages. The West displays masculine control, with Augustus firmly at the rudder, while the feminine east is symbolized by Cleopatra's ship and fleet, at the mercy of the wind. The West also represents cosmic order versus disorder, Olympian versus monster gods and permanence and reason versus flux, nature and loss of identity. Following their suicides, Anthony and Cleopatra are absorbed by the Nile, leaving no traces behind (*Aeneid* 8.790–859).

Quint (1993) boldly asserts that the East-West, male-female, division is a fundamental cultural orientation that is also central to Homer. I must respectfully dissent. While the Trojans and their allies are unquestionably Asian, they are portrayed as fundamentally similar to the Greeks in every important respect. Only Paris represents the feminized warrior, and he is scorned by other Trojans, including his own brother Hector. The Trojans and the allies are more unified than their Greek adversaries, whose commitment to sustain the struggle is severely threatened by discord between Achilles and Agamemnon. Achilles defeats Hector, as the Greeks will the Trojans, not because Hector and his countrymen and their Asian allies lack courage and discipline, but because the gods decree this outcome.

Even in the *Aeneid*, these binaries are softened. Before the intervention of Juno and Venus, Dido is positively masculine in her comportment. Like Aeneas, she has successfully brought her followers to a new land, fought and defeated local adversaries who opposed their settlement and rules in a seemingly just and decisive way, with the support of her Tyrians. She is carrying out the same kind of project that fate has decreed for Aeneas. She is transformed by divine intervention, which misogynists could read as an attempt to put this feminine upstart in her place. But there is no indication of this motive in the text, only of idiosyncratic preferences, jealousies and plots of the gods having nothing to do with Dido.

Juno is said to love Carthage above all other cities and to park her chariot and armor there. Her goal from the outset was for Carthage to rule over other nations of the earth (1.14–28, 322–88). She despises Troy and Trojans for petty, personal reasons. Their founding king was Dardanus, son of Zeus and Electra (1.35). Zeus has an erotic interest in Ganymede, a beautiful boy and son of a Trojan prince, whom he brings to Olympus to serve as his cupbearer. Most galling of all for Juno, was the so-called Judgment of Paris. Confronted by Juno, Athena and Venus, who demand that he admire and rank their charms, Paris names Venus as the most beautiful. She has promised him the love of Helen, wife of King Menelaus of Sparta, and the world's most beautiful woman (1.34). Juno is consumed by the desire to get even with her husband for his dalliances and with Paris for slighting her beauty. She sides with the Greeks in the Trojan war and does everything in her power to destroy Aeneas, or at least keep him his destiny of founding a great empire. Venus, by contrast, is the principal supporter of the Trojans and twice intervenes in the fighting to save her son Aeneas before the walls of Troy (3.557–60). She also protects Paris, presumably because of his judgment in her favor. The intervention of the gods and the malleability of human desires that it reveals undercuts any essentialist notion of fundamental differences between men and women and Asians and Europeans.

More support for this reading comes from the fate of the other woman hero of the *Aeneid*: Camilla, the fearless Volscian virgin and 'warrior queen who dares to battle men' (1.595, 7.805, 11.711). She has no strong personal presence and is described entirely in terms of her military prowess. She undercuts the grandeur of Turnus, and the sight of her in battle dress mounted on her horse leaves men stunned and gaping at her (*attonitis inhians animis*) (7.814). She has the pride and courage of a man. When the son of Aunus challenges her to hand-to-hand combat rather than from a horse, she dismounts and dispatches him without further ado (11.705). In describing the combat, Virgil uses the simile of a hawk killing a dove, who 'holds it and rips out its entrails with hooked claws while blood and torn feathers float down from the sky' (11.721–4).

The most compelling evidence for the mutability of character is the transformation of the most important 'other' of the epic: the Trojans themselves. Once again, David Quint is our point of entry. He maintains that long narrative poems like the *Iliad* and the *Aeneid* take the form of epic or romance. Epic is about victory, ordained from the outset, but only attained after numerous challenges, sacrifices and tests of their commitments, skill and endurance of their heroes. The *Iliad* is the quintessential epic. Romance in turn is circular and aimless, consists of unrelated episodes and is often associated with a defeated hero or people. For Quint (1993), the *Odyssey* is the original romance. This categorization is problematic. It is the *Iliad* that lacks teleology and ends on a somber note, before the Greeks attain victory. The eponymous Odysseus is a victor, not a loser. His wanderings appear aimless and its episodes are largely unconnected, something emphasized by the fact that most of them take place on remote islands (Fowler 1997). However, the *Odyssey* has a telos: the homecoming (*nostos*) of its hero after surviving numerous ordeals and temptations.

It is more accurate to claim, as Quint does, that the *Aeneid* combines elements of the two forms. The first half of the poem recounts the seaborne wanderings of Aeneas in a manner reminiscent of the *Odyssey*. The efforts of Aeneas and his followers to found a new Troy repeatedly fail, as they are bound to until they rid themselves of their sense of loss and victimization. In the second half of the poem, that which takes place in Italy, Aeneas and his followers recapitulate the Trojan War. From the fortress they fend off Latins and engage in collective and individual combats reminiscent of various encounters in the *Iliad*. This time they are the victors: Aeneas kills Turnus in a one-on-one combat that bears a striking resemblance to his near defeat by Diomedes in the *Iliad*.[8] As W. S. Anderson (1957) notes, the Trojans become the Greeks and their victory paves the way for the founding of Rome and the ultimate conquest of Greece by their descendants. History has come full circle.

In the course of the *Aeneid* the Trojans progress from being the Asian 'other' to the Western 'self', and not because they have physically moved west. They recover psychologically from their galling and costly defeat and, as their self-confidence returns, develop the 'Western' qualities of order, purpose, and commitment – *gravitas*, in a word – and spurn women and material comforts when they stand in the way of more 'serious' political goals. The Trojan transformation is most evident in the character of Aeneas who begins life as a Trojan and ends it as an Italian (Cairns 1989: Ch. 5). This teleology drives the epic and is introduced relatively early in Book 1 when Aeneas asserts that Italy is his true motherland (*Italiam quaero patriam*) (1.380).

The transformation of the Trojans is not enough to guarantee a successful political-military outcome. The gods must make peace among themselves. Toward this end, Juno sets aside her hatred and proposes a compromise to Jupiter. Let Aeneas wed Lavinia and Trojans plight their troth Latins, but

> never command the Latins, here on native soil,
> to change their age-old name,
> to become Trojans, called the kin of Teucer,
> alter their language, change their style of dress.
> Let Latium endure. Let Alban kings hold sway for all time.
> Let Roman stock grow strong with Italian strength.
> Troy has fallen – and fallen let her stay –
> with the very name of Troy!

(12.950–61)

Earlier, Jupiter had decreed that the kingdom of Troy would rise up again (1.341–3). Now he wisely accedes to her request and proclaims that:

> Latium's sons will retain their father's words and ways,
> Their name till now is the name that shall endure.
> Mingling in stock alone, the Trojans will subside.
> And I will add the rites and the forms of worship,
> make them Latins all, who speak the Latin tongue.

(12.967–71)

With Juno's assistance Aeneas now defeats Turnus and the epic comes to an end.

Learning from the ancients

My narratives stresses the numerous similarities between Homer and Virgil. Their differences are equally striking and critical for our understanding of identity construction. To the extent that the group of bards responsible for the *Iliad* had a political agenda it was class related. The *Iliad* and the *Odyssey* are both composed for aristocrats. They vaunt their intelligence, leadership skills and willingness to sacrifice material comforts for honor, in sharp contrast to the plebian concerns, limited cognitive abilities and lack of steadfastness of ordinary people. In the *Iliad*, common folk (*demos* or *hoi polloi*) were set up as an 'other' that justified aristocratic privilege and helped to maintain class divisions in the West for the next 2500 years. For Homer, as for nineteenth century European nobles, class cuts across and often trumps territorial, ethnic or religious divides. This may help to explain why the Trojans share so much in common with the Greeks, more than they do with their common folk. Greek and Trojan aristocrats need each other to sustain and validate their common project: the quest for *aristeia*. Thersites, as noted earlier, is put in his place by Odysseus, who hits him over the head with Agamemnon's scepter, a symbol of royal authority (*Iliad* 2.246–324). Rule by aristocrats is portrayed as natural and divinely sanctioned.

The Trojans are nevertheless the principal 'other' in the *Iliad*. They are represented in a nuanced way and not very different from the Greeks. Their portrayal is constructed from the appearance, words and deeds of individual actors; Hector, Priam, Paris, Andromache, Hecuba and Aeneas are key in developing Homer's image of the Trojans. They are certainly not essentialist in their characteristics, and neither are the Greeks. Greeks and Trojans reveal striking variation in their character, courage, values and commitments. We can draw clear distinctions in this regard between Achilles and Agamemnon and Hector and Paris.

With Virgil, epic poetry becomes politicized in the narrower sense of supporting an on-going political regime and its projects. Augustus attempted to rewrite the history of his rise to power, passing over the bloody, internecine struggles involved to emphasize, quite falsely, his republican roots. The *Aeneid* makes this message its own: the recent past – the civil wars – should be forgotten (*clementia*), but the longer past mastered and avenged (*pietas*). Virgil transforms the civil war against

Anthony and Cleopatra into one of foreign conquest. This glamorous couple are not only a threat to Augustus, but to Rome because they represent values, beliefs and practices that must be overcome if Rome is to maintain its identity and authority (*Aeneid* 8.790–859; Miles and Allen 1986; Qunit 1993: 23, 62–4). Virgil naturalizes Augustus' imperium; he has Aeneas's father Anchises describe it as the culmination of a process that begins with the Trojans' arrival in Italy (*Aeneid* 6.875–9). He hails 'Caesar Augustus!, Son of a god', as one who 'will bring back the Age of Gold to the Latin fields where Saturn once held sway …'(6.914–17). Virgil gives the Roman imperial project divine sanction. At the outset of the epic, Jove announces: 'On them I set no limits, space or time: I have granted them power, empire without end' (1.333–4).

Virgil's poem is agitprop *avant la lettre*. It nevertheless carries subtler messages and political advice for Augustus. After hailing the future Roman Empire in Book 1, Jove goes on to proclaim that after violent centuries battle will cease:

The terrible Gates of War with their welded iron bars will stand bolted shut, and locked in side, the Frenzy of civil strife will crouch down on his savage weapons, hands pinioned behind his back with a hundred brazen shackles, monstrously roaring out from his bloody jaws.

(1.351–5)

Augustus is being called upon to live up to this prediction, to rule in a restrained, but effective way to avoid provoking the kind of opposition that Julius Caesar did and the bloody internecine struggles that followed his assassination.

In the last book of the epic, Aeneas, sensing, or at least hoping, for victory, promises not to command defeated Italians to bow to Trojans nor seek the scepter of kingship. 'May both nations', he proclaims, 'undefeated, under equal laws, march together toward an eternal pact of peace' (12.225–8). This message is reinforced by Jove and Juno who ordain that Trojans blend with Latins into a stronger, hybrid people (12.950–71). Writing as an Italian Roman, Virgil is, in effect, urging Augustus to treat Roman citizens equally, regardless of their territorial origins. By doing so, he can garner support through the Empire and make Jove's prophecy self-fulfilling. Here too, Aeneas sets an example. He allies with Etruscans and various Latins and marries the Latin princess Lavinia, making it clear that [*Romanita*], from its very outset, is a multicultural project.

What do these texts tell us about the creation of 'others' and the roles they play in forming or solidifying identities? 'Others' feature in both epics. They are the Trojans in the *Iliad*, and the Greeks, Tyrians, Latins, Asians, women and the Trojans themselves in the *Aeneid*. They vary greatly in their degree of stereotypy and the extent to which the characteristics attributed to 'others' are portrayed as natural or acquired. They also vary in their plasticity. Such portrayals are invariably constructed from the appearance, words and deeds of individual characters; Hector, Priam and Aeneas help develop Homer's positive image of the Trojans. However, individuals with negative qualities can also serve as stand-ins for groups, as Pyrrhus does for the Greeks in the *Aeneid*. The most negative stereotype – of the

East in the *Aeneid* – is associated with Anthony and Cleopatra, but while they are mentioned and described, we never really encounter them as actors.

For both authors, 'others' are rarely essentialist in their characteristics. Individuals within outgroups show considerable variation in their character, courage, values and commitments. Achilles and Agamemnon, Hector and Paris and Turnus and Camilla are prominent examples. As we have seen, even the negative stereotype of women, so evident in the Aeneid, is at least in part undercut by Dido (before she is made to fall in love with Aeneas) and Camilla. The construction of the Trojans as their own 'other', from which they distance themselves in the course of the epic, indicates the possibility of transformation. Virgil appears to be suggesting by analogy that the Easterners who have now become part of Rome's Empire also have the potential to become good Roman citizens.

Identity construction in both epics stands in sharp contrast to the understandings of Kant, Hegel and Schmitt. In the *Iliad*, Trojans and Greeks are each others' 'other', but they do not need one other to become themselves. Both groups had strong identities prior to the war and there is no evidence that they achieve greater solidarity as a result of the war. If anything, it exposes just how fragile the unity of the Greeks really is and threatens, in the form of the conflict between Achilles and Agamemnon, to destroy it altogether. Greek and Trojan mutual dependence serves a different function. It allows warrior aristocrats on both sides to compete for *aristeia*. This is only possible against an adversary who shares the same values and practices. The Trojan War is a hard fought struggle, motivated initially by Menelaus' need to recover his wife and his honor. In practice, it becomes a competition for standing within the Greek and Trojan communities, where standing is a function of performance on the battlefield. Cooperation between adversaries – Priams' successful ransom of his son's body from Achilles – allows the chief Greek hero to regain his humanity when reason and affect convince him to put aside his overriding desire for vengeance.

Homer and Virgil show an understanding of identity that mirrors some of the findings of modern psychology. Identities form and become robust in the absence of others, as they do for Greeks and Trojans in both epics. Hostility and discrimination arise from the competition for scarce resources but are not necessarily accompanied by exclusion and stereotypy. In the *Iliad*, the competition is for honor, a more restricted and relational good than material resources. It is intense and generates mutual hatred in the course of the war, but little stereotypy. In the *Aeneid*, Trojans and Italians fight, also over questions of honor. Turnus is unwilling to accept Lavinia's betrothal to Aeneas because it would relegate him to a subordinate status. In both epics, Greeks and Trojans make attributions about the character of their adversaries on a purely individual basis and honor those they respect (Heredotus 1997).

Both epics emphasize distinctiveness. For Homer, Greeks and Trojans are distinctive because they conduct their affairs according to a demanding code of honor. They share this code and their warriors compete in displaying excellence. They are not troubled that their values and behavior make them all but indistinguishable as peoples. As I noted earlier, their similarities are essential because they make it possible for their warriors to compete for honor. This would be impossible against less worthy and courageous foes who did not follow the same rules of combat. This also holds true for Virgil's Trojans, Tyrians and Italians, but with two additional twists. The Trojans and Tyrians get on famously at first and largely because of their fundamental similarities. The Trojans lose sight of their Italian mission by blending with the Tyrians, symbolized by Aeneas' relationship with Dido. They must leave to found their own empire in Italy, creating a rupture with the Tyrians that becomes the basis for their future historical antagonism. Ultimately, Trojan distinctiveness derives from their god-given 'world historical' mission to found Rome and set it on its course of world conquest. As Sherif and Sherif suppose, personal and family loyalties can be consistent with and even supportive of loyalties to larger collectivities. They can also threaten them. In the *Iliad*, both armies are composites of independent forces beholden to local leaders. These lords have come to the aid of Agamemnon, Menelaus or Priam because of family, guest friendship or personal ties and obligations. The Greek alliance threatens to unravel because of Achilles' feud with Agamemnon, but in the end it is solidified because of the death of Patroclus. Personal obligation in the form of revenge seeking brings Achilles back into the fight.

Kant, Hegel and Schmitt all consider hostility to others a key component of national identity formation and solidarity. Classical texts and research in psychology and comparative politics cast serious doubt on the validity of this assumption. We have many historical examples of exclusion of others facilitating identity formation and solidarity, and at least as many of these processes were successful in its absence. Karl Deutsch (1953) describes the boundaries of national communities in terms of a 'we feeling' based on shared symbols and a narrative of a common past. He finds that though these symbols and their associated narratives may be shaped around opposition and resistance to others, it is by no means essential. Nor is it clear that many of the 'others' that are created are brought into being with identity in mind. The Soviet 'other' during the Cold War may have been necessary to garner support for a large defense budget and a quasi-imperial foreign policy but was hardly essential, or even central, to American identity. The same is true of current 'others' like illegal immigrants or international Islam, both of which for many Americans seem to have replaced the Soviet Union as the irrational and evil foreign other (Euben 1999: 43–4).

Kant, Hegel and Schmitt use historical evidence selectively, and Hegel and Schmitt in particular only cite cases where national identity and conflicts with external others appear closely coupled. Their formulations have the potential to make adversarial 'others' self-fulfilling and thus appear natural. The analogy here is to the realist conception of international relations as a self-help system. Realists maintain that international relations must always have this character, and it will to the extent that policymakers are socialized to act in accord with this assumption. The demonized 'other' and the naturally antagonistic character of the international system have the potential to create – and to some extent have created – a pernicious cycle of thought and deed. Both conceptions are mutually supporting, if not mutually constitutive. This relationship provides strong normative incentive to rethink them both.

Kant, Hegel and Schmitt do not effectively distinguish between the use of 'others' to construct identities and build internal solidarity. The two projects are not identical. Common identity must to some degree involve a feeling of solidarity, but all three writers refer to a more intense form of solidarity, deliberately mobilized by governments to inspire people to sacrifice their money, time and even lives in wars against foreign adversaries. Hegel and Schmitt view war and sacrifice positively. Hegel does so because he regards the state as a critical historical development that enables the spirit to reach fulfillment. Hegel's and Schmitt's formulations arise out of the crucible of European nationalism, for which, in different ways, they are advocates and spokesmen. Recent work on Kant and Hegel suggests that their 'othering' was part and parcel of the response by intellectuals from relatively backward parts of Europe to the challenge posed by the French Revolution (Shilliam 2006; Pinkard 2000: 61–8; Dickey 1987: 278–81). Robert Shilliam suggests that Kant and Hegel actually pursued a variant of the strategy I associate with Virgil: they sought to construct a German 'self' by incorporating important elements of the French 'other' (Shilliam 2006). Unlike Virgil, who is quite open about this aspect of his project, Kant and Hegel incorporate the other more furtively as it confounds their otherwise sharp dichotomy between a community and the 'others' against which it defines itself.

There are also good grounds for questioning the political utility of constructing identities or fostering greater solidarity by means of violent conflicts against stereotyped others. Hegel's Prussia–Germany offers the most compelling negative example. Nationalism was a root cause of the aggressive foreign policy of the Wilhelminian Reich, which led to World War I, defeat, territorial dismemberment, revanchist sentiment, the rise to power of Hitler, World War II, the Holocaust, further loss of territory and almost 50 years of division. The twentieth-century tragedies of Japan, Italy, the former Yugoslavia, Cyprus and the Indian sub-continent also arose from hyper-nationalism, fanned by leaders, and led to destructive internal or foreign wars.

Hegel, Schmitt's, and above all, Huntington's, formulations of identity would lead us to expect that the boundaries between 'us' and 'others' are relatively inflexible once they are established. As identity is defined in opposition to others, and solidarity depends on distinction and even hatred of others, both would be threatened by the inclusion of peoples who were formerly excluded. It is remarkable just how fluid categories of 'others' turn out to be in practice. With regularity, 'others' who were not only excluded and demonized, but objects of violent ethnic cleansing have subsequently been incorporated into community with no loss of national identity or solidarity. English Catholics and Irish immigrants in Britain, Jews in Germany, Irish Catholics, Southern Europeans, Jews, native Americans, Japanese-Americans and African-Americans in the United States. As racism generally has an impoverished rhetoric, it is hardly surprising that the very charges that Huntington makes against Latin immigrants – that they are unassimilatable – were routinely made against Italians, Slavs and Jews in the early decades of the twentieth century.

Once excluded groups can be made pillars of national identity, as the Maoris have in New Zealand. Maori designs grace the tails of Air New Zealand planes, New Zealand sports teams and delegations of all kinds chant hakas (Maori war chants) at the outset of matches or meetings, and school children are taught about their Maori heritage. More subdued moves have been made in the US with respect to native- and African Americans. Conversely, groups once considered at the core of a community's identity, as Britain was for colonial Americans, Australians and New Zealanders, have been expelled and to varying degrees stereotyped. In New Zealand, one not infrequently hears the British referred to disparagingly as 'pommy bastards' – a reference to the pom on their military beret.

The New Zealand case points to another interesting parallel with Homer: the possibility of excluding a group or nationality without demonizing them or treating their representatives with hostility. New Zealanders have made the British into an 'other' as part of the process of defining a separate identity. Citizens of the United Kingdom are nevertheless welcomed in New Zealand and treated with the same degree of courtesy as any other visitor or immigrant. In Canada, a similar process can be observed with respect to Québecois and Anglo-Canadians. The rhetoric of French separatism can be intense, but it rarely affects inter-personal relations. Having spent a sabbatical year in Montréal I can attest that I was treated exactly the same way in shops, cafes and social and professional encounters regardless of the language I spoke. These cases, and others, suggest, as does psychological research, that even when 'othering' is pronounced it need not be associated with the kind of stereotyping and hostility that poisons interpersonal relations.

The psychological and political science literature indicates that fundamentalist formulations of 'others' are more ideology than they are a description of reality. They are used rhetorically to advance political projects, which in the case of Schmitt and Huntington, can only be considered nefarious. Homer and Virgil offer different understandings of identity that are associated with their very different projects. Their conceptions are particularly germane to those who want to make inclusion and tolerance the norm. Homer and Virgil offer discourses that find much empirical support in contemporary psychological research, and whose starting point is the understanding that national identity and solidarity are fully consistent with, and even abetted by, policies of inclusion and non-stereotyped understandings of 'others'.

Notes

1 For critiques, see Mandler (2004 and 2006) and Cannadine (2001).
2 For an argument on how Democratic Peace advocates misread Kant, see Lawrence (2007).
3 Kant, in *Perpetual Peace* (105–08), thought that *xenia* was probably the one universal form of conduct.
4 All quotes from the *Iliad* are from the Fagles translation.
5 As they do again in Book 6, 101–18.
6 All quotes from the Fagles translation.
7 Ariosto's Angelica, Tasso's Armida and Milton's Eve (Quint 1993: 28–9, 86).
8 Contrast Book Five of the *Iliad* with Virgil, *Aeneid*, 12.903–14.

Bibliography

Abrams, D. and Hogg, M. (eds) (1990a) *Social Identity Theory: construction and critical advances*, London: Harvester Wheatsheaf.
—— (1990b) 'Social Identification, Social Categorization and Social Influence', *European Review of Social Psychology*, 1:195–228.
Allport, G. (1954) *The Nature of Prejudice*, Boston: Addison-Wesley.
Anderson, W.S. (1957) 'Virgil's Second *Iliad*', *Transactions of the American Philological Association*, 88: 17–30.
Bartelson, J. (1995) *A Genealogy of* Sovereignty, Cambridge: Cambridge University Press.
Berenskoetter, F. (2007) 'Friends, There Are No Friends? An intimate reframing of the international', *Millennium*, 35(2): 647–76.
Brewer, M.B. (1999) 'The Psychology of Prejudice: ingroup love or outgroup hate?', *Journal of Social Issues*, 55(3): 429–44.
—— (1979) 'Ingroup Bias in the Minimal Group Situation: a cognitive motivational analysis', *Psychological Bulletin* 86: 307–24.
Brewer, M.B. and Campbell, D.T. (1976) Ethnocentrism and Intergroup Attitudes: evidence from east Africa, Beverley Hills: Sage.
Brown, C. (2007) 'The Twilight of International Morality?' Hans J. Morgenthau and Carl Schmitt on the end of the *Jus Publicum Europaeum*', in M.C. Williams (ed.) *Realism Reconsidered: the legacy of Hans Morgenthau in International Relations*, Oxford: Oxford University Press.
—— (2000) 'Social Identity Theory: past achievements, current problems and future challenges', *European Journal of Social Psychology* 30(6): 778.
Brubaker, R. and Cooper, F. (2000) 'Beyond Identity', *Theory and Society*, 29(1): 1–47.
Cairns, F. (1989) *Virgil's Augustan Epic*, Cambridge: Cambridge University Press.
Campbell, D. (1998) *Writing Security*, revised ed., Minneapolis: University of Minnesota Press.
Cannadine, D. (2001) *Ornamentalism: how the British saw their empire*, New York: Oxford University Press.
Clark, I. (1989) *The Hierarchy of States: reform and resistance in the international order*, Cambridge: Cambridge University Press.
Coker, C. (2007) Personal communication, 23 June.
Colley, L. (1992a) 'Britishness and Otherness, *Journal of British Studies* , 31: 302–29.
—— (1992b) *Britons*, New Haven: Yale University Press.
Collins, D. (2004) *Master of the Game: competition and performance in Greek poetry*, Cambridge: Harvard Center for Hellenic Studies.
Connolly, W.E. (2000) 'Secularism, Partisanship and the Ambiguity of Justice', in E. Portis, A. Gundersen and R. Shirley (eds), *Political Theory and Partisan Politics*, Albany: State University of New York Press.
—— (1991) *Identity\Difference: democratic negotiations of political paradox*, Ithaca: Cornell University Press.
Dechesne, M.J., Greenberg, J., Arndt, J. and Schimel. J. (2000) 'Terror Management and Sports: fan affiliation: the effects of mortality salience on fan identification and optimism', *European Journal of Social Psychology*, 30: 813–35.
Deschamps, J.C. and Brown, R. (1983) 'Superordinate Goals and Intergroup Conflict', *British Journal of Social Psychology*, 22: 189–95.
Deutsch, K.W. (1953) *Nationalism and Social Communication*, Cambridge MA: MIT Press.
Dickey, L. (1987) *Hegel*, Cambridge, Cambridge University Press.

Dovido, J.F. and Gaertner, M.L. (1987) 'Stereotypes and Evaluative Intergroup Bias', in D. Mackie and D. Hamilton (eds.) *Affect, Cognition, and Stereotyping*, San Diego: Academic Press.

Doyle, M. (1983) 'Kant, Liberal Legacies, and Foreign Affairs, Parts 1 and 2', *Philosophy and Public Affairs*, 12(3): 205–35 and 12(4): 323–53.

Elmers, N. (2001) 'Individual Upward Mobility and the Perceived Legitimacy of Intergroup Relations', in J. Jost and B. Major (eds), *The Psychology of Legitimacy: emerging perspectives on ideology, justice, and intergroup relations*, New York: Cambridge University Press.

Euben, R.L. (1999) *Enemy in the Mirror: Islamic fundamentalism and the limits of modern rationality*, Princeton: Princeton University Press.

Feshbach, S. (1994) 'Nationalism, Patriotism and Aggression: a clarification of functional differences', in L. Huessman (ed.) *Aggressive Behavior: current perspectives*, New York: Plenum.

Finley, M.I. (1978) *The World of Odysseus*, New York: Viking.

Flockhart, T. (2006) 'Complex Socialization: a framework for the study of state socialization', *European Journal of International Relations* 12(1): 89–118.

Fowler, D. (1997) 'Story-Telling', in C. Martindale (ed.), *The Cambridge Companion to Virgil*, Cambridge: Cambridge University Press.

Freeman, M.A. (1981), 'Liking Self and Social Structure: a psychological perspective on Sri Lanka', *Journal of Cross-Cultural Psychology*, 12(1): 291–308.

Fraser, N. and Honneth, A. (2003) *Redistribution or Recognition? A political philosophical Exchange*, London: Verso.

Habermas, J. (1990) *Moral Consciousness and Communicative Action*, trans. C. Lenhardt and S. Weber Nicholsen, Cambridge: MIT Press.

—— (1984–87) *A Theory of Communicative Action*, trans. T. McCarthy, 2 vols., Boston: Beacon Press.

Halliday, F. (1994) *Rethinking International Relations*, Vancouver: University of British Columbia Press.

Hegel, G.W.F. (1999) 'The German Constitution', in L. Dickey and H.B. Nisbet (eds) *Political Writings*, trans. H.B. Nisbet, Cambridge: Cambridge University Press.

—— (1991) *Elements of the Philosophy of Right*, A.H. Wood (ed.), trans. H.B. Nisbet, Cambridge: Cambridge University Press.

Held, D. (1995) *Democracy and the Global Order: from the modern state to cosmopolitan governance*, Cambridge: Polity Press.

Herder, J.G. (1877–1913) *Ideen*, ch. 7, sec. 1, in *Herder's Sämtliche Werke*, B. Suphan (ed.) Berlin: Weidmann, vol. 13.

Herington, C.J. (1985) *Poetry Into Drama*, Berkeley: University of California Press.

Herodotus (1997), *The Histories*, trans. G. Rawlinson, New York: Knopf.

Hinkle, S. and Brown, R. (1990) 'Intergroup Comparisons and Social Identity: some implications and lacunae, in D. Abrams and M. Hogg (eds), *Social Identity Theory: construction and critical advances*, London: Harvester Wheatsheaf.

Homer (1998) *The Iliad*, trans. R. Fagles, New York NY Penguin Classics.

Honneth, H. (1996) *The Struggle for Recognition: the moral grammar of social conflicts*, London: Polity Press.

Hopf, T. (2002) *Social Construction of International Politics: identities and foreign policies, Moscow, 1955 and 1999*, Ithaca: Cornell University Press.

Horowitz, D. (1985) *Ethnic Groups in Conflict*, Berkeley: University of California Press.

Huntington, S. (1996) *The Clash of Civilizations and the Remaking of the World Order*, New York: Simon & Schuster.

Iyengar, C. Sullivan, L. and Ford, T. (1980) 'Affective and Cognitive Determinants of Prejudice', *Social Cognition*, 9: 359–80.

Jahn, B. (2006) *Classical Theory in International Relations*, Cambridge: Cambridge University Press.

Jordan, W. (1968) *White Over Black: American attitudes toward the Negro, 1550–1812*, Chapel Hill: University of North Carolina Press.

Kant, I. (1991) 'Idea for a Universal History with a Cosmopolitan Purpose', and 'Perpetual Peace: a philosophical sketch', in H. Reiss, *Kant: Political Writings*, Cambridge: Cambridge University Press.

Klosterman, R. and Feshbach, S. (1989) 'Toward a Measure of Patriotic and Nationalistic Attitudes', *Political Psychology*, 10: 257–74.

Knox, B. (2006) 'Introduction' to Virgil, *The Aeneid*, trans. R. Fagles, New York: Viking.

Lawrence, A. (2007) 'Imperial Peace or Imperial Method: skeptical inquiries into ambiguous evidence for the "democratic Peace", in R.N. Lebow and M.I. Lichbach', *Theory and Evidence in Comparative Politics and International Relations*, New York: Palgrave-Macmillan.

Lebow, R.N. (2008) *A Cultural Theory of International Relations*, Cambridge: Cambridge University Press.

—— (1976) *White Britain and Black Ireland: social stereotypes and colonial policy*, Philadelphia: Institute for the Study of Human Issues.

Lebow, R.N., Kansteiner, W. and Fogu, C. (eds) (2006), *The Politics of Memory in Postwar Europe*, Durham: Duke University Press.

LeVine, R.A. and Campbell, D.T. (1972) *Ethnocentrism: theories of conflicts, ethnic attitudes and group behavior*, New York: Wiley.

Mandler, P. (2006) 'What is National Identity?' *Modern Intellectual History*, 3: 271–97.

—— (2004) 'The Problem with Cultural History', *Cultural and Social History*, 1: 94–118.

Mansbridge, J.J. (2001) 'Complicating Oppositional Consciousness', J.J. Mansbridge and A.D. Morris (eds), *Oppositional Consciousness: the subjective roots of social protest*, Chicago: University of Chicago Press.

Miles, G.B. and Allen, A.W. (1986) 'Virgil and the Augustan Experience', in J.D. Bernard (ed.), *Virgil at 2000: commemorative essays on the poet and his influence*, New York: AMS Press.

Mill, J.S. (1964–67), 'A Few Words on Non-Intervention', in *Dissertations and Discussions: Political, Philosophical, and Historical*, Boston: W.V. Spencer.

Mouffe, C. (1993) *The Return of the Political*, New York: Verso.

Mummendey, A. and Schreiber, H. (1983) 'Better or Just Different? Positive social identity by discrimination against or by differentiation for outgroups', *European Journal of Social Psychology*, 13: 389–97.

Mummendey, A. and Simon, B. (1989) 'Better or Different III: the importance of comparison dimension and relative ingroup size upon intergroup discrimination', *British Journal of Social Psychology*, 28: 1–16.

Mummenday, A. and Wenzel, M. (1999) 'Social Discrimination and Tolerance in Intergroup Relations: reaction to intergroup differences', *Personality and Social Psychology Review*, 3: 158–74.

Nagy, G. (1996) *Poetry as Performance: Homer and beyond*, Cambridge: Cambridge University Press

—— (1990) *Pindar's Homer: the lyric possession of an epic past*, Baltimore, Johns Hopkins University Press.

Narilkar, A. (2006) 'Peculiar Chauvinism or Strategic Calculation? Explaining the negotiating strategy of a rising India', *International Affairs*, 82(1): 59–76

Onuf, N.G. (1998) *The Republican Legacy*, New York: Cambridge University Press.

Osiander, A. (2001) 'Sovereignty, International Relations and the Westphalian Myth', *International Organization*, 55(2): 251–287.

Pettigrew, T.F. and Meertens, R.F. (1995) 'Subtle and Blatant Prejudice in Western Europe', *European Journal of Social Psychology*, 25: 57–75

Pinkard, G. (2000) *Hegel*, Cambridge: Cambridge University Press.

Plato (2000) *The Republic*, G.R.F. Ferrari (ed.), trans T. Griffith, Cambridge: Cambridge University Press.

Quint, D. (1993) *Epic and Empire: politics and generic form from Virgil to Milton*, Princeton: Princeton University Press.

Said, E.W. (1978) *Orientalism*, New York: Pantheon.

Schmidt, B.C. (1998) *The Political Discourse of Anarchy: a disciplinary history of International Relations*, Albany: State University of New York Press.

—— (1976) *The Concept of the Political*, trans. C. Schwab, New Brunswick: Rutgers University Press.

Seaford, R. (1994) *Reciprocity and Ritual: Homer and tragedy in the developing City State*, Oxford: Oxford University Press.

Sherif, M. (1966) *In Common Predicament: social psychology of intergroup conflict and cooperation*, New York: Houghton Mifflin.

Sherif, M. and Sherif, C.W. (1953) *Groups in Harmony and Tension: an integration of studies on inter-group Relations*, New York: Harper.

Shilliam, G. (2006) *The Other In Classical Political Theory*, Cambridge, Cambridge University Press.

Sidanius, J. (1993) 'The Psychology of Group Conflict and the Dynamics of Oppression: a social dominance perspective', in S. Avenger and W. McGuire (eds), *Explorations in Social Psychology*, Durham: Duke University Press.

Struch, N. and Schwartz, S.H. (1989) 'Inter-Group Aggression: its distinctiveness from ingroup bias', *Journal of Personality and Social Psychology*, 56: 364–73.

Suetonius (1920) *The Lives of the Caesars*, trans. J.C. Rolfe, New York: Putnam.

Sumner, W.G. (1906) *Folkways*, New York: Ginn.

Suzuki, S. (2007) 'China's Quest for Great Power Status: three social mechanisms of delinquent gang gormation', University of Manchester, Centre of International Politics Working Paper Series, no. 29.

Tajfel, H. (1981) *Human Groups and Social Categories*, Cambridge: Cambridge University Press.

—— (1978) 'Social Categorisation, Social Identity and Social Comparison', in H. Tajfel (ed.) *Differentiation Between Social Groups: studies in the psychology of intergroup relations*, London: Academic Press.

Tajfel, H. and Turner, J. (1986) 'The Social Identity Theory of Intergroup Behavior', in S. Worchel and W. Austin (eds), *Psychology of Intergroup Relations*, Chicago: Nelson-Hall.

Tajfel, H., Billing, M., Bundy, R. and Flament, C. (1971) 'Social Categorization and Intergroup Behavior', *European Journal of Social Psychology*, 1(2):149–78.

Taplin, O. (2000) 'The Spring of the Muses: Homer and related poetry', in O. Taplin, (ed.), *Literature in the Greek World*, Oxford: Oxford University Press.

—— (1992) *Homeric Soundings: the shaping of the Iliad*, Oxford: Oxford University Press.

Taylor, C. (1992) 'The Politics of Recognition', in A. Gutmann (ed.) *Multiculturalism and 'The Politics of Recognition': an essay by Charles Taylor*, Princeton: Princeton University Press.

Taylor, D.M. (1981) 'Multiple Group Membership and Self-Identity', *Journal of Cross-Cultural Psychology*, 12(1): 61–79.

Thomas, R.F. (2001) *Virgil and the Augustan Reception*, Cambridge: Cambridge University Press.

Turner, J.C. (1975) 'Social Comparison and Social Identity: some prospects for intergroup behaviour', *European Journal of Social Psychology*, 5: 5–34.

Virgil (2006) *Georgics*, trans. J., Lembke, New Haven, CT: Yale University Press.

—— (2008) *The Aeneid*, trans. R. Fagles, New York Penguin Classics.

Xenophon (1923): *Symposium*, Trans. E.C. Merchant, and O.J. Todd, Cambridge MA: Harvard University Press.

9 Political community formation beyond the nation-state

Benjamin Herborth

Speaking of community intuitively entails two distinct, yet related, connotations. First, community conjures up a positive feeling: 'whatever the word "community" may mean, it is good "to have a community", "to be in a community" ...Company or society can be bad; but not the community. Community, we feel, is always a good thing' (Bauman 2001: 1). The positive connotation of safety and security, however, seems to work only on account of the implicit contrast with 'an insecure world'.[1] Both of these connotations are particularly visible in the everyday usage of the language of community in international life. Employed by practitioners and scholars alike, the language of community provides us with an inherently normative vocabulary, which enables us to speak of strong moral obligations in the present and provides us with a framework for normative change as a political project pointing towards the future. In the light of natural disasters or humanitarian emergencies the international community is called upon to lend their support to those in need. In turn, dissatisfaction with the capacities to provide such support leads to call for enhancing and further institutionalizing an international community capable of learning from past mistakes. Hence, getting a grasp on what constitutes a political community beyond the nation-state is a question which is by no means of purely scholarly interest.

Quite the opposite, in fact. The normative grammar of community formation is ever-present in political discourse. Kofi Annan (2002: 30), when the incumbent secretary-general of the United Nations, struggled to find an answer to the question of what constitutes a political community, and found that 'problems without passports' have already led to the emergence of an international community, even though he considered its institutions and mechanisms to be 'hardly more than embryonic'. It is precisely this in-between status, however, which is at the centre of the normative grammar of community formation. We have achieved a lot, we haven't achieved enough, we need to achieve more, and we can do that. The concept of community, one might say, is the rare instance of a social scientific idea which is quite suitable as a campaign slogan. Even the most dramatic failures, such as the failure to prevent genocide in Rwanda, can be attributed to the lack or the absence of an international community. The failure to prevent genocide does not refute the idea that there is such a thing as an international community. Rather, it is precisely the absence of an international community which accounts for crimes against humanity. The international community could have been present, but it wasn't. Its very absence lends evidence to the possibility of its existence.

Evidently, the concept of community is a tricky one for the social sciences. There is no denying its prevalence in political discourse. At the same time, political scientists routinely refer to their subject matter in terms of community – whether it is in the context of the small-scale empirical study of urban communities, inquiries into the impact of highly specialized epistemic communities in global politics, or even the most general sense of a political entity (regional, national, or global) that is to be studied. However, even though the concept of community seems to be ubiquitous in academic discourse also, it has never received a great deal of systematic attention. At least in part, this is probably due to a well-founded suspicion in the social sciences vis-à-vis feel-good concepts such as community. If the rhetoric of community constantly pulls us towards its own normative centre of gravity – if it institutes, in other words, precisely the normative bond it is purported to describe – the concept might just be ill-suited for the purpose of critical analysis. While it is important to take note of these pitfalls, it would be premature to infer that the concept of community is altogether spoiled for the social sciences. However, it is imperative to disentangle as clearly as possible the performative effects of the rhetoric of community on the one hand and the analysis of such performative effects on the other. With this distinction in hand, reconstructing its practical grammar in order to understand the performative effects of the rhetoric of community may equip us with a more powerful analytical tool-kit for understanding normative change. By analyzing what politicians, citizens and scholars do when they speak of community, we may be able to shed light on the pertinent question of the 'authorization of authority' (Walker 2002: 112).

Within the framework of anarchy, political authority was firmly located on the inside of the nation-state. Political loyalties as well as claims to produce collectively binding decisions seemed to coalesce with territorially delineated boundaries. However, to the extent that the anarchy framework is considered to be obsolescent in the light of various emerging forms of political authority beyond the nation-state (such as the process of European integration, the consolidation of international criminal law leading to the institutionalization of an International Criminal Court, or the emergence of a transnational merchant law), the question of how these new forms of political authority emerge, i.e. the question of how they are themselves authorized, has come to the fore. I contend that it is precisely the normative appeal of the concept of community, which becomes apparent in its practical usage, which makes it interesting for the purpose of studying the emergence of political authority beyond the nation-state.

In order to follow through on this hunch, the chapter will proceed in three steps. First, I will briefly sketch how the predominant literature on juridification, compliance, and legitimacy fails to address the problem of how the political spaces within which juridification and compliance may legitimately occur are constituted in the first place. Second, I will tentatively introduce a performative understanding of political community formation, which is inspired by John Dewey's pragmatist interpretation of the constitution of political spaces. Such a performative understanding of political community formation, I contend, avoids both the statist pitfalls of the literatures on juridification and compliance and the anti-modernist connotations associated with the concept of community in the tradition of German sociology. The third section attempts to substantiate the claim that a performative view of political community formation may help to better understand the emergence of political authority beyond the nation-state by presenting exemplary illustrations from the fields of transnational private law (lex mercatoria) and supranational trade law (WTO). Both cases evade categorization in terms of governance over a delineated territory (state, region, globe), thus emphasizing the conceptual independence of dynamics of political community formation and the modern state.

The limits of causal explanation: why the problem of order is not a Hobbesian one

Drawing a sharp line between the domestic and the international has allowed the discipline of International Relations to maintain an exclusive competency for the realm of international politics characterized by the distinct dynamics of interaction under conditions of anarchy. While intuitively plausible in an age of great power competition and bipolarity, a perspective conceiving of the international as a distinct realm of (power) politics is hardly suitable to account for the emergence of a regional polity in Europe, or the institutionalization of supranational jurisdiction in specific fields such as trade or crimes against humanity. As the billiard-ball model of the states system has been discredited, it became obvious that the political problems political actors are supposed to cope with – environmental, economic and security-related – do not halt at nation-state borders 'any longer'. Hence, the need for global governance – an attempt to exercise political control which has to deal with the still dominant perception of the international realm as anarchic; that is, as characterized by the very absence of government and the rule of law. Governance without government (Rosenau and Czempiel 1992) thus became the catchword of a new field of research in International Relations. First attempts to come to terms with these developments have remained descriptive and characteristic of disciplinary confusion. Concepts of governance in complex multi-layered systems are indisputably plausible. However, the mere acknowledgement of complexity and the involvement of different levels in any particular instantiation of 'governance' just re-describes the problem rather than contributing to its analysis. While acknowledging the need to overcome a political vocabulary forged to describe the sovereign nation-state, research on global governance starts with the executive problem of political steering. The challenge is then to recreate the steering capabilities of the Keynesian–Westphalian state at a higher scale. And notably, this challenge is to be faced by political scientists themselves. As Robert Keohane (2001: 1) put it in his presidential address to the American Political Science Association: 'Facing globalization, the challenge for political science resembles that of the founders of the United States: how to design institutions for a polity of unprecedented size and diversity'. Global governance as a world steering programme then

not only leaves this heroic task to political scientists, it also begins to work on political solutions before the constellation giving rise to these presumed problems has
been understood more thoroughly in the first place.

The idea of global governance as a comprehensive framework for processes of
juridification and strategies for the management of compliance thus seems to reit-
erate the core assumptions of a particular 'historical constellation characterized by
the fact that state, society, and economy are, as it were, co-extensive within the
same national boundaries' (Habermas 1998: 48). 'Global Governance' thus underestimates and overestimates the state at the same time. It underestimates the state to
the extent that it fails to conceive of the 'retreat of the state' (Strange 1996) as a
state-driven process, a new and different form of the extension of the state in a
Gramscian sense that would allow us to theorize activities in what has been dubbed
global civil society in relation rather than diametrical opposition to the state. At the
same time it overestimates the state to the extent that it uncritically (and, to some
extent unwittingly) prolongs the semantics of nation-state politics in an emerging
post-national constellation. Governance as a controlled, directed activity presupposes a pre-constituted political space to which executive steering ambitions refer,
be it the city-state, the nation-state or an unmarked global space. The legitimacy of
global governance then lies in the relation between efforts to exercise governance
and the space to be governed. By extending the semantics of nation-state politics
beyond the nation-state, by transnationalizing the executive as it were, the discourse on global governance systematically evades this question. At the same time,
it retains and reproduces an understanding of society as contained within the territorial boundaries of the modern state. Niklas Luhmann has identified four key
assumptions of this view, which he describes as 'epistemological obstacles' (a term
he takes from Gaston Bachelard) to a better understanding of modern societies.
Typically, we assume:

1   that a society consists of specific human beings and the relations between
     human beings;
2   that society is thus constituted, or at least integrated, through a consensus
     among human beings, through a correspondence of their attitudes and a com-
     plementarity of their purposes;
3   that societies are regional, territorially delineated units, so that Brazil is a dif-
     ferent society than Thailand, the USA a different one than Russia, and pre-
     sumably also Uruguay a different one than Paraguay;
4   and that societies can be observed from the outside like groups of human
     beings.

(Luhmann 1997: 24f)

Under these conditions, the problem of political order can be circumscribed as a
Hobbesian one (cf. Parsons 1968/1951: 36). Distinct individual members of society are faced with the problem of how to achieve political decisions, which are generally acceptable. Rejecting the tautological solution proposed by contract theories,
normativist social theories[2] argue that a set of shared norms and values is required,

which can diffuse into society by means of socialization and internalization. Consequently, theorists of international relations have introduced a distinction between rationalist and constructivist explanations of social outcomes. However, drawing a hard and fast line between rationalist and constructivist accounts tends to obliterate their common starting point. Both rationalists and constructivists in IR analyse trans- or supranational forms of political regulation in terms of the causal motivation of individual actors to comply. Neither addresses the question of how the political space within which such regulatory efforts take place is constituted. Using the IR literature on compliance, juridification and legitimacy as an example, I will demonstrate the shortcomings of both rationalist and constructivist perspectives on the emergence of political authority beyond the nation-state before I outline a conceptual alternative based on a performative concept of community formation.

At first glance, it seems obvious to conceive of compliance with supranational law as the central indicator for juridification. Research on inter- and supranational juridification has thus focused on identifying possible causes of compliance. Bernhard Zangl (2001, cf. List and Zangl 2003) has distinguished three major strategies to achieve compliance – representing three major strands in the scholarly debate. First, compliance can be enforced through punishment. Establishing negative incentives – effective sanctions – international organizations can alter the cost-benefit calculus of defecting states. Second, according to the management school norm-compliance can be achieved by establishing positive incentives. Assuming that non-compliance is often caused by a lack of either knowledge or capabilities to implement norms, defecting states could be supported and encouraged to comply through administrative dialogues. Third, the adjudication school posits that non-compliance is often due to the rather unspecific content of international norms. Court-like institutions can thus help to clarify the interpretation of particular norms, thus subjecting defecting states to the pressure of a global public sphere. Recently legitimacy has been suggested as a fourth perspective that emphasizes the importance of the participation of 'civil society actors'. As a global public sphere is, however, also treated as the driving force of the recognition of adjudication it seems warranted to treat this as an extension of the adjudication school, not as an entirely different perspective.

These different causal mechanisms can be discussed as strategies of norm-implementation insofar as they refer to particular characteristics of international institutions which 'make states comply' although they are not intrinsically interested in doing so. Even if we accept the heroic and somewhat technocratic assumption that these causal mechanisms could be allocated freely according to criteria of efficiency in a process of rational institutional design, the notion of external incentives as opposed to intrinsic interest points out several problems with a compliance perspective on juridification and legitimacy. All three strategies – enforcement, management and adjudication – are basically about changes in the setting within which compliance or non-compliance might occur. Even from a narrowly rationalist perspective states would be expected to change their behaviour as available options are altered. Creating incentives, however, is characteristic of traditional diplomatic strategies, not of juridification as a fundamentally different mode of organizing, or possibly overcoming, international politics.

In order to be able to grasp a transformation from diplomatic to juridical practices in global politics we thus need a conceptual apparatus that focuses on the different logics underlying these respective practices. Ironically, at a conceptual level such a differentiation is at the centre of Kenneth Waltz' (1979) classical account of the international system, as his distinction between hierarchy at the domestic level and anarchy at the international level is built on the Durkheimean distinction between organic and mechanical solidarity.[3] Domestic politics, in Waltz, is characterized by the fact that states are capable of producing collectively binding decisions; international politics is characterized by the absence of this very capability. Research on supranational juridification and legitimacy will thus succeed in challenging the reification of this distinction only insofar as it demonstrates that the legitimacy of collectively binding decisions posited by Waltz for the domestic level has been emerging at a supranational scale as well.

A major problem with the concept of legitimacy is that it is used throughout the literature in entirely different ways. It can refer to the social bond which constitutes a political community (Jackson 2002; Hurd 1999) or to procedural characteristics of institutions the democratic quality of which is questioned (Moravcsik 2002; Howse and Nicolaidis 2003). Apart from the conceptual differences between these two poles, they respond to entirely different questions. Conceptualizing legitimacy as a social fact, as a 'power reality' (Nye 1999: 30),[4] means elaborating an analytical concept which is supposed to help us to better understand how collectively binding decisions are produced. Discussing legitimacy in the context of the democratic deficit – of the European Union, for instance – means, in contrast, to engage in an explicitly normative discourse on reasonable criteria under which pooling sovereignty can be justified. I will discuss legitimacy as a social fact that is constitutive of corporate agency based on the premise that these two questions can and should be disentangled. For not any actor that is capable of producing collectively binding decisions is necessarily normatively justifiable. 'In this sense, saying that a rule is accepted as legitimate by some actor says nothing about its justice in the eyes of an outside observer' (Hurd 1999: 381). Notwithstanding this analytic distinction, however, specific concepts of justice held by those affected by the rules in question are often crucial to the narratives by which the legitimacy of a political community is constituted and maintained. Disclosing their significance – their role in processes of signification – however, does not mean engaging in such an explicitly normative discourse about their moral quality.

Legitimacy as a 'power reality' is thus supposed to explain '[w]hat motivates states to follow international norms, rules, and commitments' (Hurd 1999: 379). In the first systematic treatment of the subject, Ian Hurd discusses three ideal-typical motivations: coercion, self-interest and legitimacy.[5] As well as Max Weber's ideal types of legitimate domination these different 'currencies of power ... *recur in combination* across all social systems where rules exist to influence behaviour' (Hurd 1999: 379, emphasis added). Hurd himself, however, maintains a subjectivist conceptualization of legitimacy as 'the normative belief (held) by an actor that a rule or institution ought to be obeyed'. Hence, and despite the fact that Hurd argues the converse, his concept of legitimacy is not categorically different from either coercion or rational self-interest. For if legitimate authority can be reduced to the subjectively held belief that a particular norm be justified, it would be nothing but a normatively coloured kind of interest-based cooperation. In the case of a normative consensus cooperation becomes possible – any participant who disagrees with the given consensus may cease to cooperate. Cooperation is thus a function of the subjective predispositions of (all!) participant actors. Material and normative interests, which eventually characterize the difference, have already been disentangled in Max Weber's distinction between purposive rationality and value-rationality (*Zweckrationalität* and *Wertrationalität*) both of which are discussed as an expression of society formation (*Vergesellschaftung*), as opposed to community formation (*Vergemeinschaftung*). Analytically, Hurd's subjective concept of legitimacy can thus be situated in the literature on trans- and international norm entrepreneurs (cf. Keck and Sikkink 1998) and should be referred to, more precisely, as persuasion.

Coercion, self-interest and persuasion can then be distinguished from a non-individualist concept of legitimacy, which does not cause compliance, but constitutes a political community in the first place. A supranational actor, which cannot be reduced to its individual members, is constituted insofar as it becomes possible to produce collectively binding decisions. In analogy to what Wendt (1999: 161ff) has called 'collective knowledge', the legitimacy of a rule or institution does not depend on its recognition through single individuals. Being 'interested strictly in the subjective feeling by a particular [sic!] actor or set of actors that some rule is legitimate' (Hurd 1999: 381) therefore obscures that legitimacy, by virtue of Hurd's own reasoning, is based on an intersubjective level of collectively shared meaning, not on a merely subjective interpretation. For the internalization of a rule as legitimate 'takes place when the actor's sense of its own interests is partly constituted by a force outside itself, that is, by the standards, laws, rules, and norms present in the community, existing at the intersubjective level' (Hurd 1999: 388). If some standards, laws, rules and norms, however, are not legitimate, without being inherently different from legitimate ones except for the fact that they do not refer to the political community of a nation-state, but to a less 'densely institutionalized' (Martin and Simmons 1998: 742) international realm (think of environmental standards), legitimacy itself has to be located at the level of intersubjectivity. Legitimacy would then be reinforced by social practices and historical memory neither of which depends on beliefs held by individual actors.

These internal tensions in Hurd's argument become particularly obvious as he discusses the legitimacy of sovereignty as an empirical 'application': 'Rather than being a quality of any single state in isolation, sovereignty is a feature of the international system'; it is 'an institutional arrangement for organizing political life that is based on territoriality and autonomy' (Hurd 1999: 393). The relative stability of territorial borders, even where power asymmetries provide great chances for a quick conquest, can only be explained if the validity of sovereignty is due to its internalization by individual states. Being internalized, mutual recognition and non-intervention are a reality of international life, not the result of an eternally repeated cost-benefit calculation. 'The limits of sovereign power over neighbours would then be defined by an accepted scheme of spatially divided international authority' (Hurd 1999: 397). Pursuing a state's systemic project is, hence, not based on the material truth of a distinction between the domestic and the international, but on the historically contingent fact that legitimacy happens to be constructed predominantly at the level of the nation-state.

Hurd's position is thus somewhat paradoxical. The existence of the legitimacy of a specific norm – sovereignty and, by implication, non-intervention – at the international level implies the absence of the possibility of a more general legitimate rule of law. There can be no complete body of international law which is legitimate, for this would interfere with the legitimized principle of non-intervention. The legitimacy of non-intervention is the legitimacy of anarchy. The territorial differentiation of the state system is constituted in a bottom-up process by the legitimate rule of law within the nation-state and in a top-down process by the mutual recognition of states as sovereign actors.[6] Again, the state's systemic project can still provide a valuable focus for research, because it can, in its constructivist version, shed light on social practices by means of which the state system reifies itself. Depicting these processes does not imply that theorists themselves reify a current, historically contingent form of political organization, if they allow for change in the processes of 'legitimacy construction'.

Insofar as such processes involve less of a cooperation problem and more of a problem of political community formation, a strictly intersubjective, non-individualist concept of legitimacy needs to clarify how the capability of producing collectively binding decisions is constituted. Conceptualizing the social function of legitimacy as the 'inclusion of exclusion' Niklas Luhmann has argued that the state's legitimate monopoly on the use of violence is a potential, which is realized mostly in cases of deviance.

> In its legitimate form, violence (today as the state's monopoly on the legitimate use of force) has the function to expel illegitimate violence. With this differentiation violence is thus characterized by the inclusion of exclusion, and legitimacy is, from this perspective, not a value-laden concept, but precisely this inclusion of exclusion – a paradox the solution of which constitutes itself as the state's monopoly on the legitimate use of force (or as its functional equivalent).
> (Luhmann 1997: 414n5, my translation)

Even in the case of extreme violations of particular rules, legitimacy thus grants mechanisms by means of which a political community can address such violations internally. Legitimacy within a political community then refers to the constitution of an intersubjective space, which allows for the contestation of norms or rules by eliminating the risk that adherents to minority positions are simply excluded. As a constitutive concept legitimacy would then refer to the general possibility of producing collectively binding decisions while coercion, self-interest and persuasion seek to explain the compliance with a particular norm in a particular case. In that respect, compliance and legitimacy are conceptually independent (cf. Steffek 2003).

Such a concept of legitimacy contrasts sharply with the traditional image of a normatively integrated political community, where normative integration refers to a set of shared norms or beliefs. Not only does such a concept of normative integration, as I have attempted to demonstrate earlier, rest on the subjectivist assumption of individual recognition or 'internalization', as it were, of particular norms by every single individual, it also (and despite this latent individualism!) conceives a totality of similar individual motivations as the basis of a political community's capability to produce collectively binding decisions. Firmly centred around a normative core, citizens are conceived of as merely enacting the shared values of the community.

Legitimacy as an intersubjective space that allows for the non-exclusive contestation of norms, in contrast, is not a presupposition about citizens' sameness, but a condition of the possibility of difference.[7] While the legitimacy of the normatively integrated political community causes compliance via internalization of a specific norm, the legitimacy of an intersubjective space of contestation constitutes a political community where the continuous struggle over the interpretation of particular norms, not unlike the Gramscian war of position, serves to reproduce its boundaries. And while the normativist view presupposes a consensus on specific norms, the concept of political community suggested here is content-less insofar as it fulfils merely its constitutive function, not providing an explanation for compliance with any specific norm. A non-individualist understanding of legitimacy would thus correspond to what has been referred to as a 'generative concept of structure' (Wendt 1987). Just as speakers of the same language are not, by virtue of their shared tacit understanding of its grammar, forced to actually say the same things, citizens who share a set of symbolic references within a political community may have diverging political attitudes. In a democratic political community each citizen would be related to the political community in a specifically individuated way:

> Every individual self within a given society or social community reflects in its organized structure the whole relational pattern of organized social behavior which that society or community exhibits or is carrying on, and its organized structure is constituted by this pattern; but since each of these individual selves reflects a uniquely different aspect or perspective of this pattern in its structure, from its own particular and unique place or standpoint within the whole process of organized social behavior which exhibits this pattern – since, that is, each is differently or uniquely related to that whole process, and occupies its own essentially unique focus of relations therein – the structure of each is differently constituted by this pattern from the way in which the structure of any other is so constituted.

> (Mead 1962/1934: 202)

The mutual recognition as legal (and political) subjects, which renders possible the 'non-exclusive' contestation of norms, thus hinges on a shared set of symbolic references, not on a particular relation to these symbolic references which is collectively internalized. Producing collectively binding decisions within a political community does not refer to some kind of interest-based consensus among individual members. Conceived as an intersubjective space of (possible) contestation, the legitimacy of legal bindingness can be conceptualized as independent of individual material or normative interests.

Moreover, it should be noted that this implies a major difference to a Luhmannian understanding of politics as being solely about the production of collectively binding decisions, thereby rendering unproblematic the historical constitution and transformation of the functional spaces within which this might become possible. If producing collectively binding decisions presupposes, as I have argued earlier, such an intersubjective space, the concept of politics involves integration and contestation as two constitutive dimensions. Correspondingly, what I shall refer to as a contentious politics of legitimacy involves two distinct dimensions, for not only specific norms within political communities, but also the very process of community formation becomes subject to contestation.

To sum up, both rationalist and constructivist attempts to account for the emergence of political authority beyond the nation-state in terms of causal explanations run into a logical problem. Any causal explanation as to why individual agents comply with particular regulatory impositions presupposes what needs to be explained. An explanation that points to antecedent causes of compliance is incapable of shedding light on the emergence of these antecedent conditions. The causal dynamics commonly investigated in both the rationalist and the constructivist literature on compliance, juridification and legitimacy kick in as soon as the problem at hand is solved. They explain regularities in behaviour within a pre-constituted political space precisely because they take for granted the existence of such a political space within which regulatory efforts become possible in the first place.

Towards a performative view of political community formation

The language of community is by no means immune to any of the problems discussed earlier. On the contrary, even a brief overview of its intellectual history reveals a past that is paved with anti-modernist, anti-democratic, and even outright fascist associations. As noted earlier, the feel-good quality of the rhetoric of community entails a connotation of secureness, which presupposes an insecure world as an external precondition. This connotation, which is evoked when we speak of community, the distinction between tradition and modernization, is in fact at the centre of classical sociological treatments of the subject. 'Community' enters the stage of social thought as the antagonist of 'society', which is presented as a unifying description of the manifold transformations (differentiation, rationalization, bureaucratization) uprooting traditional forms of integration and solidarity. 'Community', one might argue, owes its positive feel to 'society' as a semantic antagonist, which encompasses a wide array of challenges to the secure life in community. Under these auspices, the evolution of society can be read as a history of estrangement, which pays for an enormous increase in the efficiency of social organization with the suppression and replacement of traditional forms of life. Depending on the temper of individual authors, such a constellation could be decried as a tragic experience of historical loss (from right-wing Hegelianism to the more conservative branch of communitarianism), as characteristic of an oppressive, yet historically necessary period, which could be overcome at higher stages of development (cf. Marx' notion of original community, the positive feel of which was to be resurrected under communism), or as an irreversible historical process, which can only be dissected by means of sober analysis.[8] However, the main reason to rebuff the language of community, especially in the context of German social theory, has been a normative one. While the English 'community' still resonates positively in most contexts, the German *Gemeinschaft* is inevitably reminiscent of the homogenized vision of a *Volksgemeinschaft* (popular community, a community of the people in the singular), which pervaded fascist political rhetoric. Ferdinand Tönnies, who had coined the distinction between *Gemeinschaft* and *Gesellschaft* (community and society) in German sociology, while clearly inspired by a romantic zeitgeist, by no means joined the choir of cultural pessimists and conservative nationalists which provided a fertile ground for a discourse of totalitarian homogenization. He invested his own political hopes in the emergence of new forms of solidary association and gradual transformation, which led him straight into German social democracy (Joas 1992). Yet what is at stake here is not the political views of a classical German sociologist, but rather the problematic implications of the rhetoric of community. Tönnies himself was acutely aware of the unintended consequences of his conceptual choice. There is no denying, he writes in a letter to his son, that the concept of community was successfully instrumentalized by the Nazi party (cf. Kaesler 1991: 517).

Against this backdrop, resorting to the concept of community in order to overcome conceptual and normative problems with common ways of theorizing the emergence of post-national forms of political authority seems to be highly counterintuitive. However, from the analytical perspective which I have assumed by approaching the concept of community from the perspective of its practical usage in everyday language, this is not a matter of conceptual choice. There is no denying that the rhetoric of community is still very present in political discourse. Hence, political scientists ought to analyze its implications and consequences, i.e. the practical grammar of the language of community. This involves pointing out how the concept of *Gemeinschaft* has been used in history, and it cautions us against advocating particular processes of community formation without being meticulously aware of the unintended consequences it may have. The 'dark side of the concept of community' may then provide us with a twofold caveat. On the one hand, it serves as a negative foil to explicate what is not meant. On the other, it points to the fact that whenever we speak of a particular political community, the particularity of which becomes evident by demarcating it from others, we inevitably face a problem of exclusion. The reflexive mode of political community formation which I have tentatively introduced before explicitly addresses this problem by focusing on the inclusion of exclusion, i.e. the recursive reference to the exclusionary consequences of any particular act of collective self-regulation – be it the exclusion of particular groups, individual, or topics. Such a performative view of political community formation, which focuses on the consequences rather than causes of the exercise of political authority is much more in line with the pragmatist understanding of community.

The traditional German distinction between *Gemeinschaft* (community) and *Gesellschaft* (society) introduced by Tönnies had assumed that *Gemeinschaft* constitutes a primordial, yet normatively superior mode of social integration through shared values and lived traditions which is superseded in the course of modernity by *Gesellschaft* as a mode of co-ordination rather than integration which is based on purposive rationality. The resulting tale of modernity consequently bemoans the loss of primordial modes of integration as too high a price for an increase in social rationality alongside a trajectory leading straight into the Weberian iron cage. A second tradition, which seems to be more prevalent in the Anglo-American context, allows for the possibility of communities to be constructed, i.e. to occur as the result of particular social processes rather than as a precondition of social integration that has been 'always already there' and needs to be defended against the encroachment of modernity (cf. Joas 1992, Buzan 2004: 111). Less sceptical about modernization as such, some scholars in the second tradition have even reversed the sequence, arguing that the international system may in fact be superseded not only by an international society of states providing a basic normative framework that goes beyond pure balancing, but also by an inclusive international community encompassing individuals as citizens of a global proto-polity.[9]

Both accounts depict their evolutionary trajectories in rather teleological terms. While I side with the latter account when it comes to rejecting the primordial character of community, the idea of thinking political community formation in terms of a 'contentious politics of legitimacy', which I have proposed earlier, allows us to account for contingency and openness in processes of post-national community formation. Rather than stipulating a particular macro-historical trajectory, such a performative view on political community formation is meant to remain sensitive to historical reconfigurations. This is, in fact, very much in line with Dewey's notion (2004) of the public (and the state) as a continuous experimental practice, which he presents as an explicit critique of literature that seeks causal origins in terms of individual motivations.[10] 'Appeal to a gregarious instinct to account for social arrangements is the outstanding example of the lazy fallacy. Men do not run together and join in a larger mass as do drops of quicksilver, and if they did the result would not be a state nor any mode of human association' (Dewey 2004/1927: 36).[11] The concrete circumstances of human association, however, are different at different times and in different places. The attribution of causal motifs inevitably produces a vast array of competing explanations, which remain incommensurable as they merely reflect their respective contexts of origin. Dewey thus proposes replacing the quest for causal origins with a focus on practical consequences. 'We take then our point of departure from the objective fact that human acts have consequences upon others, that some of these consequences are perceived, and that their perception leads to subsequent effort to control action so as to secure some consequences and avoid others' (Dewey 2004/1927: 12). To the extent that such consequences remain confined to those immediately involved, they can be dealt with in private, i.e. among the participants of a particular situation. However, to the extent that others are affected, dealing with consequences becomes a problem of the public – and the public, in turn, constitutes itself precisely by addressing this problem. Hence, the 'quality presented is not authorship but authority, the authority of recognized consequences to control the behaviour which generates and averts extensive and enduring results of weal and woe' (Dewey 2004/1927: 19).

The pragmatist focus on practical consequences has often been misunderstood as a mere affirmation of a given status quo. However, from a pragmatist point of view the success of any particular transaction hinges not on its conformity with externally given expectations, but simply on what follows successively after the fact. What is 'objective' in Dewey's account is the mere fact that some kind of consequence can be observed. The 'recognition' of particular consequences – as well as the neglect of others – remains subject to the subsequent process of communication. All we can say about the public act of self-regulation is that based on the recognition of particular, possibly unintended, consequences of action, those who are affected constitute themselves as a public which manifests itself in the institutionalization of contextually specific forms of self-regulation. The specific kind of public that we refer to as the state

> is the organization of the public effected through officials for the protection of the interests shared by its members. But what the public may be, what the officials are, how adequately they perform their function, are things we have to go to history to discover ... And since conditions of action and of inquiry and knowledge are always changing, the experiment must always be retried; the State must always be rediscovered.
>
> (Dewey 2004/1927: 33f)

The ongoing reconstitution of what the public performs cautions against the absolutization of particular problems once recognized to be pertinent, or the uncritical perpetuation of institutional responses once deemed suitable. By permanently refocusing public attention, i.e. by permanently revising the decision of what ought to be addressed in public and what needs to be left out for the moment, the inclusion of exclusion thus becomes the organizing principle of political community.

The politics of global trade

Global economic activity seems to be a prototypical case of society formation, structured in terms of purposive rationality. Searching for instances of community formation in the politics of global trade thus means tackling a 'hard case'. However, it is hardly innovative to point to the social, legal, and political preconditions of economic action. Adam Smith underpins his outline of the benefits of self-interest for public wealth with a theory of moral sentiments. Max Weber himself traces the macro-historical process of rationalization back to a Protestant work ethic, and the sociological theory of Talcott Parsons is built in no small part on a critique of the rationalist model of economic action. Within the framework of nation-state politics, the community within which economic activity could unfold has been taken for granted. Rational economic action was firmly embedded in the political community of the nation-state which provided it with all necessary legal and political institutions. Hence, a distinct community of merchants emerges only where such a framework is lacking. This had been the case with medieval merchant law, and it might again be the case to the extent that global economic activity is increasingly decoupled from the regulatory efforts of the nation-state. The nation-state can provide the community framework within which rational economic activity can unfold, and it has done so for the most part of the last couple of centuries. However, the modern state is by no means necessary as a provider of such a framework. To the extent that a regulatory framework dealing with the consequences of economic transaction beyond the nation-state is deemed necessary, distinct and relatively secluded publics may emerge which provide for such a framework. The new transnational merchant law, and the institutional thickening of the WTO framework are two cases in point.

Lex mercatoria: a transnational legal order?

'When I tried to explain the subject of this article to one of my partners', renowned international lawyer, Keith Highet reports, 'he at first thought that Lex Mercatoria was a once-famed linebacker for the Chicago Bears' (Stein 1995: 6). Is the *lex mercatoria* – the idea of an emerging transnational law of commerce beyond the regulatory framework of the nation-state – just an academic construction, detached from legal practices 'in the field'?

As a matter of fact, the *lex mercatoria* can hardly be described as a consistent fully-fledged transnational legal order. There are no means of enforcement except for the pressure of the 'public sphere' of globally operating companies, which are interested in an efficient way of handling conflicts in which national law, favouring always one of the contracting parties and often lacking specific clauses on the issues at stake, is increasingly dysfunctional. Mutual recognition as legal subjects, however, can be interpreted as the very foundation of legitimacy at the nation-state level as well. If contracting parties do recognize each other as subject to a transnational law of commerce, and if they state in their contracts, as demanded by the International Chamber of Commerce (ICC), that the contract may be abrogated, but not the declaration to authorize an arbitrator to 'finally settle' (International Court of Arbitration 1998: 8) the dispute, this does to a certain extent correspond to state authority in the settlement of private law suits within the nation-state.

The somewhat antiquated overtone of the denotation *lex mercatoria*, Felix Dasser (1989: 32) argues, is a matter of purpose. It sheds light on the parallels to established, traditional legal orders such as medieval customary merchant law and the Roman *jus gentium*, which had been developed as a response to the incapacity of local legal orders to cope with the excessive demands for regulation in the context of an upcoming intensification of foreign trade. 'The merchants themselves created the rules and regulations they needed' and thus created the trading practices which were later incorporated by the legal institutions of the state (Dasser 1989: 32). The *jus gentium*, rejecting strict regulatory forms of civil law by invoking a transnational norm of *bona fide* then allowed more flexible responses and could serve as a rudimentary legal framework for Mediterranean trade. The same transformation of customary trade practices into judicial law was repeated in the High Middle Ages, when foreign trade reoccurred in Italy in the eleventh and twelveth centuries in the context of rural legal orders and canon law which was explicitly hostile to the intensification of trade (cf. Dasser 1989: 33ff, Stein 1995). In this context the concept of a *lex mercatoria* was coined, depicting the merchant law, which had been developed and increasingly harmonized alongside major routes of commerce. 'Cosmopolitan in nature and inherently superior to the general law, the merchant law by the end of the medieval period had become the very foundation of an expanding commerce throughout the Western world' (Schlesinger, quoted in Dasser 1990: 35). When in early modern times trade gained a significance which could not be ignored any longer by the rulers, the *lex mercatoria* was absorbed by the legal orders of the mercantilist and absolutist state, thus losing its autonomous character and being replaced by the mercantilist codifications beginning with Colbert's laws in the late seventeenth century. The subsequent waves of liberalization, however, have set the stage for yet another reoccurrence of an autonomous commercial law. Beginning with trade associations in the late nineteenth century which provided model contracts including arbitration clauses, the institutionalization of the International Chamber of Commerce in Paris in 1923, the conclusion of large-scale contracts between major companies from the 'industrialized world' and non-industrialized states (particularly in the oil and petroleum business), and the increasing importance of private arbitration in the domestic realm, the raw material of a new *lex mercatoria* has been produced. A major debate among legal scholars was launched in the early 1960s, dividing the field mainly into two still predominant camps: adherents of a rather traditional, positivist perspective regarding international trade law as a mere catchment basin for quite similar clauses within national legislations on the one hand, and adherents of an autonomist approach observing an 'anational, autonomous, self-generating system of laws articulated by the international commercial community to regulate its activities' on the other (Wiener 1999: 161; cf. Dasser 1989: 41; Mustill 1987).

More specifically, the 'raw material' for the academic debate was largely produced in a series of contracts between oil companies and Arab states. In a case in September 1951, Petroleum Development Ltd. v. Sheikh of Abu Dhabi, for instance, the arbitrator, Lord Asquith of Bishopstone, faced the problem of how to apply a legal order containing no specific clauses on international trade to a complex decision on oil concessions. On the basis of the general clause in the contract that 'the ruler and the company both declare that they intend to execute this agreement in a spirit of good intentions and integrity, and to interpret it in a reasonable manner' (Dasser 1989: 180), the arbitrator decided to apply general principles, partly taken from English Municipal Law, but compatible with other modern legal orders as well, which are 'in my view so firmly grounded in reason as to form part of this broad body of jurisprudence – this "modern law of nature"' (Dasser 1989: 180). The decision, attracting a great deal of attention among jurists, helped to pave the way towards a new *lex mercatoria*. While cases in which arbitration is explicitly accepted as part of the original contract do not seem to provide strong evidence that the applied law has a transnational character, where and how to choose arbitration was often part of the dispute. The trials of the Iran–US Claims Tribunal provide an instructive example. In the original contract the parties had chosen Iranian law, the Iranian party thus claimed that the interest on compensation should be decided according to Iranian law – i.e. denied – as well.

In both cases the new *lex mercatoria* was invoked not as a mere confirmation of what had been stated by the parties in their contract anyway, but as a genuine source of law, applicable in cases where other sources were unavailable, or grossly incompatible with the interests of one party and the circumstances under which the contract had been concluded. The question as to how these steps can be justified is contested among jurists.

Clive M. Schmitthoff, the 'principal advocate' (Wiener 1999: 164) of the positivist position, admits that the *lex mercatoria* is rooted in the customary rules of medieval merchant law and tends to constitute quasi-autonomous legal practices, based on principles the universality of which transcends particular national legal systems.[12] He maintains, however, that the legitimacy of the not so transnational law of commerce is entirely due to its acceptance through the nation-state. If this tacit support is withdrawn, national law could easily override the sentences of private arbitrators. The *lex mercatoria* 'does derive its authority from the sovereign power of national lawgivers' (Schmitthoff 1988: 231). Hence, the *lex mercatoria* is conceived not as an autonomous legal order, but rather as a vehicle for the unification of national laws on international trade, gradually decoupling it from stricter domestic regulations (Wiener 1999: 167; Dasser 1989: 45; Schmitthoff 1988: 20ff.). The positivist interpretation is widely acknowledged and became effective, for instance in the institutionalization of the United Nations Commission on International Trade Law (UNCITRAL) in 1966, which aims not only at the co-ordination of work of the different organizations active in the field, but also at the harmonization of international trade law through model and uniform laws and the promotion of new international conventions.[13]

Proponents of the autonomist approach largely agree with the positivist characterization of the *lex mercatoria* as a set of universalistic legal norms which serve to facilitate international trade. They differ, however, as to what the sources of legitimacy are. 'The autonomous order is "spontaneous", because it rests upon the will of the parties who create rules best suited to their particular needs' (Wiener 1999: 162). The 'community of merchants' invents a specific legal order, binding themselves to practices they have continuously reinforced in their trade practice. Berthold Goldman, one of the leading proponents of the autonomist perspective in the debates in the early 1960s, contends that – at a scale different from national law – the *lex mercatoria* emerges as an autonomous legal order not beyond, but beside, national law. What is of interest in the present context is not which of these accounts is substantively correct. More importantly, the mere fact that there is a process of contestation within which the boundaries of the *lex mercatoria* are explicitly negotiated is sufficient to observe a process of political community formation at work.

Discussing the emergence of the *lex mercatoria* in a social science context and relating it to the question of how the emergence of legal and political authority beyond the state is possible and how it affects the competences of the nation-state, means to forbear from the discussion of abstract principles of legitimacy, focusing instead on the social practices by which it can be produced.

In a sociological study on the subject, Dezalay and Garth (1996) address precisely this question. Attempting to understand international commercial arbitration in the light of Bourdieu's notion of social fields, they argue that it is neither a 'quasi-mechanical effect of the intensification and acceleration of circulation and exchange' nor an expression of the imperialist impetus of great powers instrumentalizing legal means for their advantage (Bourdieu 1996: vii). Unpacking the *lex mercatoria* in terms of an analysis of the legal field producing it, allows us to 'recapture the global logic of the new world legal order without resorting to generalities as vague and vast as their object' (Bourdieu 1996: viii). The legitimacy of international commercial arbitration is the product of a specific set of practices, competition and conflict among jurists, who, educated in their different national traditions, attempt to globalize *their* legal order, but unwittingly produce a global legal field which again transforms the national legal practices as well as it is reinforced and reshaped by them.

Only specific jurists, renowned scholars or judges, were chosen as arbitrators in the 1960s and early 1970s. They were not tied to one of the few institutions dominating the competition in the field, most importantly the ICC, but 'rather handle[d] arbitrations under the auspices of multiple institutions or as ad hoc proceedings' (Dezalay and Garth 1996: 10; cf. 18ff). The resulting 'mafia', a closely related international arbitration community, was a surprisingly small circle of individuals (Dezalay and Garth 1996: 10, cf. Sassen 1996: 104n22).[14] These individuals, largely educated in the continental European legal tradition, did not regard arbitration as a genuine profession. As one of Dezalay and Garth's interviewees contends: 'Arbitration is a duty, not a career' (Dezalay and Garth 1996: 34). For the independence of the arbitrator can only be guaranteed if he has no self-interest in promoting a personal career. Confining arbitrations to these prominent figures had the positive effect of giving the arbitrators a specific charisma, which helped in creating the legitimacy of the decision through the unquestioned integrity of the arbitrator. The notion of a new *lex mercatoria*, independent from state law, was developed among these scholars and arbitrators, mainly the French and Swiss representatives (Dezalay and Garth 1996: 38ff). It was the charismatization of their decisions, which, at first, helped to create the space, the legal field, in which arbitration could gain legitimacy. With the increase of cases and the growing recognition through corporations and public institutions, however, legitimacy based on such an arcane charismatization could not be sustainable. Charisma, as Dezalay and Garth (1996: 37) note in Weberian terms, needs to be routinized. And the routinization of charisma occurred through the opposition of European grand old men, invoking the *lex mercatoria*, and younger American technocrats, emphasizing their technical skills and specialization and perceiving arbitration rather as US-style offshore litigation. They promoted 'the rationalization of arbitration know-how' (1996: 37).

This opposition, however, is rather a manifestation of competition in a symbolic field, a strategic distribution of roles than of permanent positions. 'It is not at all clear that these young technocrats are ready to renounce completely the attractions of charismatic arbitration, which present advantages both for the arbitrators and for the parties in conflict' (Dezalay and Garth 1996: 40). In their attempts to enter into a field governed by the 'arbitration mafia', however, the 'newcomers' emphasized precisely those rather technical skills, which allowed for a further recognition of arbitration as a legal practice. In this respect an American arbitration expert commented on the *lex mercatoria*:

> The question is ... whether commercial parties feel that it provides sufficient security and predictability – and how well arbitrators who don't have the abilities of [Berthold] Goldman [a senior French professor and the 'father' of the *lex mercatoria*] are able to apply the theory and come up with suitable answers that are perceived as fair and reasonable by both parties.
>
> (Dezalay and Garth 1996: 40)[15]

Particularly the institutionalization of the International Chamber of Commerce as a major site of international arbitration can be regarded as a 'microcosm' of the creation and institutionalization of the legal field as such.

> We see first the legal *honoratiores*, embodying the wisdom of law and the social legitimacy necessary to the management of social conflicts. We then find institutionalization and the creation of a division of labour, which permits the development of a collective legitimacy dependent not on individual notables but rather on 'the ICC' or even 'law' or 'international commercial arbitration'. (Emphasis in orginal)
>
> (Dezalay and Garth 1996: 46)

The pioneering distinguished scholars and senior judges had reinvented, promoted, and institutionalized international commercial arbitration, providing the 'technology', such as the *lex mercatoria*. The ICC as a major site of institutionalization guaranteed its acceptance in the world of business and the reputation of the professional notables advanced recognition through the official justice system.

The second phase of routinization of the legal field thus created is characterized by the conduct of arbitration as 'offshore litigation', looser ties with academic law, and the rejection of the *lex mercatoria* as an internally consistent transnational law of commerce. Younger American lawyers, the main protagonists of the transformation, did not only have to enter the closed community of ICC arbitration, they also had to 'impose a redefinition of the rules of the game' (Dezalay and Garth 1996: 51). The Americanization coincided with an increasing bureaucratization, rejected by the senior notables as 'treason'. Rather than emphasizing their neutrality, the litigators perceived the service to the client as their fundamental duty. Satisfying big clients means to ascend in the hierarchy of the law firm. The competition in the legal field is thus also a competition over the definition of key characteristics of the profession. Despite the general tendency towards Americanization, adjourning the legal field from learned law to routine litigation and disputing, and from seniority and notability to facilitations for new entrants, the senior arbitrators still play an important role, especially in big, non-routine cases. The legal field is produced not by the domination of a single logic of arbitration, but, unwittingly, as a result of their competition.

The autonomy of law within the legal field, however, does not imply that questions of power are excluded. As a matter of fact, Dezalay and Garth (1996: 100) argue that the transformation from arbitration in the European tradition to litigation in the American tradition 'can best be understood as part of a new and more competitive market in legal services created by transformations originating in the business world'. In a case between a US company and Algeria on construction projects in the context of the boom in oil revenues in the early 1970s, the Algerian side, knowing the ICC arbitration system on account of 'experiences' with French companies after Algerian independence, originally seemed to have an advantage. At a time when major law firms started their engagement in big litigations and the potential damage in the particular case investigated were as high as $ 650 million (for 'the project would have to be finished at considerable expense' and the 'Algerians sued not only the construction company but also the parent company'), a clash of the legal traditions seemed to be inevitable (Dezalay and Garth 1996: 103). Interestingly, the litigator of the construction company had big problems in finding a law firm to take the case. Despite the high value, the lack of familiarity with the largely French system of ICC arbitration apparently had a deterrent effect. In fact, the aggressive skills of American lawyers, 'intense document production, aggressive fighting, huge amount of paperwork and pretrial skirmishing' (Dezalay and Garth 1996: 103) proved to be largely inefficient during the arbitration process. The US company thus hired two of the most important figures in the ICC arbitration community, Berthold Goldman and Pierre Lalive, a move which was countered by the Algerian side by hiring one of the most renowned students of Goldman. The arbitration, a top-level dispute about elements of the French legal tradition, held in English, finally led to a 'substantial award that was only a portion of the requested damages'. Withal, the *lex mercatoria*, invoked by Goldman and Lalive 'facilitated the avoidance of local law in favor of principles favorable to the Western construction company' (Dezalay and Garth 1996: 109). This case can serve as an example of the 'raw material' causing the increase in international commercial arbitration since the 1960s, and as an illustration of the importance of national legal traditions in the structuration of and proceedings in the legal field. Most importantly, however, the very autonomy and indeterminacy of the applied transnational law produced outcomes advantageous for the Western industrial states. The autonomy of transnational merchant law is, as Dezalay and Garth (1996: 98) conclude, closely related to its 'subordination to economic and political power'.

WTO: the constitutionalization of world trade?

The principal target of protests against such a perceived subordination has been the WTO. Protests which are, as the organization's official publications unsurprisingly maintain, hardly substantiated by the efforts of a 'member-driven' organization to foster the rule of law in the global economy, i.e. establishing rules that are fair, transparent and legally binding.

Dispute settlement is advertised in this context as 'the central pillar of the multi-lateral trading system, and the WTO's unique contribution to the stability of the global economy. [It] underscores the rule of law, and it makes the trading system more secure and predictable'. Unlike the dispute settlement procedure under the old GATT[16] the system is, in fact, 'based on clearly defined rules'. Under the GATT any participant, including the charged party, could block procedure rulings. WTO dispute settlement has reversed the procedure; now rulings are adopted unless there is a consensus among all members to reject it. Hence, while GATT procedures involved a long process of bargaining where a consensus among all parties needed to be achieved, the new architecture requires both court-like procedures and a strict timetable. Technically, states are still encouraged to settle disputes without a panel decision as the first stage of the dispute settlement procedure involves up to 60 days for consultation. If consultation fails, at the second stage a panel is to be appointed within 45 days. The creation of a panel can be blocked once, but avoided only through a unanimous decision of the Dispute Settlement Body. The panel is given six months to conclude, formally 'helping' the Dispute Settlement Body to make rulings or recommendations. In order to overturn the panel's conclusions, however, again a consensus is required. Hence, panel decisions *de facto* acquire the status of court rulings. Appeals are possible on the basis of technical issues such as legal interpretation, but 'they cannot reexamine existing evidence of examine new issues' (WTO Website accessed May 5, 1999). Three of seven members of the Appellate Body (appointed for four-year terms) decide on the appeal, upholding, modifying or reversing the panel's ruling within a maximum of 90 days. The Dispute Settlement Body then needs to 'accept or reject the appeals report within 30 days – and rejection is only possible by consensus' (WTO Website accessed January 12, 2006).

Replacing the diplomatic procedure under GATT with a formalized juridical process entails a 'legal paradigm shift' (Weiler 2000: 2). As a matter of fact, with a decision by the Appellate Body a dispute is not settled but won or lost. It has been argued that the only reason why the Appellate Body is not called 'World Trade Court' – a more appropriate depiction of its actual competencies – is to avoid irri-tations in some parts of the US congress that are notoriously hesitant to support any kind of supranational court.

Among legal scholars, however, the juridical rigor of a factually binding mech-anism has triggered a debate about the 'constitutionalization' of global economic governance. 'Normatively, the proponents of a constitutional understanding of the WTO aspire to greater legal certainty for private economic rights against the risk of depredation of powerful domestic-interest groups'. (Howse and Nicolaidis 2003). Interestingly this libertarian stance, articulated most prominently by Ernst-Ulrich Petersmann, a former member of the Appellate Body, adopts a position of legal positivism, which in the case of the *lex mercatoria* was held by those defending the exclusive authority of the nation-state. What can in a rough categorization be referred to as the anti-constitutionalist camp (Howse and Nicolaidis 2003; v. Bogdandy 2001) tends to highlight the lack of transparency and democratic accountability of WTO procedures. With the exception of a minority position that advocates constitutionalization in order to include additional, non-economic issues such as environmental standards or labour regulations, and despite the more nuanced differences in legal interpretation, a major dividing line between 'constitutionalists' and 'anti-constitutionalists' seems to be their perspective on the relation between law and politics. While Petersmann enthusiastically endorses not only the virtues of the free market but primarily the rule of law by which these virtues are made possible in the first place, Armin von Bogdandy, for instance, criticizes the 'decoupling' of law and politics in the WTO system. While the classical separation of powers allows us to conceive of law and politics as structurally coupled, insofar as political actions are constrained by the legally binding text of the law which is based on a political decision of the legislative power, WTO law is fairly explicit about jurisdiction while the political task of the legislation remains, at best, vague and indirect as a function of international treaties.

The question of whether the democratic quality of WTO jurisdiction is deficient vis-à-vis the long-established institutions of popular sovereignty within the nation-state should be disentangled, however, from the question of whether it can be described adequately as some (potentially undemocratic) kind of constitutional order. Does the criticism that law and politics are decoupled through the WTO system imply that the WTO is 'about law' while domestic politics is 'about both law and politics'? Obviously, the opposite is the case. While law and politics are interwoven through a system of the separation of powers in order to make juridical decisions independent from political influences, a deficient separation of powers will, paradoxically, make WTO procedures more political. Only if we follow the conceptual sloppiness of identifying politics with the currently predominant form of democratic politics in Western states – that is, if the concept of the political starts from a normative appreciation of a specific kind of political practice – could WTO activities be described as lying 'beyond politics'.

Insofar as it is capable of producing collectively binding decisions at the supranational level, WTO rulings are an immensely political activity. As John Greenwald (2003: 114) has noted, '[w]hen panel and/or Appellate body decisions narrow the ability of member states to restrict trade in ways that go beyond the negotiated limits placed on the use of trade measures, they are not applying WTO law, but are legislating it'.

Moreover, the dynamic development of WTO jurisdiction, replacing the old diplomatic '"5–4-mentality" (finding an agreement which should be acceptable to all parties) with the "new ethos" of "getting it (legally) right" and/or "making it appeal-proof"'(Weiler 2000: 8), has established a standard for what is conceived of as a successful international agreement, which can be counterproductive. Abbott (2001: 293) argues, for instance, that the WTO's failure to address issues such as bribery and corruption (which other organizations such as the OECD did address) can be explained at least in part by the high barriers of binding jurisdiction. At the same time, Weiler (2000) notes that the diplomatic culture of secrecy and intransparency prevails especially in the Secretariat, thus blocking off the emergence of more public political procedures within the organization.

Even if there is, as practitioners concede, a tension between 'the strong (quasi-judicial) and the weak political structures' (Ehlermann 2002: 632ff), which leads to a lack of political accountability, it doesn't make WTO activities less political. The fact that 'WTO-plus' obligations are imposed exclusively on China by virtue of the WTO Accession Protocol, covering areas 'ranging from the administration of China's trade regime (transparency, judicial review, sub-national governments and transitional review), to the Chinese economic system (market economy commitments), to new WTO disciplines on investment (investment measures and national treatment of foreign investors)', seems to suggest that the WTO rule of law appears to know that some members are more (or rather less) equal than others (Ya Qin 2003: 483). Again, what is at stake here is not to adjudicate which of the competing takes on WTO constitutionalization is substantively correct. Rather, the existence of such diverging views indicates that the discussion of the consequences of self-regulatory efforts is at the centre of the process of institutionalization.

Community formation, society formation, and the problem of market regulation

At first glance *lex mercatoria* and the WTO dispute settlement don't seem to have much more in common than the fact that they are legal institutions regulating international trade. While the WTO was designed as a formal international organization that is supposed to provide a forum for the trade policies of states, the *lex mercatoria* emerged, spontaneously as some legal scholars contend, as a transnational legal field regulating disputes among private actors. While the development of the *lex mercatoria* was fostered by the specific legal practices of its practitioners, WTO dispute settlement is a purposeful attempt at re-embedding global trade (cf. Howse and Nicolaidis 2003).

On the other hand, both *lex mercatoria* and the WTO system share 're-embedding markets' as a common theme. Apparently, the dissolution of the co-extensiveness of political community and society (including economic activities) within the nation-state creates an empty space, the lack of a regulatory framework that is firmly established at the nation-state level. Such a regulatory framework cannot intervene into the operations of the economic field, but it serves to institutionalize its autonomy in the first place. In the case of the *lex mercatoria*, private actors, lacking these public functions, institutionalized their 'own' public sphere, a space where the necessary regulatory embedding could take place. Similarly, WTO dispute settlement can be interpreted as the provision of a regulatory framework that is supposed to maintain free trade in the light of possibly protectionist national policies.

As both *lex mercatoria* and WTO dispute settlement provide regulatory frameworks in favour of the autonomy of the global economy, they are fundamentally different from the legitimacy of political communities at the nation-state level. For both *lex mercatoria* and WTO dispute settlement address legal problems as well as political issues from a distinctly economic perspective. In that respect *lex mercatoria* and WTO dispute settlement cannot be described in terms of a trans- or internationalization of political communities beyond the nation-state, but as a particular kind of quasi-political community formation within a functionally differentiated world society. Even if the WTO should become more responsive to demands to address extra-economic issues such as labour rights or environmental standards more carefully, it *prima facie* does so 'from within' the global economic field. In the US-shrimp/turtle case, for instance, banning the import of shrimp from countries which did not employ fishing techniques that protected endangered sea turtles, was addressed as a case of hidden protectionism, not as an environmental issue. Similarly, US governments have been trying to integrate labour standards into WTO regulations, which were challenged by developing countries as an attempt to impose an indirect trade barrier on their exports. Dynamics of successful public mobilization that might have an effect on WTO policies are thus unlikely to occur.

Beyond these immediate political effects of 'differentiated community formation', the emergence of quasi-judicial functions in the supranational realm is an instructive example of how the distinction between society formation and community formation introduced above plays out at a global scale. In Weber's original formulation society formation referred to either purposive rationality or value-rationality. Both types of action involve persons as role-takers pursuing, in their role, specific material or normative interests. The proposition that functional systems address (through communication) not individuals but persons in their specific roles in modern systems theory – which, starting from the idea of world society and its process of functional differentiation rather than from a territorially differentiated international system (Albert 2002, Stichweh 2001), provides an instructive framework for 'thinking beyond nation-states' – is a modern version of the same argument. It replaces Weber's latent individualism with a strict focus on the operational autonomy of social systems and differentiates between their respective operational codes instead of positing two broadly defined concepts of rationality. At the same time modern systems theory has ousted Weberian or other concepts of political community, rejecting primarily the idea of society as being normatively integrated on account of collective identities. While the classical idea that communities involve individuals, not role-takers (i.e. 'whole persons') can be disputed, the reconceptualization of political community formation which I have suggested earlier is an attempt to maintain a categorical difference between systemic rationalities, on the one hand, and, on the other, the intersubjective recognition of legal subjects by means of which producing collectively binding decisions becomes possible. While society is constituted merely through communication, political communities involve, in addition, a shared set of symbolic references, which allows for its 'imagination' as community.[17]

Such a distinction allows us to conceive of problems of global governance as dissimilarities insofar as community formations – instantiated, for instance, through the invocation of founding myths such as the people conquering the Bastille – tend to stick to the established level of aggregation, the nation-state, more tightly than societal activities involving persons-as-role-takers. Phenomena of global governance could then be described as an attempt to trigger supranational processes of political community formation in the context of a functionally differentiated world society. Temporal metaphors – catching up with society formation – would, however, be too simplistic. WTO dispute settlement and the *lex mercatoria* do not provide evidence of an extension of political community beyond the nation-state, they rather indicate that functional equivalents for regulatory functions – the institutional embedding which is a precondition for the autonomy of the economic at the national level – can emerge from the distinct context of transaction beyond the nation-state.

The process of differentiated community formation described above thus creates a fundamental paradox of global governance. While institutions that are capable of governing – that is, producing collectively binding decisions – begin to emerge beyond the nation-state, their scope of governance remains predicated on the logic of the particular field from which they have emerged. In that respect the way in which law, politics and economics are 're-coupled' beyond the nation-state might not increase but rather decrease both the possibility of political accountability and the public control of legislative functions.

Conclusion

This chapter has attempted to give a straightforward answer as to why political scientists and students of international politics in particular should care about the problem of political community formation. They should care because the language of community formation provides us with an analytical tool-kit capable of analyzing the emergence of trans- and supranational political spaces without conceptually presupposing the modern state. From the point of view of processes of political community formation, the authorization of authority beyond the nation-state, i.e. the factual legitimacy of claims to political regulation, does not hinge on any antecedent condition of legitimacy. Legitimacy is not some kind of substrate that needs to be present before a political community can constitute itself. Building on John Dewey's performative understanding of the constitution of public spheres, I have conceptualized political community formation as a recursive process of self-imposition and self-regulation (cf. also Honneth 1999, Schmalz-Bruns 2007). Whether or not such an attempt at self-regulation is successful then hinges on a threefold process of recognition. It hinges on the question of whether particular consequences of action are recognized as being of public relevance and thus requiring regulatory efforts, of whether the participants recognize each other as legitimate political subjects, and of whether these two process taken together eventually lead to the recognition of a particular act of authorization. Any of these dimensions of recognition is subject to an open process of contestation. Hence, deviance and non-compliance do not lend evidence to a crisis of legitimacy. To disagree with a particular decision is not a sign of a legitimation crisis, but simply an expression of opposition within the political process. Whatever is excluded within a particular political community at a given time is not excluded *per se*. For it is precisely the ongoing actualization and re-negotiation of a community's boundaries, i.e. the inclusion of exclusion, through which it is performatively integrated.

In conclusion, a cautionary note seems in order. When I emphasize the conceptual independence of processes of political community formation from the modern state this does not entail a substantive claim about the future of the modern state. None of the arguments presented here prejudge the empirical question of how the state is going to relate to emerging transnational forms of political authority. Unthinking the state is a conceptual task, not an empirical proposition.[18] In fact, it is helpful for a better understanding of how the state may react in the light of emerging competitors in the field of political authorization. As the exemplary illustrations from the field of global trade have indicated, such competitors may well arise from the systemic rationalities of the global economy rather than from a normative criticism of the present interstate system. While they employ the normative appeal of the language of community in the course of their respective processes of authorization, this does not imply that such a normative appeal needs to be plausible to an outside observer. Thinking beyond the nation-state may enable us to imagine more inclusive forms of political community at the global level (e.g. Linklater 1998). However, it also sheds light on emerging forms of political authority, which may curtail rather than enhance the prospect of democratic self-legislation in comparison to the nation-state. From a point of view that posits the state as a necessary precondition of political authority and thus confines the political imagination to the organizational form of the modern state, such a competition for authority falls into a blind spot. Only to the extent that we begin to acknowledge that the nation-state as a particular kind of political community is itself the outcome of a historical process in which it successfully superseded alternative imperial, municipal, and confederational forms of political organization, we will be able to understand the present challenges to the nation-state as expressions of an open historical process of contestation.

Notes

1 The title of Bauman's study of the concept is instructive in this respect: 'Community: Seeking Safety in an Insecure World'. Cf. also Brown (1995: 90).
2 Many of the proponents of what is dubbed 'constructivism' in contemporary IR theory in fact subscribe to such a normativist social theory. One might argue that IR is still being haunted by the long shadows of the Parsonian orthodoxy.
3 For a critical interpretation of Waltz' reading of Durkheim see Barkdull (1995).
4 In the context of Nye's discussion of soft power, however, legitimacy again becomes a steering tool designed to achieve desired political outcomes. For a powerful critique see Bially Mattern (2005).
5 Corresponding to Wendt's (1999: 268ff) triad of force, price and legitimacy.
6 For a particularly rigid version of the top-down argument see Meyer *et al.* (1997).
7 For a critique of a behaviourist conception of norms which emphasizes the aspect of contestation, cf. Wiener (2004, 2007).
8 The latter perspective has been perfected by Niklas Luhmann, who rejects the concept of community as a foremost expression of old-European thought, utterly inadequate to grasp anything but romantic prejudices in a modern, i.e. functionally differentiated, society.
9 Cf. the solidarist branch of the English school as well a much of the 'global governance

as good governance type of literature'. Buzan (2004: 108–117) provides an interesting discussion.

10 For a discussion of Dewey's *The Public and its Problems* in the context of cosmopolitan democracy, cf. Cochran (2002).

11 More generally, Dewey (2004: 36) refers to such an 'appeal to *special* forces outside the series of observable connected phenomena' as 'no different in kind to the occult forces from which physical science had to emancipate itself'.

12 In a critical account, Mustill (1987), a British Lord Justice, has enumerated these principles. Most importantly contracts are to be fulfilled (*pacta sunt servanda*), substantial changes of the circumstances can provide legitimate reasons to revise the contract (*rebus sic stantibus*), the contracting parties should deal with each other in *good faith*, and in case of a fundamental breach of the contract through one party the other party may be released from its obligations.

13 UN General Assembly resolution 2205 (XXI), (www.uncitral.org/en-index.html).

14 To become an international arbitrator then means first of all to establish a base in this field and learn the rules of the game – to build symbolic capital which can then be transformed 'into substantial cash value' (Dezalay and Garth 1996, 6; cf. 29).

15 This is the friendly version. Other newcomers contend that the old mafiosi are a major problem, 'probably just more full of themselves than other people', feeling that, on account of their charisma, they do not really 'have to explain things' (Dezalay and Garth 1996: 36).

16 By GATT I refer to the 'pre-Uruguay' agreement that was originally concluded in 1947 as a compensation for the failed attempt to found an International Trade Organization. Technically, a revised GATT is still the legal basis of the WTO Agreement.

17 Cf. Anderson 1991. The positive connotations stirred up by the concept of community can be considered as a part of these symbolic references. See also Dewey (2004/1927: 142).

18 Cf. Bartelson (2001), as well as Dewey (2004/1927: 8): 'The moment we utter the words "The State" a score of intellectual ghosts rise to obscure our vision. Without our intention and without our notice, the notion of "The State" draws us imperceptibly into a consideration of the logical relationship of various ideas to one another, and away from facts of human activity'.

Bibliography

Abbott, K.W. (2001) 'Rule-making in the WTO: lessons from the case of bribery and corruption', *Journal of International Economic Law*, 6: 275–96.

Albert, M. (2002) *Zur Politik der Weltgesellschaft*, Weilerswist: Velbrück Wissenschaft.

Anderson, B. (1991) *Imagined Communities: reflections on the origins and spread of nationalism*, London: Verso.

Annan, K. (2002) 'What is the International Community? Problems without passports', *Foreign Policy*, 132: 30–1.

Barkdull, J. (1995) 'Waltz, Durkheim, and International Relations: the international system as an abnormal form', *American Political Science Review* 89: 669–80.

Bartelson, J. (2001) *The Critique of the State*, Cambridge: Cambridge University Press.

Bauman, Z. (2001) *Community: seeking safety in an insecure world*, Cambridge: Polity Press.

Bially Mattern, J. (2005) 'Why Soft Power Isn't So Soft: representational force and the sociolinguistic construction of attraction in world politics', *Millennium*, 33: 583–612.

Bogdandy, A. v. (2001) 'Verfassungsrechtliche Dimensionen der Welthandelsorganistion. 1. Teil: Entkoppelung von Recht und Politik', *Kritische Justiz* 34: 264–81.

Bos, M. and Brownlie, I. (1987) *Liber Amicorum for The Rt. Hon. Lord Wilberforce*, Oxford: Clarendon Press.

Bourdieu, P. (1996) 'Foreword', in Y. Dezalay and B.G. Garth (eds) *Dealing in virtue: international commercial arbitration and the construction of a transnational legal order*, Chicago: Chicago University Press, vii–viii.

Brown, C. (1995) 'International Political Theory and the Idea of World Community', in K. Booth and S. Smith (eds) *International Relations Theory Today*, Cambridge: Polity Press, 90–109.

Buzan, B. (2004) *From International to World Society? English School theory and the social structure of globalisation*, Cambridge: Cambridge University Press.

Cochran, M. (2002) 'A Democratic Critique of Cosmopolitan Democracy: pragmatism from the bottom-up', *European Journal of International Relations*, 8: 517–48.

Dasser, F. (1989) *Internationale Schiedsgerichtsbarkeit und lex mercatoria: Rechtsvergleichender Beitrag zur Diskussion über ein nicht-staatliches Handelsrecht*, Zürich: Schulthess Polygraphischer Verlag.

Dewey, J. (2004/1927) *The Public and its Problems*, Athens: Ohio University Press.

Dezalay, Y. and Garth, B.G. (1996) *Dealing in virtue: international commercial arbitration and the construction of a transnational legal order*, Chicago: Chicago University Press.

Ehlermann, C.-D. (2002) 'Six Years on the Bench of the World Trade Court: some personal experiences as a member of the appellate body of the World Trade Organization', *Journal of World Trade*, 36: 605–39.

Finnemore, M. and Sikkink, K. (1998) 'International Norm Dynamics and Political Change', *International Organization*, 52: 887–921.

Greenwald, J. (2003) 'WTO dispute settlement: an exercise in trade law legislation?', *Journal of International Economic Law*, 6: 113–24.

Habermas, J. (1998) *Die postnationale Konstellation: Politische essays*, Frankfurt: Suhrkamp.

Honneth, A. (1999) 'Demokratie als reflexive Kooperation: John Dewey und die Demokratietheorie der Gegenwart', in H. Brunkhorst and P. Niesen (eds) *Das Recht der Republik*, Frankfurt: Suhrkamp, 37–65.

Howse, R. and Kalypso, N. (2003) 'Enhancing WTO Legitimacy? Constitutionalization or global subsidiarity', *Governance* 16: 73–94.

Howse, R. and Nicolaidis, K. (2003) 'Legitimacy through "higher law": why constitutionalizing the WTO is a step too far', in T. Cottier and P.C. Mavroidis (eds), *The Role of the Judge in International Trade Regulation: Experience and Lessons for the WTO*, Ann Arbor MI: University of Michigan Press.

Hurd, I. (1999) 'Legitimacy and authority in international politics', *International Organization*, 53: 379–408.

International Chamber of Commerce (2001) 'ICC International Court of Arbitration – Facts and figures on ICC arbitration'.

International Court of Arbitration (1998) 'Rules of Arbitration', in force as from 1 January 1998.

Jackson, P.T. (2002) 'Rethinking Weber: towards a non-individualist sociology in world politics', *International Review of Sociology*, 12: 439–69.

Joas, H. (1992) 'Gemeinschaft und Demokratie in den USA. Die vergessene Vorgeschichte der Kommunitarismus- Diskussion', *Blätter für deutsche und internationale Politik* 37: 859–69.

Kaesler, D. (1991) 'Erfolg eines Mißverständnisses? Zur Wirkungsgeschichte von 'Gemeinschaft und Gesellschaft' in der frühen deutschen Soziologie' in L. Clausen and C.

Schlüter (eds) *Hundert Jahre 'Gemeinschaft und Gesellschaft'. Ferdinand Tönnies in der internationalen Diskussion*, Opladen: Leske+Budrich.

Keck, M.E. and Sikkink, K. (1998) *Activists Beyond Borders: advocacy networks in International Politics*, Ithaca: Cornell University Press.

Keohane, R.O. (2001) 'Governance in a Partially Globalized World: presidential address to the American Political Science Association, 2000', *American Political Science Review*, 95: 1–13.

List, M. and Zangl, B. (2003) 'Verrechtlichung internationaler Politik', in G. Hellmann, K.D. Wolf, and M. Zürn (eds) *Die neuen Internationalen Beziehungen. Forschungsstand und Perspektiven in Deutschland*, Baden-Baden: Nomos.

Linklater, A. (1998) *Transformation of Political Community: ethical foundations of the post-Westphalian era*, Cambridge: Polity Press.

Luhmann, N. (1997) *Die Gesellschaft der Gesellschaft*, Frankfurt: Suhrkamp.

Martin, L. and Simmons, B. (1998) 'Theories and Empirical Studies of International Institutions', *International Organization*, 52: 729–57.

Mead, G.H. (1962/1934) *Mind, Self, and Society*, Chicago: University of Chicago Press.

Meyer, J.W., Boli, J., Thomas, G.M., and Ramirez, F.O. (1997) 'World society and the Nation-State', *American Journal of Sociology*, 103: 144–181.

Moravcsik, A. (2002) 'Reassessing Legitimacy in the European Union', *Journal of Common Market Studies*, 40(4): 603–25.

Mustill, M. J. (1987) 'The New Lex Mercatoria: the first twenty-five years', in Bos, M. and Brownlie, I. *Liber Amicorum for the Rt. Hon. Lord Wilberforce, P.C., C.M.G., O.B.E., Q.C.*, Oxford: Clarendon Press.

Nye, J.S. (1999) 'Redefining the National Interest', *Foreign Affairs*, 78: 22–35.

Parsons, T. (1968/1951) *The Social System*, New York: Free Press.

—— (1969) *Politics and Social Structure*, New York: Free Press.

Rosenau, J.N., Czempiel, E.-O. (eds) (1992), *Governance without Government: order and change in world politics*, Cambridge: Cambridge University Press.

Sassen, S. (1996) *Losing Control? Sovereignty in an age of globalization*, New York: Columbia University Press.

Schmalz-Bruns (2007) '"An den Grenzen der Entstaatlichung. Bemerkungen zu Jürgen Habermas" Modell einer "Weltinnenpolitik ohne Weltregierung"', in P. Niesen and B. Herborth (eds) *Anarchie der kommunikativen Freiheit: Jürgen Habermas und die Theorie der internationalen Politik*, Frankfurt: Suhrkamp, 269–94.

Schmitthoff, C. (1982) 'Nature and Evolution of the Transnational Law of Commercial Transactions', in N. Horn and C. Schmitthoff (eds) *The Transnational Law of International Commercial Transactions*, Antwerp: Kluwer.

—— (1988) *Clive M. Schmitthoff's Select Essays on International Trade Law*, ed. C-J. Cheng, Dordrecht, Boston, London: Martinus Nijhoff Publishers/Graham & Trotman.

Steffek, J. (2003) 'The Legitimation of International Governance: a discourse. approach', *European Journal of International Relations*, 9(2): 249–75.

Stein, U. (1995) *Lex mercatoria: Realität und Theorie*, Frankfurt am Main: Klostermann.

Stichweh, R. (2001), 'Systems Theory Versus the Theory of Action: communication as a theoretical option', *Metapolitica* 5(20), 52–67.

Strange, S. (1996) *The Retreat of the State*. Cambridge: Cambridge University Press.

Walker, R.B.J. (2002) 'Alternative, Critical, Political', in F.P. Harvey and M. Brecher (eds) *Critical Perspectives in International Studies*, Ann Arbor: University of Michigan Press.

Waltz, K.N. (1979) *Theory of International Politics*, Reading: Addison-Wesley.

Weiler, J.H.H. (2000) 'The Rule of Lawyers and the Ethos of Diplomats: reflection on the internal and external legitimacy of WTO dispute settlement', *Harvard Jean Monnet Working Paper* 9/00, Cambridge: Harvard Law School.

Wendt, A. (1987) 'The Agent-Structure Problem in International Relations Theory', *International Organization*, 41: 335–70.

—— (1999) *Social Theory of International Politics*, Cambridge: Cambridge University Press.

Wiener, A. (2004) 'Contested Compliance: interventions on the normative structure of world politics', *European Journal of International Relations*, 10: 189–234.

—— (2007) 'Demokratischer Konstitutionalismus jenseits des Staates. Perspektiven auf die Umstrittenheit von Normen', in P. Niesen and B. Herborth (eds) *Die Anarchie der kommunikativen Freiheit: Jürgen Habermas und die Theorie der internationalen Politik*, Frankfurt: Suhrkamp.

Wiener, J. (1999) *Globalization and the Harmonization of Law*, London and New York: Pinter.

WTO World Trade Organization Online, available http://www.wto.org/ (accessed May 5, 1999)

Ya Qin, J. (2003): '"WTO-plus" obligations and implications for the World Trade Organization Legal System', *Journal of World Trade* 37: 483–522.

Zangl, B. (2001) 'Bringing Courts Back In: Normdurchsetzung im GATT, in der WTO und der EG', *Swiss Political Science Review*, 7: 49–80.

Epilogue

Community rethought?

Gideon Baker and Jens Bartelson

One of the greatest challenges faced by the social sciences today is to rethink the concept of community in order to handle the many moral and political issues of a globalized world. Responding to this challenge, the contributors to this volume have all had to face the same basic philosophical problem; how to rethink the concept of community without thereby simply reproducing a particularistic social ontology? Since most of our inherited conceptions of community carry implicit connotations of boundedness and homogeneity, attempts to project these conceptions onto a world which lack those characteristics are likely to generate paradoxes that cannot be resolved within the same conceptual framework. Thus it seems as if the concept of community must be rethought wholesale and the entire framework for its articulation restated. But getting rid of the core connotations of boundedness and homogeneity leaves us with little else. What could possibly constitute a multitude of people into a community in the absence of both borders and shared attributes among its prospective members? What could the concept of community possibly mean without boundaries, common political institutions, or a common cultural identity? And where do we look for inspiration when we have been forced to admit that modern social theory is part of the problem rather than a source of possible solutions?

Those are some of the questions that have kept the contributors to this volume busy. While their responses differ widely, they have all been willing to explore a range of alternatives, in the past as well as in the present. In this epilogue, we will not dwell so much on individual contributions, but will rather try to identify some crucial dimensions within which the rethinking of community is currently taking place in the hope of providing a preliminary framework for a more systematic analysis of the possibilities of political community. We believe that three such dimensions are especially salient: *space, time* and *language*. All of these concepts stand in an intimate yet ambiguous relationship to our different conceptions of community. Rethinking community wholesale must therefore entail a preparedness to question the meaning and function of those basic categories within existing accounts of political community, as well as the implications of understanding them differently. Let us start with time and space. In contemporary attempts to rethink the idea of community, we believe it is possible to detect at least two different ways of understanding the relationship between our spatiotemporal categories and the possibility of a life in common between human beings.

First, it seems plain that every human community necessarily occupies a slice of timespace, and that its identity to some extent is constituted by the symbolic meaning attributed by its members to its historical past and its territory. Some analyses in this volume seem to accept this basic contention, but simultaneously try to dispute the necessity and desirability of such attributions for a life in common. If we accept that the categories of time and space not only exist independently of the meaningful experience of a life in common, but also are indispensable to its creation and reproduction, we will also be tempted to conclude that human communities have to be spatiotemporally bounded in order to be sufficiently cohesive and viable. Such an argument would be based on the idea that time and space are objective preconditions of human existence, even if their meanings happen to be socially constructed and mediated. This view assumes that although spatiotemporal categories are man-made, their referents are not: time and space exist independently of our changing conceptions of them. Time and space together thus constitute the backdrop against which the drama of human community can unfold, as well as the most basic resources available when making sense of this drama.

Second, it seems equally obvious that the very categories of space and time themselves are constructed by human beings in order to make sense of their habitat, and that they thereby provide the most basic coordinates necessary for a life in common. From this point of view, spatiotemporal categories are expressions of communal life, rather than given requirements of its very possibility. Some analyses of human community in this volume seem to imply that spatiotemporal categories are constructed all the way down in an effort to bestow shared meanings on what otherwise should remain a disorganized and fragmented experience. If we accept this view, we will be equally tempted to conclude that human communities are what human beings make of them by tailoring their cosmological beliefs to fit their needs, and thus that demarcating human communities spatiotemporally is but one historically specific way of making and maintaining them. This is a much more radical belief, since it posits that time and space themselves are constructed by us, rather than merely our meaningful experience of them. Time and space are thus but manifestations of the perpetual quest for community, being co-constituted rather than constitutive.

Hence, rethinking spatiotemporal categories amounts to rethinking community, as well as conversely. But this process itself invariably takes place within some *other* time and space whose making always is unaccounted for by the same account. Although every effort to reconcile the above views seems to result in paradoxes, each seems to presuppose what the other takes for granted. Therefore, as we would like to suggest, the tension between these views is productive in the sense that it is exactly what allows community to be rethought, in the past as well as in the present. Ultimately, the way of handling this tension is to admitt that time and space are real – and therefore both enable and constrain the creation of human communities – only by virtue of being constructed by their inhabitants. Hence what makes a mere multitude of individuals a community is the fact that they inhabit a slice of timespace of their own device. So while the regeneration of community always takes place within a pre-constituted spatiotemporal framework, the reconstitution of that very framework is what allows for both regeneration and transformation. Defining ourselves is a way of building our habitat out of the cosmological resources at our disposal, and building such a habitat is a way of defining ourselves as members of a community, whether universal or particular in scope. But how is this connection forged in practice?

As some contributions to this volume suggest, the typical way in which this regeneration and transformation takes place is through the use of *language*. Language might thus be thought of not only as constitutive of particular communities or expressive of their shared meanings, but also as the universal medium by means of which the tension between what is given and what can be created can be provisionally resolved. Not only is the capacity to use language necessary in order to form the communicative bond integral to any human community, but also in order to create the web of cosmological belief necessary for a life in common. Not only are communities spoken into being through rhetorical performances that provide the mythical foundations of political authority and cultural identity, but also because language itself contains those resources needed to transform the spatiotemporal framework within which human communities are situated, and through its use, the relationship between human communities and the corresponding cosmological beliefs finds mediation.

In finishing, let us remind ourselves why such a framework for re-thinking political community is important. Contemporary accounts of the future of political community are often highly normative invocations of a boundless cosmopolitan political community in which identity and difference in world politics are finally resolved. The contributions to this collection have sought to resist the temptation to see things this way. They have shown in different but complementary ways that the related inside-outside and identity-difference problematics at the heart of political community are perhaps not so amenable to resolution, and instead need to be creatively re-engaged. Various such re-engagements have been proposed here, engagements which remain true to the critical impulse behind the liberal cosmopolitan vision of the transformation of political community while questioning its idealisation of boundlessness and identity in political community. They include: pluralizing our accounts of the time of political community in world politics in order to resist ethnocentric and teleological assumptions of convergence on a shared or global time of political community; de-nationalising our conception of democracy so as to get around the seemingly intractable problem of identity and difference in accounts of global democracy; challenging simplistically pejorative readings of the inside-outside of political community through a reconsideration of the place of hospitality in cosmopolitan ethics; de-nationalizing but not de-territorializing political community (Nietzsche's 'good Europeans'); re-habilitating particularistic communal belonging by way of the development of an idea of *critical* belonging; re-habilitating territory – the local rather than the global – as a privileged site of political community; refocusing attention away from the transformation of political community to the more ancient concern of how to maintain justice in the political community; revisiting and questioning the assumption that the 'other' in political community formation must necessarily be demonised in the process; and re-articulating political community formation at the global level in more sociological and less normative ways. Perhaps Chandler, in his chapter, identifies the overarching concern expressed here most starkly when he wonders aloud whether political community today might involve bypassing the empty space of global politics, a space which tempts us to project our longing for identity onto the world at large, and instead experimenting with building up social bonds in ways that limit our freedoms and develop our sense of responsibility and accountability to others.

In something like this spirit, this volume seeks to stand as a small corrective to the reification of the global, and to narrowly pejorative readings of territory, belonging and boundaries. In seeking to avoid these ruts in particular, the contributions here do not seek to identify with an anti-cosmopolitan position, to array themselves on the side of the communitarians in political theory and academic international relations. In a much less partisan fashion, the hope is simply that this text will stand as a reminder that thinking the future of political community needs to be approached from as many angles as possible while avoiding as many sacred cows as possible. In short, re-thinking the future of political community is difficult. It is to be hoped that contributions which take this as their starting point may thereby prove more enduring than blueprint-driven speculation on the future of political community.

But rather than finish on such a cautious note, it is worth ending with a reminder of why such a careful re-thinking of the future of political community is important in the first place. The future of political community is important because community, despite all the aforesaid problems in accounting for community today, cannot be detached from our understanding of the political. And, to be blunt, in some ways this is a shame, or at the very least an inconvenience. Having lost much of his extended family in the Holocaust, Emmanuel Levinas had more reason than most to remind us that a communal bond established between the same and the other constitutes a totality which is always in danger of becoming a 'totalization' or tyranny of the worst kind. Community is dangerous; as anyone who has ever inhabited one knows, the totalizing tendency is real even in the most outwardly benign communities. And yet it is only in the context of the (political) struggle for recognition in a society of equals, Levinas tells us, that a non-totalizing bond between the same and the other can be glimpsed: 'Beyond the State in the State' as he put it in the title of a late essay. In other words, even an ethics of otherness or alterity needs political community – 'transcending' the reduction of otherness to identity which is the hallmark of community must nevertheless occur within political community. Even Levinas, with his profound suspicion of political community 'where the stranger is assimilated; where the other is reconciled with the identical in everyone' concedes that not only does political community *not* contradict the ethics of responsibility for the other, but is even 'called by it'. Identity and difference might not be resolvable, and seeking such 'resolution' in political community might be the most dangerous thing of all, but political communities that manage this tension as justly as they can will be as important to us in the future as they are now.

Index

Abbott, K.W. 195
Achilles 152–3, 154, 156–7, 160, 161
Actium, Battle of 161
adjudication 179
advocacy 117–18, 124
Aeneas 158, 159, 160–1, 162, 163, 164, 165
Aeneid, The (Virgil) 10, 157–64, 164–7, 169
Afghanistan 145
Agamben, G. 29, 33, 114, 116, 118–19, 131; apocalyptic time 22–7
Agamemnon 152–3, 154
Ajax 155–6
Algeria 193
Algerians, non-status 64
Allport, G. 149–50
Americanization 192–3
anarchy 176
Anderson, B. 81–2
Anderson, W.S. 163
Andromache 154
animals 23
Annan, K. 175
Anthony, Mark 157, 161, 165
anti-constitutionalism 195
anti-globalization movement 113–14
Aphrodite 155
apocalyptic time 22–7
Appellate Body 194
arbitration 189–90, 191–3, 200
Archibugi, D. 113
Arendt, H. 22, 132, 133, 137–8
aristocrats 164
Aristotle 133–4, 135, 138, 140
ars topica 129, 130, 131
artificial nationalism 83
Athena 155
Augustus 157, 158, 159, 164–5

autonomist approach to international trade law 189, 190

Bankovsky, M. 57
Baudrillard, J. 123, 125
Bauman, Z. 175
becoming, political temporality of 28
being, politics of 28, 33
Benhabib, S. 40
Benjamin, W. 22, 23, 25, 32, 33
Berenskoetter, F. 148
binary oppositions 5–6
biopolitical neo-liberal global governance 116
bios 23
Birmingham, P. 91, 99, 101, 102–3, 104, 105
Bodin, J. 43
Bogdandy, A. von 195
Booth, K. 113
Bosnia 63
boundaries 7, 45, 46; and consent 40–2; politics of hospitality 7, 51–69
boundedness 2
Bourdieu, P. 191
Brewer, M. 149, 150
Brown, W. 30
Brubaker, R. 144–5
Buchanan, A. 38–9
Bulley, D. 63

Camilla 159, 162
Campbell, D. 63
Canada 64, 169
Carr, K.L. 78
Carthage 160, 162
causal explanation, limits of 177–84
causation 16, 32
charismatization of arbitration 191–2

China 196
Christianity 73, 74–81, 82
chronos 15–17, 23, 33
Cicero 9, 129, 131–2, 135, 137
Cities of Refuge North America 67–8
city republic 41
civilization 131–2
Cleopatra 161, 165
coercion 180–1, 182
coherence with oneself 138
co-historising 94
Cold War 21
collective learning processes 18–19
collective memory 151
collectively binding decisions 182–4
Comité d'Action des Sans-Statuts (CASS) 64
communication 123, 134
communicative action 32
community 175; concept of 1–5; constitution of 8, 90–111; formation and society formation 196–8; individuals and 4, 120–5; and society 184–5, 186
compliance 179–80, 182
conditional hospitality 52–3, 56, 60–1
conflict 145
Connolly, W. 33, 86, 131, 137, 147, 148; political time 27–9
consent 37, 40–2, 45, 46
consequences, practical 186–7
constitution of community 8, 90–111; critical belonging 8, 91, 97–104, 105–7, 206; Heidegger's politics 92–7; poiesis, praxis and politics 105–7
constitutionalization: of international law 18–22; of world trade 193–6
constructed communities 4
construction project case 193
constructivism 179–84
contestation 11, 40, 47–8
contingent, the 133
Cooper, F. 144–5
cooperation 181
cosmopolitan democracy 38–9
cosmopolitan futures 18–22
cosmopolitanism 1–2, 6, 10; ethics and sovereignty 54–5, 65–6; post-territorial political community 9, 112–26
cosmopolitanism 'to come' 124–5
Critchley, S. 64, 96
critical belonging 8, 91, 97–104, 105–7, 206; tradition, repetition and destructive retrieve 98–104
critical mimesis 91, 101–4, 105–6

critique 130–1
Cruz, C. 102

Dardanus 162
d'Argenson, Marquis 44
Dasein (there-being) 91, 92–3; critical belonging 97–104
Dasser, F. 188, 189
Davis, W.A. 93
De Beistegui, M. 95, 96, 99, 100, 101, 102
'death of God' *see* secularisation
decisionism 53–4, 55–7
deliberative democracy 39–40
democracy 6–7, 36–50, 206
democratic legitimacy, paradox of 40–5, 47–8
Democratic Peace 146
Derrida, J. 8, 22, 45, 51–2, 52–3, 63, 65, 67, 68, 131; comparison of views on ethics and sovereignty with Schmitt's 55–7; 'double law' of hospitality 60–3; views compared with neo-Kantians' 57–60
destiny 94, 96, 100
destructive retrieve 98–104
Deutsch, K. 167
Dewey, J. 186–7
Dezalay, Y. 191–3
diachronic temporalities 22–3
dialectics 134, 140
dialogue 138, 147
dichotomy 90
Diderot, D. 41
Dido 158, 160–1, 162
difference, paradox of 131
Dikec, M. 64–5
discrimination 150
Dispute Settlement Body 194
distinctiveness 150–1, 166–7
Doty, R.L. 64
'double law' of hospitality 53, 60–3
Douzinas, C. 116, 119, 124
Duffield, M. 116, 124
Durkheim, E. 3

Eagleton, T. 133
East-West binary 161–2
Ecologues, The (Virgil) 157–8
Edkins, J. 63–4
education 137
Elias, N. 3
eloquence 131–2, 135–6, 139–40
empirical history 22
enemy 53–4, 56

enforcement 179
Enlightenment 130
environmental protests 113–14
environmental standards 197
epic poetry 151–69; *Aeneid* 10, 157–64,
   164–7, 169; *Iliad* 10, 151–7, 161–2,
   163, 164–7, 169
epistemological obstacles 178
Erwiderung 101–3, 108
Esposito, R. 131
essentialism 90
ethics 32; as hospitality 52–3, 63–5;
   sovereignty and 51–69
ethos 134
Europe 146, 168
European Charter of Cities of Asylum 60
European Constitution 73–4, 76, 84
European political community 8, 73–89;
   'good Europeans' and experience of
   freedom 84–6, 87; nationalism as a
   'metamorphosis of the cross' 81–4;
   secularisation 74–81, 85
European Union (EU) 21
exclusion 131; inclusion of 24, 185–7,
   198–9; inclusion of formerly excluded
   groups 168–9
exigency 25
existential analysis (*Daseinanalytik*) 92–7

factionalism 43
Falk, R. 113
fantasy 129
fate 100
female-male binary 161–2
feminization of the other 161
Fish, S. 133
foreign policy 112
fortune 17
Foucault, M. 22, 44, 114, 116, 130, 131,
   147
France 74
freedom 57, 87–8; 'good Europeans' and
   the experience of 84–6, 87
friendship 138; guest friendship (*xenia*)
   152, 169
Fritsche, J. 94–5
Fronteras Compasivas 64

Gadamer, H. 135
Gaonkar, D.P. 133
Garth, B.G. 191–3
GATT 194, 200
Gelven, M. 93
Gemeinschaft 185, 186

general will 41, 43–4
generalized international 63–4
genocide 175
Georgics, The (Virgil) 157, 158
Gesellschaft 185, 186
global citizenship 114
global civil society 6, 115, 117–18, 120–1
global *demos* 36–7, 39–40, 45; mankind as
   46–8
global governance 116; political
   community formation 10–11, 175–203,
   207
global justice 30
globalization 21, 30; of the democratic
   community 6–7, 36–50, 206
'God, death of' *see* secularisation
Goldman, B. 190, 193
'good Europeans' 8, 73–89, 206; and the
   experience of freedom 84–6, 87;
   nationalism 81–4; secularisation
   74–81, 85
governments 112
Greeks 154–5, 159–60, 164, 166; Trojan
   War 152–7, 166
Greenwald, J. 195
Grotius, H. 146
groups 149–51
guest friendship (*xenia*) 152, 169

Habermas, J. 27, 29, 32, 95–6, 113, 144,
   147, 178; and the 'Kantian project'
   18–22
Hadrian 159
Hardt, M. 114, 116, 117, 121, 122, 123
hate 152–3
Hayes, C. 81
Hector 152, 153–4, 155–6
Hecuba 154, 156
Hegel, G.W.F. 17, 144, 145, 147–8,
   167–8
Heidegger, M. 8, 80, 90–111; critical
   belonging 98–104; Heidegger's politics
   and thought of community 92; mapping
   the debate on Heidegger's politics 92–7;
   rhetoric 134–5
Held, D. 37, 113, 146
Helen 152, 154, 155, 162
Herder, J. 147
hermeneutic 135, 140
heterotemporality 27–31
Highet, K. 188
historising 94
history: historical tradition 94, 97–104;
   progress in 6, 15–35

Hobbes, T. 43, 146
Homer: The *Iliad* 10, 151–7, 161–2, 163, 164–7, 169; The *Odyssey* 151, 157, 163, 164
homo sacer 24–5
homogeneity 1–2
Honig, B. 40
Honneth, A. 148
honour 166–7
hospitality 7, 51–69, 206; ancient Greece 152; 'double law' of 53, 60–3; ethics as 52–3, 63–5
hostility 150–1, 167
Howse, R. 194
Hoy, D.C. 99, 100
hubris of intellectualism 29
humanism, liberal 57–9
humanitarian intervention 21, 24, 30
Huntington, S. 145, 146
Hurd, I. 180–2

ideal type 152
identification *see* mimesis
identity 10, 144–74, 207; The *Aeneid* 157–64; comparative analysis of Homer and Virgil 164–7; The *Iliad* 151–7; ingroups and outgroups 149–51; learning from the ancients 164–9; philosophy of 144–9
Iliad, The (Homer) 10, 151–7, 161–2, 163, 164–7, 169
incentives 179–80
inclusion 131; of exclusion 24, 185–7, 198–9; of formerly excluded groups 168–9
individuals: and collectively binding decisions 183–4; postmodern individual 8; relationship to community 4, 120–5
ingroups 149–51
institutional memory 151
internal dialogue 138
International Chamber of Commerce (ICC) 188, 189, 191, 192
International Cities of Refuge Network (ICORN) 67–8
International Commission on Intervention and State Sovereignty 5
international law: constitutionalization of 18–22; *lex mercatoria* 188–93, 196–8
International Network of Cities of Asylum (INCA) 60, 67
International Parliament of Writers (IPW) Network of Cities of Asylum 60
international system 146

intersubjectivity 181
inventio 129, 131
Iran–US Claims Tribunal 190
Iraq 145
irreducibility of the 'problematic of sovereignty' 63–5

Jabri, V. 116, 121, 124
James, W. 140, 141
Judgment of Paris 162
Juno 158, 159, 162, 163–4, 165
Jupiter (Jove) 158, 159, 164, 165
juridification 179–80
jus gentium 188–9
justice 57–8, 206–7; global 30; responsibility, hospitality and 62

kairos 15–17, 23, 31, 33
Kaldor, M. 113, 116, 117
Kant, I. 17, 55, 58, 66–7, 130, 144, 145, 147–8, 167–8; Habermas and the 'Kantian project' 18–22
Keane, J. 120–1
Keohane, R.O. 38–9, 177
knowledge 139–40
Kohn, H. 81
Kosovo 113

La Caze, M. 67
labour standards 197
Lacoue-Labarthe, P. 90, 95, 96, 97, 100, 101, 107–8
Lalive, P. 193
language 23, 139, 141, 204, 206; and hospitality 61–2
Lavinia 158, 165
law: international *see* international law; state of exception 118–19
laws of hospitality 61
legal field, routinization of 191–3
legitimacy: paradox of democratic legitimacy 40–5, 47–8; political community formation 179–84, 198
Levinas, E. 51, 57, 58, 59, 207
lex mercatoria 188–93, 196–8
liberal cosmopolitanism *see* cosmopolitanism
liberal humanism 57–9
liberalism 146–7
limited hospitality 52–5, 56, 60–1
Linklater, A. 55, 113
Llobera, J. 82
logos 134
Löwith, K. 97, 108

Lucan 157
Luhmann, N. 178, 182, 199

Macedonia 160
Machiavelli, N. 17, 32
male-female binary 161–2
management school 179–80
mankind 46–8
Mansbridge, J. 150
Maoris 168–9
market regulation 196–8
Marx, K. 17
Mead, G.H. 183
Menelaus 152, 155
merchant law, medieval 188–9
messianic time 25–6
'metamorphosis of the cross' 81–4
Mezentius 159
Mill, J.S. 146
mimesis 96–104; critical 91, 101–4, 105–6
Mitsein (being-with) 92–4, 95–6
modernity 3, 18–22
moral action 133
morality 32; Christian 78
Mouffe, C. 131, 148
multiculturalism 1, 2
multi-level authority system 19–20
multiple *demoi* 39–40
multitude 114, 117–18, 121, 122
mutability of character 162–3
mutoli 139, 141

Nagel, T. 45
Nancy, J.-L. 107–8
Näsström, S. 36, 39, 42
nation 40–5; *see also* state
nationalism 38, 168; European political community 81–4; Heidegger 100
nationalization 3
Nazism (National Socialism) 92, 94–7, 107–8, 185
Neaman, E. 95
necessary, the 133
Negri, A. 114, 116, 117, 121, 122, 123
neo-Kantians 54–5, 65–6; comparison with Derrida 57–60
neo-liberalism 116
Netherlands, The 74
networked actors 120–1
New Zealand 168–9
Newell, R.N. 96
Newton's theory of time 16
Nicolaidis, K. 194

Nietzsche, F. 138, 144, 147, 148; 'good Europeans' 73–89
nihilism 75
non-governmental organizations (NGOs) 115, 146
non-intervention 182
non-status Algerians 64
normative view 175–6, 178–9, 183
Nussbaum, M. 28–9
Nyers, P. 64

Octavia 158
Octavian *see* Augustus
Odysseus 153, 163, 164
Odyssey, The (Homer) 151, 157, 163, 164
opinion 132–3
oppositional consciousness 150
oratory 135–7; *see also* rhetoric
order, problem of 177–84
other/otherness 8, 9, 10, 90, 106, 207; fluidity of category of other 168–9; hospitality *see* hospitality; and identity 10, 144–74, 207
outgroups 149–51
Owen, D. 79

Pallas 159
Pandarus 155
paradox of democratic legitimacy 40–5
paradox of difference 131
Paris 152, 154, 155; Judgment of 162
Parsons, T. 187
particular vs universal 4, 6
pathos 134
Patroclus 152, 156, 167
Paul 25, 33
peace 19, 145, 163–4, 165
performative view 176, 184–7
persuasion 132–3, 134, 181, 182
Petersmann, E.-U. 194, 195
Petroleum Development Ltd. v Sheikh of Abu Dhabi 189–90
philosophical history 20, 22
philosophy: of identity 144–9; rhetoric and 132–3
pity 156
Plato 73, 77, 132–3, 134, 140
pleasure 23
plurality 106–7
Pocock, J.G.A. 16–17
political community formation 10–11, 175–203, 207; community formation, society formation and market regulation

196–8; *lex mercatoria* 188–93, 196–8; limits of causal explanation 177–84; performative view 176, 184–7; politics of global trade 187–8; WTO 193–8
political engagement 122–4
political order, problem of 177–84
political steering 177–8
political time 15–17, 26–7
politics 8–9, 26; of global trade 187–8; and hospitality 62–3; of peace 124
population 44
positivism 189, 190
postmodernism 7–9; postmodern individual 8
post-structuralism 7–8; radical and post-territorial political community 9, 112–26
post-territorial political community 9, 112–26, 206; individuals and the community 120–5; political community without political subjects 118–20; political project of 115–18
power 116–17, 147
practical consequences 186–7
presentness 29
Priam 152, 154, 155, 156–7, 159–60
'problematic of sovereignty', irreducibility of 63–5
procedural co-presence 90
progress 6, 15–35
prophecy 25
protest, individualized 124
Prussia–Germany 168
public, the 186–7
Pufendorf, S. 146
punishment 179
Pyrrhus (Neoptolemus) 159–60

Quint, D. 157, 161, 162–3
Quintilian 135–7

radical post-structuralism 9, 112–26
Rajchman, J. 87–8
Ramírez, J.L. 134, 135
rationalism 179–84, 187–8
Rawls, J. 147, 148
reactionism 102
real communities 4
realism 167
reason 136
recognition 198
regulation, market 196–8
religion 147; European political community and 73, 74–81, 82

repetition 98–104, 105
representation 43; advocacy vs 117–18
responsibility 57–60
revaluation of values 84–6
rhetoric 9, 129–43
rifts in time 28
rights 118–20
Roiz, J. 136
romance, epic and 162–3
Rousseau, J.-J. 17, 19, 41–2, 43, 45
routinization of the legal field 191–3
Rundell, J. 66
Rushdie, S. 60
Rutulians 158–9

Schmitt, C. 53–4, 65–6, 67, 108, 115–16, 144, 145, 147, 148, 167–8; comparison with Derrida 55–7
Schmitthoff, C.M. 190
Schofield, M. 3
Schuman, R. 73
science 75–81
secularisation 74–81, 85; nationalist response 81–4
self, coherence within 138
self-esteem 149
self-formation 137
self-interest 180–1, 182
self-regulation 186–7
shame 156
Sherif, C.W. 150
Sherif, M. 150
Shilliam, R. 168
Sieyès, E. de 42, 43
silence 138–9
singularities 26
Smith, A. 75–6, 187
Smith, J.E. 16
sociability 46–7
social identity theory 149
social movements 146
social relations, changing 117
society 184–5, 186; formation and community formation 196–8
sociocultural homogeneity 1–2
Socrates 132–3, 137–8
solidarity 168; without community 121
Sophists 132–3
sovereignty 5, 6, 24–5, 146, 181–2; and ethics 51–69; irreducibility of the problematic of 63–5; paradox of democratic legitimacy 40–5
space 204–6

state: autonomy, globalization and
democracy 37–8; as continuous
experimental practice 186–7; global
governance and 178; and global policy
community formation 199; philosophy
of identity 145–6; sovereignty *see*
sovereignty
state of exception 118–19
strategic action 32
subjects, political community without
118–20
subtle racism 150
Suetonius 158
Sumner, W.G. 149
supranational institutions 38; constitutions
19–20
synchronic temporalities 22–3

Tajfel, H. 149
Taylor, C. 148
telos 21–2
territorial boundedness 2
territorial politics, hollowing out of
112–13
Thersites 153, 164
thinking 28
time 6, 15–35, 204–6, 206; apocalyptic
22–7; cosmopolitan futures 18–22;
political 15–17, 26–7; thinking time
differently 27–31
timeliness 16, 31
Tönnies, F. 3, 185
totalization 207
Toynbee, A. 81
trade 187–98; *lex mercatoria* 188–93,
196–8; politics of global trade 187–8;
WTO 193–8
trade associations 189
tradition 94, 130; critical belonging 94,
97–104
Trojan War 152–7, 166
Trojans 153–5, 164, 166, 167;
transformation of 162–3
truth 76–81; rhetoric and truthfulness
137–8
Turnus 158–9, 163, 164
tyranny 26
Tyrians 160–1, 167

unconditional hospitality 52–3, 56, 60–1,
66
unconditionality without sovereignty 52
undecidability 53, 57–60

United Nations Charter 21
United Nations Commission on
International Trade Law (UNCITRAL)
190
United States of America (USA) 116, 145,
197
unity in diversity 84
universalism: ethics and sovereignty 55,
57–60; mankind as global *demos* 46–8;
universal vs particular 4, 6

values, revaluation of 84–6
Van Roermund, B. 36
Vattel, E. de 146
Venus 159, 162
verbalism 136
Vico, G. 129, 139–40, 141
violence, state monopoly on use of 182
Virgil: The *Aeneid* 10, 157–64, 164–7,
169; The *Ecologues* 157–8; The
Georgics 157, 158
Virilio, P. 28–9
Virno, P. 122
virtù 17, 32
virtue 139–40
Vogel, L. 106
Vulcan 159

Waltz, K. 180
war 145
war on terror 113, 145
Weber, M. 79, 180, 181, 187, 197
Weiler, J.H.H. 195–6
Wendt, A. 39
West-East binary 161–2
will of all 43–4
will-to-truth 77–81
withness 92–3
Wokler, R. 41, 42
Wolin, R. 94
Wolin, S. 28, 129–30
women, in epic poems 154, 161, 162, 166
Wood, D. 96, 101
world republic 19
WTO 193–8

Ya Qin, J. 196

Zangl, B. 179
Zapatistas 122
Zehfuss, M. 63–4
Žižek, S. 103
zoë 23

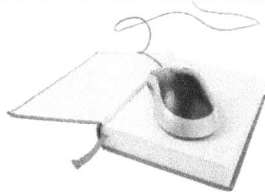

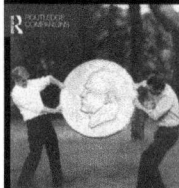

For Product Safety Concerns and Information please contact our EU
representative GPSR@taylorandfrancis.com
Taylor & Francis Verlag GmbH, Kaufingerstraße 24, 80331 München, Germany

www.ingramcontent.com/pod-product-compliance
Lightning Source LLC
Chambersburg PA
CBHW050428280326
41932CB00013BA/2031

9 780415 847872